1,111 Idioms

1,111 Idioms

With 190 Worksheets

Marco Antonio Bussanich

iUniverse

1,111 IDIOMS
With 190 Worksheets

iUniverse books may be ordered through booksellers or by contacting:

iUniverse
1663 Liberty Drive
Bloomington, IN 47403
www.iuniverse.com
1-800-Authors (1-800-288-4677)

Because of the dynamic nature of the Internet, any web addresses or links contained in this book may have changed since publication and may no longer be valid. The views expressed in this work are solely those of the author and do not necessarily reflect the views of the publisher, and the publisher hereby disclaims any responsibility for them.

Any people depicted in stock imagery provided by Thinkstock are models, and such images are being used for illustrative purposes only. Certain stock imagery © Thinkstock.

ISBN: 978-1-4917-7133-4 (sc)
ISBN: 978-1-4917-7132-7 (e)

Library of Congress Control Number: 2015910839

Print information available on the last page.

iUniverse rev. date: 12/08/2016

Personal Introduction

Marco has been teaching since 1997. He has taught English in Vancouver, Tokyo, Taiwan, Shanghai, Beijing, Zhuhai and Bangkok over a 16 year period. Marco has 2 TEFL certificates and 2 TESOL certificates. The TESOL certificates were issued in China, and were a pre-requisite for working as an IELTS English Examiner.

Marco first developed his unique IDIOM teaching concept early in his teaching career. Noticing that his students could not find a suitable, or easy to use text for idioms (i.e. a text that included practical examples, or worksheets that would help his students practice using idioms), Marco developed the concept of placing idioms into groups, as appears in the text, 1,111 idioms. Marco developed his system in over one decade of use with his students, receiving extremely positive feedback from them on his Idiom teaching method. The text, 1,111 idioms, is presented to readers as a fun and easy way to learn idioms.

As well as teaching English, Marco has also taught Engineering, Physics, Math, Engineering Math and Chemistry, in Asia and Vancouver. Marco was employed as computer programmer for over a decade, and is acknowledged in the American Journal of Anatomy for developing a Mathematical, Computer Model of the Jaw, for the Faculty of Dentistry, at the University of British Columbia. Marco also hosts a weekly Astronomy talk show, Astrotalk, at www.citr.ca. at U.B.C.'s campus radio station.

Additional sample sentences and other idiom material for the book 1,111 Idioms, will appear on Marco's Facebook page. Look for Marco on www.marcosastrotalk.com for more free material on idioms.

Use of the Book

The exercises in the book **1,111 Idioms**, are organized in the following way:
- 6 idioms are shown on the top of each page
- the meanings of the 6 idioms are then shown at the bottom of the page
- the idioms are organized in this way for an important reason: the author encourages the reader to first attempt to deduce the meaning of the idioms, before looking up the idiom's meaning on the bottom of the page.
- Paraphrasing Albert Einstein: "The value of an education should not just be about the learning of many facts, but in training the mind to think". The author believes that if the reader thinks about the idiom before looking up its meaning on the bottom of the page, this will develop their ability to understand the idioms, rather than just memorizing the meanings of the idioms.

1. **If the book is taught by a teacher**:
   The teacher should discuss the idioms in a lesson with the students, so as to help them deduce the implied meaning of the idioms. Students should also try to figure out the meaning of an idiom by using it in context in the practice sentences. If the readers cannot quickly deduce the general meaning of an idiom, they can always then refer to the bottom of the page.

2. **If the book is used by the reader**: the reader can attempt to guess the meaning or the proper context of each idiom. For the idiom, **Raining cats and dogs**, for example, the reader should be able to figure out that the idiom probably implies, **It is raining heavily**. For the idioms, **The eyes of an eagle,** or, **Watch someone like a hawk**, the reader would most probably assume that these idioms describe a person with very good eyesight.

   By allowing the reader the option to first attempt to guess or surmise the meanings of the idioms, the reader, in the long run, will come out ahead. The reader will be developing a skill, rather than just memorizing the meanings of idioms.

TABLE of CONTENTS

SECTION 1 – ANIMALS AND LIVING THINGS

AMPHIBIANS and REPTILES

A. 1. **Frog** in <u>your</u> throat
    2. A **snake** in the grass
    3. **Snake** oil salesman
    4. The **worm** has turned
    5. Pissed as a **newt**
    6. Big **frog** in a small pond

B. Place the idioms correctly in the sentences below

1. The PTA at our school is small, but its boss, Sue, is so very influential. She's a _____because she could be working for a much bigger organization, given her talents.

2. Teacher: "I will no longer put up with your bad behavior, students. _____ _____, so I will now enforce stricter discipline

3. Thomas is such _____. He says that he's my friend, but then he says bad things about me to other people.

4. I can't talk right now, I have a _____ <u>my</u> _____.

5. Fred is _____ tonight. I've never seen him drink so much.

6. Don't buy anything from that man who sells things on the street. He's a _____. He sells nothing of value.

C. Discussion

1. Have you ever felt like a big frog in a small pond?
2. Have you ever bought anything of little value from a snake-oil salesman?

D. Meanings

1. Find it difficult to speak, usually because you are coughing.
2. Refers to a person who pretends to be your friend, but who says bad things to others about you, or that secretly tries to cause you harm
3. Someone who tries to persuade you to buy something that has no value
4. A situation where someone puts up with bad treatment without complaining, but then decides they won't accept the bad treatment anymore.
5. Refers to a person who has become very, very drunk
6. The most important person in a small group, or a person who has outgrown a situation, and be more suitably placed in a larger, more important situation

ANIMALS 1

A. 1. Smell a **rat**
   2. Like a **pig** in mud
   3. A **whale** of a story
   4. **Cat** nap
   5. Have/had a **cow**
   6. A sacred **cow**

B. Use the idioms correctly in the sentences below

1. Pam _____ right away when Joseph was hired for the new job. She knew from the beginning that he was dishonest, and that he would try to steal money.

2. I didn't believe Stan when he told us that he wrestled a bear on the the mountain. That sure was _____.

3. My mother _____ when I came home late last night. She was very, very angry.

4. I feel _____ when I'm in the shopping mall. I just love to shop.

5. We can't abolish the subsidies for the free Christmas dinner. That program is like _____ for our community.

6. I was very tired when I got home from work at 4 PM. I wanted to have a long nap, but I had to cook dinner at 6 PM, so I had a _____.

C. Discussion

1. Describe a story you heard, which was a whale of a story.
2. Have you smelled a rat before, and then had your suspicions confirmed?

D. Meanings

1. To have a premonition that someone is trying to deceive or harm you
2. To be in an ideal situation, so that a person is very happy
3. A story that is too incredible, so it is hard to believe
4. A short nap
5. To become extremely upset, or very, very angry
6. Something that people are unwilling to criticize or change, because it has a long-standing tradition

ANIMALS 2

A. 1. No spring **chicken**
   2. Call off the **dogs**
   3. **Donkey** years   ***   **A British Idiom**
   4. See the **elephant**
   5. A white **elephant**
   6. **Swan** song

B. Use the idioms correctly in the sentences below

1. The orchestra conductor performed his _____ tonight. Its too bad that he's retiring, because he's such a wonderful conductor.

2. Gladys shouldn't stay up so late. She's _____.

3. The men on the battlefield have _____ for much too long now. They've been fighting for two years.

4. Scott and Beth have paid more for repairs to their home than they did to buy it. I think they now realize they bought _____.

5. Bret's mother told the dad to _____ and stop criticizing Bret's study habits. The criticism was only making Bret upset.

6. They've been saying that they'll fix the transit system for _____ _____, but they've never done anything to make it better.

C. Discussion

1. Talk about something you know that has been happening for donkey Years, but that should have been stopped or changed long ago.
2. Has anyone in your family bought something that was a white elephant?

D. Meanings

1. Refers to a person who is no longer young
2. To stop criticizing or attacking someone
3. Refers to something that's being happening for a long, long time
4. To do something considered especially extreme, especially if it is engaging in war
5. Something that is completely useless, even though it cost a lot of money
6. The very last performance in a person's long career

BIRDS

A. 1. **Birds** of a feather flock together
   2. As the **crow** flies
   3. Eat **crow**
   4. The eyes of an **eagle**
   5. Watch <u>someone</u> like a **hawk**
   6. **Parrot** fashion

B. <u>Place the idioms correctly in the sentences below</u>

1. I was so happy when Tom finally had to _____, and admit the accounting errors were his fault. He had been blaming me for a long time

2. When students learn something _____, it's possible They won't really understand its true meaning.

3. We can't cheat in Mrs. Huntley's class. She _____ everyone _____, so it's easy to get caught cheating.

4. Tim and Jen spend a lot of time together. They both like swimming and Hiking, so I guess it's true that _____.

5. The driving distance between Seattle and Vancouver is about 142 miles, but it's actually about 110 miles _____.

6. Farah has _____. I couldn't spot the planet in the telescope, but she found it right away.

C. <u>Discussion</u>

1. Has anyone ever watched you like a hawk? How did it feel?
2. What kind of subjects are good to learn parrot fashion? Why is that?

D. <u>Meanings</u>

1. People who have similar likes and inclinations will meet, congregate, and then spend time together, often doing the things that they both like
2. Refers to the shortest linear distance between two points
3. To admitting your wrongdoing in a humble way
4. Watch things very carefully, and be good at analyzing or noticing things
5. To pay very close attention to someone, with the aim of making sure that they do not make mistakes, or do something wrong
6. Refers to something that is learned by repetition, but which is also only memorized, without really understanding its meaning

BUGS

A.
1. The **bee's** knees
2. A **fly** in the ointment
3. A **bee** in <u>your</u> bonnet
4. Bitten by a **bug**
5. Get **butterflies**
6. Snug as a **bug** in a rug

B. <u>Place the idioms correctly in the sentences below</u>

1. I feel as _____ in my new apartment. I don't think I could've found another place where I'd be more comfortable.

2. I've been _____ by this video game. I can't stop playing it.

3. Jessica's _____ in English. She always aces the tests.

4. I _____ before giving the speech at the banquet last night. I became very nervous, and my palms were sweaty.

5. Alba has _____ her _____ over the proposal to build a new daycare center. She never stops talking about it.

6. John was a _____ at the meeting last night. We couldn't make decisions because he raised objections to every proposal.

C. <u>Discussion</u>

1. Have you ever been a fly in the ointment? Why did you do this?
2. Describe a time when you were bitten by a bug.

D. <u>Meanings</u>

1. Someone, or something, that is very good at something
2. A bothersome person, who prevents something from happening, or from being successful
3. To feel strongly about some thing, and to talk continuously about it
4. Become very eager or enthusiastic to do something. After being bit by the bug, the person will start doing this thing a lot
5. Become nervous
6. To be very comfortable and warm

BULLS and OXEN

A. 1. As strong as an <u>ox</u>
    2. As stupid as an <u>ox</u>
    3. A **bull** in a china shop
    4. A red flag to a **bull**
    5. Take the **bull** by the horns
    6. Don't take any **bull** from <u>someone</u>

B. Place the idioms correctly in the sentences below

1. It would be advantageous, Jeff, to _____ on this issue and show everyone that you have leadership material.

2. I _____ anyone, John. Just because Sam is your boss, that doesn't mean you have to take abuse from him.

3. I couldn't believe Jody scored the touchdown, even though 3 men tried to bring him down. Jody truly is _____.

4. It's _____ if you try to discuss Bob's problems in Math with him. He doesn't take kindly to criticism about his Math ability.

5. Bill is _____. I can't believe that he doesn't realize that Sonia has no intention of dating him.

6. Tim was like _____ last night. He got very drunk, got into a fight, and destroyed a lot of tables and chairs in the bar.

C. Discussion

1. Discuss a time when you saw someone act like a bull in a china shop.
2. Discuss an incident where you took the bull by the horns

D. Meanings

1. Someone, or something, that is very strong
2. Someone, or something, that is very stupid
3. Refers to a person that says or does things very rashly or quickly, without considering the damage this will cause → an insensitive and rash person
4. Refers to something that always makes a particular person angry
5. To act swiftly, and with determination, to take control of a situation
6. To not take any abuse or maltreatment from someone, or to not accept their lies

CATS

A. 1. The **cat's** whiskers
   2. Has the **cat** got <u>your</u> tongue?
   3. Let the **cat** out of the bag
   4. There's more than one way to skin a **cat**
   5. Who's she, the **cat's** mother?
   6. **Fat** cat

B. Use the idioms correctly in the sentences below

1. Bob: "I talked with your mother today, but I didn't tell her about her surprise birthday party".
   Sue: "Thanks, Bob. I'm glad you didn't _____".

2. I was surprised when Alma didn't say hello to me at the party, so I said to her, "What's wrong Alma _____ <u>your</u> _____?

3. Daisy was the best dressed model in the pageant tonight. She really was _____.

4. "Why do you continue to refer to Pam as she? _____ _____?"

5. The _____ in the senate are getting rich by abusing their powers.

6. Tracy taught me a new way to answer this math question, so I learned that _____.

C. Discussion

1. Has the cat ever got your tongue when someone asked you a question?
2. Talk about a friend of yours who you feel is the cat's whiskers.

D. Meanings

1. Something that is very popular, appealing or desirable
2. Something that is said to someone when they are quiet, when they should be talking or saying something
3. To reveal a secret that was not intended to be told to someone
4. There is more than one way to do something, rather than the traditional or most used way
5. This saying is used to show that you think it is rude when someone refers to someone as **"she"**, instead of using the person's real name
6. A description of a politician or a businessman, who it has been concluded, unfairly uses their wealth or their power

Marco Antonio Bussanich

CATS, DOGS, MICE and BIRDS

1. Raining **cats** and **dogs**
2. Play a game of **cat** and **mouse**
3. When the **cats** away the **mice** will play
4. Put the **cat** amongst the **pigeons**
5. Fight like **cats** and **dogs**
6. Like the **cat** that ate the **canary**

B. Use the idioms correctly in the sentences below

1. Tom only goes to the bar with us when his girlfriend Pam is out of town.
   _____.

2. I got soaked on my way to work. Its _____ outside.

3. Mrs. Smith _____ when she asked the principal to sit in on her class. No one misbehaved when this happened.

4. Amy's avoiding me, even though she knows I've got an important question to ask her. I don't why she's _____.

5. Brenda looks _____. I suppose she's quite proud of being the top salesperson this month.

6. I don't know why Jim and Sue are still together. Whenever I see them, they _____.

C. Discussion

1. Discuss a situation where you saw the mice play when the cat was away.
2. Is it easy to spot someone who looks like the cat that ate the canary?

D. Meanings

1. Describes when it rains very heavily
2. This occurs when one person attempts to deceive or confuse someone else, in order to gain advantage over them, so they can defeat them
3. People will behave mischievously when their boss, or a person of authority, is absent
4. If the cat is put amongst the pigeons, then the cat causes a lot of angst for a group, specifically referred to as pigeons
5. Refers to two people who fight a lot, and who often fight violently
6. To feel satisfied when you accomplish something you are proud of

8

CHICKEN

A. 1. **Chicken** and **egg**
   2. Run around like a **chicken** with <u>its</u> head cut off
   3. **Chicken**
   4. **Chickens** (have) come home to roost
   5. **Chicken** out
   6. **Chicken** feed

B. Place the idioms correctly in the sentences below

1. My pay is _____. I barely make enough money to survive.

2. We all went skiing on the big ski hill, but Joe _____ in the end and didn't go. Going down the big hill scared him too much.

3. Our team can't win because we don't have good players. We can't afford to get the good players, because so few fans pay to see us play. It seems we're in a _____ situation.

4. Lee wants to spend more time with his children, but they don't want to spend time with him. He was an uncaring father, so his _____ have _____ _____.

5. The people at work were _____ their _____ _____ after the earthquake hit. Everyone panicked and ran for the door.

6. You are such a _____ Joe. You should have stood up to that bully and fought him, instead of running away.

C. Discussion

1. Have your chickens ever come home to roost?
2. Describe a situation you have been in that was a chicken and egg scenario.

D. Meanings

1. A situation where it is impossible to know which of two events came first, or which of the events caused the other
2. Refers to a situation where a person is acting illogically or irrational, and is therefore not thinking in a clear or calm manner
3. Refers to a person who is a coward, or who is afraid
4. This happens when all of your bad karma, mistakes and bad returns pile up, leading to bad luck, or to bad consequences
5. To become so afraid and intimidated that you will not do a certain thing
6. A very small amount, especially in comparison to something else

DOGS

A. 1. A **dog's** life
   2. In the **dog** house
   3. Put on the **dog**
   4. Every **dog** has its day
   5. Let sleeping **dogs** lie
   6. A **dog's** dinner

B. Use the idioms correctly in the sentences below

1. Tom's having success recently, but there comes a time when everyone has some type of success. _____.

2. Our reunion party was _____. I have never attended any event that was that badly organized.

3. At times, it's _____ being a teacher.

4. I wish you wouldn't talk about my ex-girlfriend anymore. It is better to _____.

5. Jeremy's mother punished him and put him, _____, so he can't go out for 2 weeks.

6. I don't like coming to these re-union parties because many people _____ _____ and brag about things that aren't even true.

C. Discussion

1. Has a parent or teacher ever put you in their doghouse.
2. Is it better to discuss past mistakes, or to let sleeping dogs lie?

D. Meanings

1. An unpleasant or difficult life
2. To be punished by someone else
3. To act as if you are rich or important
4. Everyone will be successful at one point in their life
5. To not talk about problems or issues that have happened in the past
6. Something that is very unappetizing, and that looks so bad that it should only be fed to dogs

FISH 1

A. 1. A big **fish**
   2. A big **fish** in a small pond
   3. A cold **fish**
   4. A **fishing** expedition
   5. There are more **fish** in the sea
   6. Neither **fish** nor fowl

B. Place the idioms correctly in the sentences below

1. Troy always felt like _____ in our small town. He's much happier now that he moved to the big city.

2. I can't figure out whether Sue likes to go out and have fun, or whether she just stays home at night. She seems to be _____.

3. Don't worry about not dating Tom anymore, Tanya. _____
   _____ to choose from.

4. Don's _____ here because his uncle owns the company.

5. The police are on _____. They will never find the evidence they want if they try to secretly snooping around here.

6. Duncan is _____. He dumped his girlfriend without showing any emotion.

C. Discussion

1. Has anyone ever gone on a fishing expedition and try to dig up some of your personal information?
2. Has there ever been a time when you felt like a big fish in a small pond?

D. Meanings

1. An extremely important or powerful person or individual
2. An important person that is a member of a small group, and that would perhaps be better suited to be placed in a situation of greater importance
3. A person that is uncaring, or that has no feelings
4. To secretly try to find out facts about someone else
5. There are many more people that you can have a relationship with, rather than the person you are now dating, or no longer dating
6. Something that's in between two extremes, making it difficult to categorize

FISH 2

A. 1. Like a **fish** out of water
   2. Drink like a **fish**
   3. Have bigger **fish** to fry
   4. A **fishing** expedition
   5. **Fishy**
   6. Like shooting **fish** in a barrel

B. Place the idioms correctly in the sentences below

1. Debbie doesn't like her new job. She feels _____.

2. The reason the coach gave for his team's bad performance sounds _____ to me. He's trying to take the pressure off his players by not blaming them.

3. The test was too easy. Writing it was _____.

4. Mark from accounting was on _____ today. He came to our department, trying to find out some information about our methods.

5. I didn't talk to James about his work habits yet, because I _____ _____ right now. I have to deal with Elsa's continued absence first.

6. Martha _____. I wouldn't be surprised if she was an alcoholic.

C. Discussion

1. Have you neglected to do one thing, because you had bigger fish to fry?
2. Have you ever gone on a fishing expedition?

D. Meanings

1. Refers to a person that is in an unfamiliar situation, or in a situation where he/she is not comfortable in, or a situation where they cannot do well in
2. To drink a lot of alcohol, quite regularly
3. Ignoring one situation, or doing nothing about one particular thing, because you have another, or other, more important things to do
4. Trying to secretly find out facts, without letting others know what you're doing
5. Something or someone that is suspicious, hard to believe, or untrustworthy
6. Competing in something where it is very easy to win

FLOWERS

A. 1. Pushing **daisies**
2. **Flower** power
3. Gild the **lily**
4. Everything is coming up **roses**
5. No bed of **roses**
6. A shrinking **violet**

B. Place the idioms correctly in the sentences below

1. My life has been _____ since those 2 car accidents.

2. Pete's dad has passed away. He's been _____ for 2 years now.

3. Max is _____. There's no way he'll confront the boss on the issues of overtime pay and seniority.

4. _____ for Stan lately. He married his dream girl, and he got a big payout from his investments as well.

5. The ice-cream sundae I make is simply the best, but Tony's _____ _____ by adding pecans to it.

6. There's too much conflict and war in the world today. Every world leader should start believing in _____, and then all will be well.

C. Discussion

1. Is the idiom "Pushing daisies", too crude a way to describe death?
2. Do you have "rose-tinted glasses" on, or do you believe that life is "No bed of roses"?

D. Meanings

1. Refers to someone who is dead
2. A saying from the Hippie era, where the emphasis was on love and peace
3. To try to improve something, even though it is already very good: the improvements are often seen as unnecessary, though
4. A description of someone whose life is very successful
5. A situation which is not all pleasant
6. A reference to a person who is very shy, or who wilts when confronted or when under pressure

13

Marco Antonio Bussanich

FOWL

A. 1. Get <u>your</u> **ducks** in a row
2. Golden **goose**
3. Cook <u>your</u> own **goose**
4. Rare as **hen's teeth**
5. A **turkey** shoot
6. Talk **turkey**

B. Place the correct idioms in the sentences below

1. Robert _____ his _____ by handing in a sub-par report. Now he surely won't get the promotion.

2. I haven't seen anyone using a Walkman to play their music anymore. Walkman's are as _____.

3. I'm going to give the biggest account to Jane. I know she'll do a good job on it because she's always so well organized, and _____ <u>her</u> _____ before executing her plans.

4. When I turned down the low offer from the insurance company, they got serious and said they wanted to _____ now.

5. We know we can't win against Templeton because they're undefeated for 2 years now. The game will be _____ for them.

6. The wheat crop is the _____ for farmers in our area. Without wheat, the farmers would not make any profits.

C. Discussion

1. Does someone you know own something that is as rare as hen's teeth?
2. Discuss a situation where you have cooked your own goose.

D. Meanings

1. To have everything well organized and under control
2. An important source of money
3. To do something which spoils your chances for success
4. Something that is extremely rare
5. A contest where one side, or one opponent, is so much stronger than the other side or opponent, meaning the stronger side will surely win out
6. To discuss something openly and in a very serious manner, so as to avoid running into a problem

FROM THE WATER

A.
1. A red **herring**
2. **Crocodile** tears
3. Neither **fish** nor **fowl**
4. **Crabby**
5. Slippery as an **eel**
6. Shut up like a **clam**

B. Place the idioms correctly in the sentences below

1. The student's _____ when the principal tried to talk with them, because their mean teacher had made them very upset.

2. Tim's story sounds like a _____. I didn't believe his excuse. It seems as if he's just trying to hide the truth.

3. Virginia has a _____ disposition during exam time. She is very often in a bad mood during exams.

4. The guard on the other basketball team is as _____. It is very difficult to stop him from scoring.

5. I can't say for sure whether James likes to eat at restaurants, or to eat at home. In this case, it seems that he is _____.

6. Candy always sheds _____ when she does poorly in an exam. She cries because she wants the teacher to give her a higher grade.

C. Discussion

1. Is it good to clam up over an issue, or is it better to openly discuss it?
2. Is it noticeable when a person tried to shed crocodile tears?

D. Meanings

1. Something that is used to take people's attention away from something else, or to divert attention away from the real issue
2. Refers to someone who pretends to shows sadness about a situation, or who cries over something, but does not really care about the situation or the thing
3. Refers to something or someone that is difficult to classify
4. Someone who is cranky, or usually in a bad mood
5. Something, or someone, that is difficult to take hold of, or catch
6. Become quiet and stop talking to others, usually because you are mad or angry about something

15

HOGS AND PIGS

A.
1. In **hog** heaven
2. Be living high on the **hog**
3. Go the whole **hog**
4. Make a **pig's** ear of <u>something</u>
5. A **pig** in a poke
6. A **pig** in the middle

B. <u>Place the idioms correctly in the sentences below</u>

1. I felt like _____ when I stuck in between Jane and Lisa during their argument.

2. Joan has _____ after she won the big lottery.

3. Tom's _____ now that he's retired and living in Hawaii.

4. I _____ when I renovated my house. It cost a lot of money to renovate, but I don't have to fix anything up for a long time now.

5. Jim _____ <u>the dinner</u>. He didn't cook anything very well at all.

6. Sid's car is _____. It broke down soon after he bought it.

C. <u>Discussion</u>

1. Talk about something that you made a pig's ear out of.
2. Have you had to be the pig in the middle between two people that were arguing?

D. <u>Meanings</u>

1. To be extremely happy, due to your own personal situation
2. To have a lot of money, and to live a good life
3. To do something to the fullest extent possible
4. To do something very, very badly
5. To buy something that is of very poor quality, because you failed to examine its quality before buying
6. To be caught in a situation where you are in between two people that are having an argument, and you have to try to settle the argument

HORSES

A. 1. One **horse** race
   2. Get on <u>your</u> high **horse**
   3. Dark **horse**
   4. One **horse** town
   5. Trojan **horse**
   6. Hold <u>your</u> **horses**

B. <u>Place the idioms correctly in the sentences below</u>

1. I thought that Amanda was the _____ to get the new job, but the boss hired her right after he interviewed her.

2. The election is a _____. The Liberal candidate will win for sure.

3. _____ your _____ Kate. Stop saying things that aren't true.

4. This place is a _____. I can find nothing of interest in it.

5. Cliff _____ his _____ much too often. He seems to think he knows more about everything than anyone else.

6. The mayor's proposal to replace these small stores with a shopping mall sounds good, but I think it is just a _____. I believe that the mayor and the developers want to build apartments there in the future.

C. <u>Discussion</u>

1. Were you ever fooled by a Trojan horse.
2. What are the advantages of living in a one horse town?

D. <u>Meanings</u>

1. Describes a situation where a person, or a thing, is much better than anything or anyone else, and will surely win
2. When someone gets on their high horse, they behave as if they know more about a particular thing, (or many things) than everyone else
3. A person or thing that wins something, when they are not expected to do so
4. A town that is very small and not interesting
5. Describes something, like a proposal or an idea, that seems to have a specific purpose, but one that really is put forward to deceive, or to achieve a larger purpose, or that is meant to harm something in the future
6. When you are being told to hold your horses, you are being told to pause, and reflect on your course of actions, or on what you are saying, because you have not thought them through adequately

17

LION

A. 1. Fight like a **lion**
   2. The heart of a **lion**
   3. Put your head into the **lion's** mouth
   4. The **lion's** share
   5. Thrown to the lions **OR** Throw someone to the **lions**
   6. Walk into the **lion's** den

B. Place the idioms correctly in the sentences below

1. I was _____ when the boss made me explain to the shareholders why we lost money this year.

2. Tim has _____. He will wrestle any challenger, even if the challenger is much bigger than he is.

3. Todd _____ in the ring, as he beat a better opponent.

4. Our company does very well as it gets _____ _____ of the total sales and total customers in the cruise ship industry.

5. I hate going to the director's meeting on Mondays. Its like _____ my _____ when I face them and their questions.

6. The guards at the prison seemingly _____ _____ every day they work. It's a very dangerous place to work.

C. Discussion

1. Name a situation where you had to fight like a lion, or where you had to show the heart of a lion.
2. Is their someone in your family or at your work that seemingly always gets the lion's share of the goodies, or the attention?

D. Meanings

1. To fight very bravely, fiercely or aggressively
2. Refers to someone who has a lot of courage, heart or determination
3. To deliberately place yourself in a dangerous or difficult situation
4. Refers to the largest part, or largest share, of something
5. To subject someone to danger, or to place them in a difficult situation
6. To enter into a situation, where you will either have to face danger, or where you will be exposed to difficulty

A MONKEY'S UNCLE

A. 1. **Monkey** around
2. A **monkey** on/off <u>your</u> back
3. **Monkey** business
4. Make a **monkey** out of <u>someone</u>
5. If you pay peanuts, you get **monkeys**
6. **Monkey** see, **monkey** do

B. <u>Place the idioms correctly in the sentences below</u>

1. Ulf still carries _____ his _____ from when Sarah left him.

2. Our company pays the lowest wages, and then our bosses wonder why the workers are not motivated. _____.

3. Some people have the worst fashion, but what is more surprising, is that other people copy them. _____.

4. I _____ Sid on the basketball court. He guarded me all night, but I scored more points than anyone else.

5. I suspected _____ when the books weren't balanced, and I was right because Ted was caught embezzling money

6. The children were _____ with each other today, but I didn't mind, because it gave me some free time to use to relax.

C. Discussion

1. Has anyone ever tried to make a monkey out of you?
2. In terms of fashion sense these days, do you feel that it is a case of monkey see monkey do?

D. Meanings

1. To act or behave silly, foolish or inane
2. An emotional burden a person carries. When the burden is finally lifted, then the person has taken the monkey **off** their back.
3. Dishonest or suspicious activities
4. To do something that makes someone else look stupid, silly or idiotic
5. If low wages are paid, the quality of the staff will be low
6. A critical remark used when commenting on someone who copies another person's actions, without thinking through what actions they are copying

SHEEP AND GOATS

A. 1. **Scapegoat**
   2. Act the **goat**
   3. Get someone's **goat**
   4. Black **sheep** (of the family)
   5. Separate the **sheep** from the **goats**
   6. Like a **lamb** to the slaughter

B. Place the idioms correctly in the sentences below

1. Bob always _____ at parties, but I think that the parties would not be as enjoyable without him.

2. We had to _____ at the first basketball practice. Only the most talented boys were asked to come to the next practice.

3. The school's basketball team will be _____ when they play Rydal this weekend. Rydal hasn't lost a game in 2 years.

4. I became the _____ for the failures of the company because I was the one that the boss blamed at the last meeting.

5. Sarah is the _____. Her parents disapprove of how she neglects schoolwork, and everyone else does not like her choice of boyfriend.

6. Riley _____ my _____ most of the time. He really knows how to annoy me.

C. Discussion

1. Have you ever become the scapegoat for something that was not your fault?
2. Have you ever had to separate the sheep from the goats?

D. Meanings

1. A person that is unfairly blamed for something, even though he or she may not be at fault
2. To behave in a silly or inane way
3. To annoy someone
4. A person who is considered to behave badly, or to have their acts or actions disapproved of by the others in a group
5. To examine something, and then separate the good parts of it from the bad
6. To go somewhere unpleasant or dangerous, in a gentle way, and without protest, either because the person is not aware where he or she is being led, or because the person has no power to prevent the situation

SECTION 2 – CLOTHING

BOOTS

A. 1. Get the **boot**
   2. Put the **boot** in
   3. Be quaking in one's **boots**
   4. **Boots** and all
   5. Fill your **boots**
   6. Lick someone's **boots**

B. Place the idioms correctly in the sentences below

1. Tom _____ at work yesterday when he insulted the boss.

2. Jethro _____ the teacher's _____ for the whole semester.
   That's why he got the best mark in the class.

3. John kept _____ me for a long time, so that's why we
   fought the other day.

4. Organizing our class re-union was a big task, so the four of us had to get
   involved, _____.

5. We were _____ our _____ on the hiking trail when
   a large bear approached us.

6. Bob _____ his _____ at the buffet yesterday. He ate more
   food than anyone else.

C. Discussion

1. Has anyone or anything ever made you quake in your boots?
2. Name a time when you got totally involved in something, boots and all.

D. Meanings

1. To lose your job
2. To say something that is very critical or unkind
3. To be very frightened about something
4. To do something with a lot of energy and enthusiasm
5. To get as much of something as a person can
6. To suck up to a powerful person, or to say something nice to them, because
   you want to please them

21

CLOTHING 1

A. 1. **Button** your lip
    2. Have something up your **sleeve**
    3. Set your **cap** at someone
    4. Dead men's **shoes**
    5. The **gloves** are off
    6. Ride someone's **coattails**

B. Place the idioms correctly in the sentences below

1. Josh is quite fortunate because his uncle is the boss. He's therefore been able to _____ his uncle's _____ to the top.

2. Sid finds it difficult to _____ his _____ in sensitive situations, so she often gets into trouble.

3. When Thomas insulted me at dinner the other night, I told him _____ _____. I don't think anything can stop a fight between us now.

4. I never worry about Jane. You were all worried because you thought Jane wouldn't hand in the proposal on time, but I knew she would because Jane always _____ something _____ her _____.

5. I've been walking in _____ ever since I've started working here. It's time for me to move on and work for another company.

6. Sarah _____ her _____ at James the first time they met, so I'm not surprised that he finally proposed to her.

C. Discussion

1. Is it wise to ride someone's coattails in a place of work?
2. Name someone you know who was caught with his or her pants down.

D. Meanings

1. To keep silent, although there is a great urge to say something
2. To have a secret that can be used to gain an advantage over someone
3. Refers to a situation where a woman wants a man to notice her, and especially if she wants him to marry her
4. A situation where a person cannot make progress in their career
5. A reference to two people or two groups, who are prepared to fight or compete aggressively, often after a compromise has failed to be reached
6. To use a person, or a person's success, to get success for yourself

CLOTHING 2

A. 1. Tough as old **boots**
   2. On the **button**
   3. Put on your thinking **cap**
   4. Get your **knickers** in a twist
   5. By the seat of your **pants**
   6. On a **shoestring**

B. Place the idioms correctly in the sentences below

1. Uncle Bob is _____. He faced hard times growing up and in fighting in the war, so he has a very strong character.

2. I travelled Europe _____ and spent a lot less money than John. He travelled first class, but I think I had more fun than he did.

3. I passed the year _____ my _____. If I had scored any lower in any of my tests, then I would have failed the year.

4. Sarah's analysis was right _____.
   She summarized the problems with our firm very well.

5. I had to _____ my _____ for the Math test. It was the most difficult test I'd ever taken.

6. Joshua _____ his _____ whenever he sees his girlfriend talking with another guy.

C. Discussion

1. What thing makes you get your knickers in a twist?
2. What thing have you done on a shoestring?

D. Meanings

1. A person with strong character who does not get easily upset
2. Something that is exactly on time, or is the right amount of cash
3. To think deeply about a problem in order to solve it
4. To become very upset about something, or to worry too much about it
5. To achieve something, or to win something, by the thinnest of margins
6. To do undertake an activity, or to do something that requires the spending of money, while at the same time using very little money

23

HAT 1

A. 1. Eat your **hat**
   2. Go **hat** in hand to someone
   3. Picked out of a **hat**
   4. Throw your **hat** into the ring
   5. Old **hat**
   6. Pull a rabbit out of the **hat**

B. Place the idioms correctly in the sentences below

1. Our horse doesn't has no chance of winning the race. The odds for him to win is about the same as having his name _____.

2. I _____ at the meeting when my proposal won out over the boss's proposal. This shocked everyone, including me.

3. I hate to _____ to my relatives for money, but I have no choice now because I'm totally broke.

4. This music is _____. I wish they'd played more current songs.

5. I will _____ my _____ if our hockey team makes the playoffs.

6. He _____ his _____ when he announced that he was running for the mayor's office in the coming election.

C. Discussion

1. Have you ever pulled a rabbit out of your hat in one of your courses?
2. Would it be difficult for you to go hat in hand to one of your relatives?

D. Meanings

1. A reference to a particular thing that someone thinks will not happen. As an example, a person can say, "I will eat my hat if Jim passes the test", means that the person believes Jim has no chance of passing the test.
2. To very humbly ask someone else for help or for money
3. Refers to a random event, where the chance of any particular person winning or being chosen is completely random
4. To enter or take part in a contest or competition
5. Something that is out of date and not very original
6. To do something with the result that something is unexpectedly solved, or something is unexpectedly achieved

HAT 2

A. 1. All **hat** and no cattle
   2. Keep <u>something</u> under <u>your</u> **hat**
   3. Knock <u>something</u> into a cocked **hat**
   4. Pass the **hat** (around)
   5. Be talking through <u>your</u> **hat** **OR** Talk through <u>your</u> **hat**
   6. Take <u>your</u> **hat** off to <u>something</u>

B. <u>Place the idioms correctly in the sentences below</u>

1. I _____ my _____ to Kyle after the semester ended. I didn't think he'd do well in school, but he studied very hard, and he did very, very well.

2. We _____ the other team _____ because we beat them badly, even though their goalie kept them in the game early on.

3. We _____ at work to collect money for the flood victims.

4. Tom is _____. He looks like he an impressive athlete, but when he has the ball, he doesn't know what to do with it.

5. I told Alisha some secrets, but everyone knows about them now because Alisha can never _____ a secret _____ her _____.

6. The other team brags about what they have done, but they are just _____ their _____ because we always beat them.

C. <u>Discussion</u>

1. Talk about someone you know who is all hat and no cattle.
2. What do you think about people who often talk through their hat?

D. <u>Meanings</u>

1. To talk about something which at first seems impressive, but then you later realize that this thing is not as impressive as first thought
2. To keep something a secret, and not tell anyone else about it
3. When one thing knocks a 2nd thing into a <u>cocked hat</u>, then the 1st thing is much better than the 2nd thing
4. To collect money for something
5. To say silly or nonsensical thing
6. To express admiration for something that someone has done

PANTS and SHIRTS

A. 1. Caught with <u>your</u> **pants** down
   2. Beat the **pants** off <u>someone</u>
   3. Wear the **pants**
   4. Keep <u>your</u> **shirt** on
   5. The **shirt** off <u>your</u> back
   6. A stuffed **shirt**

B. <u>Place the idioms correctly in the sentences below</u>

1. My mom _____ in our family. She makes all of the important decisions.

2. The senator was _____ his _____ when the media exposed his affair with his secretary.

3. Our boss is _____. He should lighten up.

4. My son is extremely important to me. If he were in trouble, I would give him _____ <u>my</u> _____.

5. Andy has to learn to _____ <u>his</u> _____ in the meetings. He always gets angry, so he'll probably be fired if he doesn't stop.

6. I _____ <u>Sam</u> in tennis. I beat him in every game.

C. <u>Discussion</u>

1. Is there anyone you would give the shirt off your back for? Why?
2. Talk about one of your former teachers who is a stuffed shirt.

D. <u>Meanings</u>

1. To be caught in an embarrassing situation
2. To totally defeat another person in a competition or contest
3. To make all of the important decisions, usually in a relationship
4. To stop being angry and calm down
5. Signifies everything that a person owns
6. A formal and boring person

POCKETS

A. 1. Dig into <u>your</u> **pocket**
    2. In <u>someone's</u> **pocket**
    3. Have deep **pockets**
    4. Line <u>your</u> **pockets**
    5. Live in <u>each other's</u> **pocket**
    6. Out of **pocket**

B. Place the idioms correctly in the sentences below

1. I had to pay for the hotel _____ on my last business trip, but the company reimbursed me as soon as I got back.

2. The judge was _____ the mobster's _____. That's why most of them didn't receive jail time after the big trial.

3. I had to _____ my own _____ to pay for the X-mas decorations, because the boss said the company wouldn't pay for them.

4. The owner _____, so that's why we all got big X-mas bonuses.

5. The politicians who _____ their _____ illegally with taxpayer money are now all going to trial.

6. Cyd and Tim are an example of a couple who _____ each other's _____. They work together, and also golf and swim together.

C. Discussion

1. What do you think of others who put people in their pockets?
2. Does anyone in your family have deep pockets? Do they share their wealth?

D. Meanings

1. To pay for something with your own money
2. To control someone so they do whatever you want them to do
3. To have a lot of money
4. To make a lot of money dishonestly or unfairly
5. Refers to two people who spend a lot of time together
6. Refers to something that a person has to pay for at first, but then is reimbursed for later by their company, or their place of work

Marco Antonio Bussanich

SHIRT

A. 1. Bet your **shirt** on something
   2. The **shirt** off your back
   3. A stuffed **shirt**
   4. Keep your **shirt** on
   5. A hair **shirt**
   6. Lose your **shirt**

B. Place the idioms correctly in the sentences below

1. You don't have to wear _____, Jeremiah. Just because you're trying to save money, it doesn't mean that you can't have any fun.

2. Edgar finds it hard to _____ his _____ when he sees Bob. Edgar still cannot get over that fact that Bob bankrupted their business.

3. I know Jim's horse will win tonight, so I'm going to _____ my _____ his horse to win.

4. Jim loves his kids so much, he'd give them _____ his _____.

5. Tanya went to Las Vegas last week and _____ her _____. She lost so much money, so now she's in debt.

6. Our boss is _____. He's always much too serious.

C. Discussion

1. Has anyone in your family ever lost their shirt on an investment?
2. Talk about a former friend or teacher who was a stuffed shirt.

D. Meanings

1. To risk a lot of money on something, because you are certain it will succeed
2. Everything that a person owns
3. A boring or formal person
4. Something that is said to someone to calm them down, when they are upset or angry
5. If a person wears a hair shirt they choose to make their life unpleasant by not experiencing anything that can give them pleasure
6. To lose everything you have, either in an investment or through gambling

28

SHOES

A. 1. Waiting for the other **shoe** to drop
   2. Drop the other **shoe**
   3. If the **shoe** fits
   4. A goody two **shoes**
   5. In someone's **shoes**
   6. Step in someone's **shoes**

B. Place the idioms correctly in the sentences below

1. I don't know how I'd react if I was _____ Tom's _____. He handled the bad news about his uncle very well.

2. Many workers lost their jobs, so others are nervously _____ _____, as they fear everyone will lose their jobs when the new quarterly data on the company's performance comes in.

3. Elsa _____ into the boss' _____ admirably when he got sick.

4. I was upset when Sid criticized me for gossiping too much, but when Sue told me _____, I realized I had gossiped too much.

5. I _____ and finally completed the repairs to my kitchen.

6. No one likes how Ed sucks up to Ms. Lee to get better grades. He shows her he's _____, but he usually behaves poorly.

C. Discussion

1. Are people who behave as goody two shoes sincere?
2. Have you ever told someone, "If the shoe fits", when they were surprised by criticism that was leveled at them?

D. Meanings

1. To be waiting for a bad thing to happen, after another bad thing has already happened
2. To complete a task or chore by doing the last part of it
3. To tell someone, that unpleasant or unflattering remarks that have been made about them, are reasonable or truthful
4. To attempt to please a person in authority, often in a way that is looked on disapprovingly by other people
5. To describe how you might feel or act if you were in the same situation as another person
6. To do someone else's job

SOCKS

A. 1. Put a **sock** in it
   2. **Sock** it to someone
   3. Knock the **socks** off someone
   4. Knock someone's **socks** off
   5. Pull up your **socks**
   6. Work your **socks** off

B. Place the idioms correctly in the sentences below

1. I had to tell Todd to _____ last night because he was very drunk and was saying nasty things to people.

2. Tara _____ our boss's _____ with her presentation, so that's why she got a raise.

3. Jim had no choice put to _____ his _____. He failed all his courses last semester, so he has to have a different attitude now.

4. The Eagles _____ us last night. They beat us badly.

5. My father _____ his _____ all his life, so his pension pays very well.

6. The new movie is so good, so it _____ everybody's _____ when they see it.

C. Discussion

1. Does someone in one of your classes talk so much, that you wish you could tell that person to put a sock in it?
2. Has there ever been a time in your life when you were told to pull your socks up?

D. Meanings

1. To tell someone, in an abrupt way, to stop talking
2. To do something to someone in a very forceful way
3. To impress someone else
4. To be impressed by someone else
5. To imply that someone that they must improve their behavior
6. To work extremely hard

SECTION 3 – COLORS

BLACK

A. 1. Not as **black** as painted
   2. **Black** and **blue**
   3. **Black** and **white**
   4. In the **black**
   5. The new **black**
   6. A **black** cloud

B. Place the idioms correctly in the sentences below

1. Our company is now making profits. We're finally _____.

2. _____ has been hanging over Stanley lately. He's encountered a terrible streak of bad luck.

3. I was quite clumsy at home. I fell down the stairs and received a lot of bruises. My body is all _____.

4. Two door sports car are _____. They're so popular now.

5. When a person judges all things as being either _____ _____, then there is no way to make compromises with them.

6. When I learned about all the nice things that Sheila has done for other people, I realized that she was _____.

C. Discussion

1. Have you ever held a bad opinion about someone, only to later find out that the person was not as black as painted?
2. Does anyone you know judge things as being either white or black? Why do you think this person judges things this way?

D. Meanings

1. Refers to someone who is not as awful as other people think they are
2. To have a badly bruised body
3. To judge something in an extreme sense. The thing is either at one extreme or the other. There is no middle ground or mid point of view.
4. To be free of debt or to not owe any money to anyone
5. A thing or color is the new black if it is now fashionable
6. To be encountering a string of bad luck

BLUE

A. 1. Feel **blue**
   2. A bolt from the **blue**
   3. **Blue** blood
   4. Till you're **blue** in the face
   5. **Blue** collar
   6. Cuss a **blue** streak   ***   **A British Idiom**

B. Place the idioms correctly in the sentences below

1. Tony has been _____ ever since he lost his job.

2. It is very rare for a _____ to marry a commoner.

3. The news that Tom is not going to law school was like _____
   _____ for us. We always thought he'd become a lawyer.

4. The East side of town is a _____ neighborhood, so
   they usually vote for the Liberal candidate in elections.

5. I told Ed that he can ask us to raise his allowance _____ he's
   _____, but we will not raise his allowance.

6. When Bob gets drunk, he tends to _____.

C. Discussion

1. What things make you feel blue?
2. Talk about a situation when something hit you like a bolt from the blue.

D. Meanings

1. To feel sad or depressed
2. Something that happens unexpectedly, coming as a complete surprise
3. Refers to someone with royal or aristocratic blood or upbringing
4. Refers to a situation where a person tells someone something over and over
   again, without it having an effect on the other person
5. A person from the working class
6. To curse a lot

COLORS 1

A. 1. **Whiter** than **white**
   2. Out of the **blue**
   3. **Green** as grass
   4. In the **pink**
   5. See **red**
   6. A **red**-letter day

B. Place the idioms correctly in the sentences below

1. I _____ when Bob put his hand on my wife's shoulder.

2. I know that Tommy is _____, but he's bound to learn more as he gets older. Don't be so hard on him when he makes mistakes.

3. Tara is always _____. She's the healthiest person I know.

4. June 6 will always be a _____ for me, because that's the day I got married.

5. The news concerning Tim and June, and their pregnancy, is a shocker. It just came _____.

6. I've always suspected Sid of not being _____. I don't think he's as honest and moralistic as he paints himself to be.

C. Discussion

1. Can any one person really be whiter than white?
2. Is there a specific date that is a red-letter day for you?

D. Meanings

1. Refers to a person whose actions are completely moral and honest
2. Refers to something that happens unexpectedly
3. To have little experience, and to too easily trust what is told to you
4. To be very healthy
5. To become extremely angry, very suddenly, over something that has just taken place
6. Refers to a day when something important happens

COLORS 2

A. 1. Sailing under false **colors**
   2. Nail <u>your</u> **colors** to the mast   *******   **British Idiom**
   3. With flying **colors**
   4. **Color** <u>me something</u>
   5. Tickled **pink**
   6. In **black** and **white**

B. Place the idioms correctly in the sentences below

1. I _____ my _____ early on, when I threw my support behind the mayor. I've been loyal to him since day one.

2. I passed the test _____. I almost aced it!

3. Stan has been _____. He deliberately gave everybody false information so that he could win the contest.

4. _____ me a Seattle Seahawk. They're my favorite team.

5. The outcome of this game is laid out _____. There's no way the last place team will beat last year's champions.

6. I'm _____ that I have a new granddaughter. I love her so much. She's the cutest thing I've ever seen.

C. Discussion

1. Why do you think some people have to sail under false colors?
2. Can there be some danger in nailing your colors to the mast so obviously?

D. Meanings

1. To deliberately deceive other people
2. Refers to a person who states their opinions or beliefs very clearly and openly
3. To achieve something or accomplish something very easily
4. To state your preference quite clearly
5. To be extremely pleased about something
6. Refers to something that is so extremely and plainly obvious

COLORS 3

A. 1. **Brownie** points
   2. **Brown** as a berry
   3. **Green** with envy
   4. **Rose** tinted glasses
   5. **Silver** lining
   6. **Yellow** belly

B. Place the idioms correctly in the sentences below

1. I earned _____ with the locals. I took part in their traditional festival, so they were very appreciative of this.

2. The _____ in our loss was the unpopular coach was fired.

3. Tabatha's _____. I made the cheerleading squad and she didn't, even though she practiced much harder than I did.

4. Heath is a _____. I knew he would run away when we were confronted by the other gang last night.

5. I don't view the world in the same way as June does. She has _____ _____ on, and thinks everything will always turn out well.

6. Matilda has just returned from her Hawaiian vacation. She looks just fabulous. She's as _____.

C. Discussion

1. Is it a natural thing to feel green with envy over what others have, that you don't have?
2. If a student is helpful to the teacher, and receives brownie points, do you think the teacher will always give that person a better grade?

D. Meanings

1. To receive praise or admiration for doing something
2. To have skin that is very tanned, because you stayed out in the sun
3. To really covet something that another person has, so as to be very envious of this thing, or this person
4. A person whose viewpoint is unrealistic because he or she only notices good things, and not the bad things around them
5. One good thing, or one good aspect, of something, or of a situation, that is otherwise generally very bad
6. Refers to a person who is a coward, or who behaves in a cowardly way

SECTION 4 – DIRECTIONS

IN AND OUT

A. 1. **Out** of line
   2. **In** a flash/ **In** a jiffy
   3. **Out** of the woods
   4. **In** good with <u>someone</u>
   5. **Out** on a limb
   6. **In** good faith

B. <u>Place the correct idioms in the sentences below</u>

1. I'm _____ <u>Bob</u>. He shares all company secrets with me.

2. "I'm giving this loan to you _____. I hope you'll pay it back soon. The last time I lent you money, you didn't pay it back for 6 months".

3. Samantha: "Susan, I need those reports right away".
   Susan: "Ok, Samantha. I'll get them for you _____ ".

4. Tom has put himself _____. He parties too much and spends all his money. If he gets fired, he won't have money to support himself.

5. Jody was _____ at dinner last night. He was very drunk, and said many rude things to Christine.

6. Jackie is _____ now. She paid off all of her credit cards, and she's doing well on her other payments.

C. <u>Discussion</u>

1. How often do you see people get out of line when they get drunk?
2. Talk about someone you are in good with.

D. <u>Meanings</u>

1. To speak or behave outside of the boundaries of good taste
2. Something done very, very quickly
3. A person that has solved most of their problems, so that they are no longer in a precarious, difficult or dangerous situation
4. To have a relationship where a person trusts you, and because of this, the relationship may be beneficial to you
5. In a dangerous, precarious or untenable situation
6. When you do something in good faith, this means that you will be trusted to do what you say you will do

LEFT, RIGHT and CENTER

A. 1. Take **center** stage
2. Have two **left** feet
3. Out in **left** field
4. **Left, right** and **center**
5. **Right** as rain
6. **Right**-hand man

B. Place the idioms correctly in the sentences below

1. Jason really believes that aliens are going to come to Earth and destroy us. Jason's views on this are really _____.

2. I depend on Edgar more than anyone else realizes. Edgar is the best _____ I've ever had.

3. It's good to see that dad is _____ now, because he was very ill for a long time.

4. The post office has been losing customers _____ ever since the internet came out.

5. The view of the scientists who fear global warning are now being heard, and are _____.

6. Sue: Why did you turn Tom down when he asked you to the dance?
Pam: Tom's a nice guy, but I like to dance a lot. I couldn't have danced much with Tom because he _____.

C. Discussion

1. How many people in your family have two left feet?
2. Describe someone you know whose views on a particular matter are out in left field.

D. Meanings

1. To become the most significant person in a situation
2. Refers to someone who is not a good dancer
3. Refers to someone whose perceptions, expectations or outlooks are completely unrealistic or unattainable
4. A statement used to show that something is being done a lot
5. Refers to a person who is now healthy, after this person has gone through a long illness
6. A close assistant who is trusted by the boss

UP AND DOWN

A. 1. On the **up** and **up**
   2. **Up** and running
   3. **Up** against it
   4. **Down**
   5. **Down** and dirty
   6. **Down** the tubes (drain)

B. Use the idioms correctly in the sentences below

1. Our new business will do very well once it is _____.

2. Our economy is _____. I don't think it will recover.

3. I trust Sam completely. He's always _____.

4. Michelle is _____ with our plan. She will support it.

5. I think I am really _____ this semester. I haven't studied very much, so I do not think I'll do well on the exams.

6. I did not like the tone of the last election campaign. Too many of the politicians were _____.

C. Discussion

1. What important issues are you down for?
2. Describe a person you know who is always on the up and up.

D. Meanings

1. A person or thing that is honest or legal
2. Something that has started, and is functioning well
3. To have a very difficult situation or problem to deal with
4. To be supportive of something
5. A person that behaves in a rude, dishonest or unpleasant manner
6. Something that keeps getting worse, and that will not recover

WAY

A. 1. The easy **way** out
   2. Go back a long **way**
   3. Look the other **way**
   4. No **way**
   5. Pave the **way**
   6. Rub <u>someone</u> the wrong **way**

B. Place the idioms correctly in the sentences below

1. I can't abandon Jack, now that his wife has left him. We _____
_____, so I have to be there so that he has a friend to lean on.

2. You can't just _____ when your son steals money from
your purse. You have to talk with him and tell him to stop stealing.

3. There was _____ that I was going to help Tony cheat on the test.

4. Tom has a knack for _____(ing) <u>people</u> _____.
Everyone at work finds it difficult to deal with him.

5. Instead of trying to solve our problems, Johnny left me. It was cowardly for
Johnny to take _____.

6. People like Jackie Robinson _____ for people from visible
minorities to play in professional sports.

C. Discussion

1. Can you think of someone who went through difficult times, only to pave the way
for others to be successful.
2. Do you believe that it can become a habit to take the easy way out?

D. Meanings

1. Choosing an easy way to get out of a situation, even though this may not solve
the problem
2. Refers to two people who have been friends for a very long time
3. To ignore a bad situation, instead of dealing with the problem, in order to find a
solution to it
4. An emphatic way to say, "definitely not"
5. Refers to a first thing that has happened, making it easier for a second thing to
happen
6. Refers to a person who annoys someone else, often purposely

SECTION 5 – DIRTY

DIRT and DIRTY

A. 1. Dig up **dirt**
    2. Dish the **dirt** on <u>someone</u>
    3. Treat <u>someone</u> like **dirt**
    4. **Dirt**
    5. Do the **dirty** on <u>someone</u>
    6. Air your **dirty** linen in public

B. Place the idioms correctly in the sentences below

1. What's the _____ on the new guy? I've heard a lot of bad things so far.

2. Too many politicians _____ <u>on other politicians</u>. That's why I don't like election campaigns.

3. I don't like how Pamela was asking around about me. She's trying to ____ _____, so she can spread rumors and ruin my reputation.

4. Sheila _____ <u>on me</u> by spreading false rumors. Now I'm going to find it hard to get a date for the prom.

5. I don't like it when Tim _____ <u>his</u> _____. He always tells people his problems, but they don't want to hear about them.

6. Ken _____ his girlfriend _____. She should do the right thing and break up with him. It will be much better for her in the long run.

C. Discussion

1. Do some people enjoy spreading dirt about other people? Why is this so?
2. It is appropriate for someone to air their dirty laundry in public?

D. Meanings

1. To look for harmful information on someone
2. To tell other people harmful information about someone else
3. To treat someone very badly, or to betray them
4. Unpleasant or bad personal information
5. To betray someone, or treat them badly
6. To publicly talk about private matters that should be kept private

DUST

A. 1. Bite the **dust**
   2. The **dust** settle
   3. Eat someone's **dust**
   4. Gather **dust**
   5. Not see someone for the **dust**
   6. Shake the **dust** of some place off your feet

B. Place the idioms correctly in the sentences below

1. I'm happy I finally _____ my hometown _____
   _____. This city is more lively, and there are more jobs to be found.

2. Cam left town so fast, that I did _____ his _____.

3. His ideas were just _____ until he published his book.

4. Nearly all life forms will _____ if a big asteroid hits Earth.

5. Its good that we let _____ before talking about the
   breakup between Zack and Jill. Now we can think with clearer minds.

6. The Jamaican sprinter ran so fast, that all of the other competitors were
   _____ his _____ at the end of the race.

C. Discussion

1. Is better to let the dust settle after an argument, before trying to make peace with another person?
2. Have you ever shaken the dust of a place you didn't like to live in, off of your feet?

D. Meanings

1. Something that stops existing, fails or dies
2. To allow a pause or time of reflection after an argument or a big change
3. To be thoroughly defeated, or to be a long ways behind, a competitor
4. Something that sits unused or is not talked about for a long period of time
5. Refers to a person who has left a certain place very quickly
6. To leave a place behind forever

MUD

A. 1. Clear as **mud**
   2. Dragged through the **mud**
   3. Like a pig in **mud**
   4. **Mud** that sticks   **OR**   **Mud** has stuck
   5. A stick in the **mud**
   6. Throw **mud**

B. Place the idioms correctly in the sentences below

1. I'm _____ in my new job. I love it so much.

2. The politician had his personal life _____ because it was found that he had a number of affairs.

3. The old mayor was just _____. He never wanted to initiate any new programs, or change his philosophies.

4. I don't like Bret's attitude. He too often _____, and says bad things about nearly everyone.

5. People were saying bad things about Tom, so the _____.
Now most of us feel bad because all of those things were untrue.

6. The solution to this Math problem is as _____. Even the teacher does not know how to solve it.

C. Discussion

1. In which situations do you feel like a pig in mud?
2. Talk about an old teacher who you felt was a stick in the mud.

D. Meanings

1. Something that is very difficult to understand or comprehend
2. This happens when someone says bad things about a person, in an effort to ruin their reputation
3. Refers to someone who is extremely happy when doing a particular thing
4. Refers to a situation when something bad is said about someone, leading people to believe that it is true, even though it is not
5. A person who is dull, boring and doesn't not like to have fun, or try anything new or interesting
6. If a person throws mud, they say bad or harmful things about another person

SECTION 6 – EMOTIONS, FEELINGS AND PAIN

I'M ANGRY!

A. 1. Go **ballistic**
   2. Like a red flag to a **bull**
   3. Blow a **fuse**
   4. **Fury** drop
   5. **Lose** your **head**
   6. Go **postal**

B. Place the idioms correctly in the sentences below

1. Talking to Mike about his drinking and spending is _____
   _____. He doesn't like to discuss these things.

2. Bart did a _____ when he threw his remote at the TV,
   but he calmed down after that.

3. Ulf _____ on me when I tried to tell him that I saw his
   girlfriend on a date with another guy.

4. Ben exploded and _____ when his antique car was vandalized.

5. Many people in the building _____ their _____, and started to
   panic when the earthquake hit.

6. Ryan _____ at work when Vick accused him of theft.

C. Discussion

1. Why is difficult to keep her head when you are betrayed by a friend?
2. Do you feel that it is sexist to use the idiom, "Hell hath no fury like a woman's scorn"?

D. Meanings

1. To become very angry
2. Something that always makes a person, or an entity, very angry
3. To become angry and then be unable to control your anger
4. To throw or drop something in order to relieve stress
5. To lose your calm, and to panic, in a difficult situation
6. To express anger and lose control of your emotions

43

Marco Antonio Bussanich

OUCH, THAT HURTS 1!

A. 1. **Break** a leg
   2. **Bite** your lip
   3. **Belly-ache**
   4. **Fall** flat on your face
   5. **Take it** on the chin
   6. **Twist** my arm

B. Place the idioms correctly in the sentences below

1. Nobody had to _____ my _____ to convince me to go to the concert.

2. John usually _____ about the rain, but when it's hot, he starts to complain about that as well.

3. I _____ my _____ during exam period. I failed every exam!

4. Tommy _____ his _____ when the teacher asked him who broke the window, because Tommy did not want to be a rat.

5. Sean _____ when he learned he wasn't accepted to medical school. I was surprised how well he took the news.

6. I told Wilma to _____ before she went on stage, and my advice seemed to work, because she performed very well.

C. Discussion

1. Have you ever had to twist someone's arm to get what you wanted?
2. When was the worst time that you had to bite your lip, even though you really wanted to say something about the matter?

D. Meanings

1. To wish an actor or performer good luck, before he or she goes on stage
2. To be quiet about something, especially when you want to express your opinion on the matter
3. To consistently complain about something or someone
4. To fail embarrassingly when attempting to do something
5. To accept criticism or defeat in a very brave way
6. To try hard to persuade someone to do something

44

OUCH, THAT HURTS 2!

A. 1. **Ball** someone out
   2. **Bite** your head off
   3. **Bite** your tongue
   4. **Bust** your balls
   5. **Busting** your chops
   6. A taste of your own **medicine**

B. Place the idioms correctly in the sentences below

1. Why are you _____ my _____ Ted? I told you I wouldn't go to the prom with you. Could you please stop harassing me?

2. Jamie _____ his _____ when his father criticized him in front of everyone today, but I wouldn't have just stood there and said nothing.

3. My mother _____ me _____ last night for doing poorly in school. She yelled at me, and then she grounded me.

4. Kate got _____ her _____ when she heard others say bad things behind her back. She always does that to everyone else.

5. Shania _____ my _____ when I made fun of her in class. I didn't realize that what I did was doing was so hurtful to her.

6. Our competitor is trying to _____ our _____ by lowering their prices to the point that we can't compete. They're trying to make us go under.

C. Discussion

1. Talk about a time when you were given a taste of your own medicine.
2. Do you believe that it is a good or bad thing to ball children out when they do poorly in school?

D. Meanings

1. To castigate someone for something they did, by scolding them
2. To angrily reprimand someone for something they have done
3. To stop short of saying something that you really want to say
4. To harass someone with the intention of breaking their spirit
5. To say something to someone so as to harass them
6. To give someone the same bad treatment they have been giving you

Marco Antonio Bussanich

OUCH, THAT HURTS 3!

A. 1. Add **insult** to **injury**
  2. No **pain**, no gain
  3. A **pain** in the neck
  4. A **shot** in the arm
  5. A **slap** on the wrist
  6. Rub salt on old **wounds**

B. Place the idioms correctly in the sentences below

1. Tim added _____ when he tried to blame me for the car accident. I was injured, and it was his fault.

2. Ed's being _____. He won't stop teasing me about my grades.

3. I was fortunate when my parents only gave me _____ for coming home late. I thought they'd ground me but they only took away my phone privileges for a few days.

4. I work-out 7 days a week to stay fit. My motto is _____.

5. It _____ when people talk about my ex-girlfriend and how she dumped me.

6. Bob talked to me about my poor grades and gave me encouragement. It was _____ that made me feel better.

C. Discussion

1. Has anyone ever tried to rub salt in your wounds?
2. Discuss the difference between the idioms "a shot in the arm" and a slap on the wrist". Can they both achieve the same goal? Why or why not?

D. Meanings

1. Make a bad situation worse by doing another bad thing to someone
2. A person cannot achieve things unless they toil or work hard to get them
3. An annoying person
4. Give someone encouragement or help, for a difficult situation they are in
5. Punishment that is very mild, given the severity of the offence
6. Make a bad situation worse by talking about the difficulties in someone's past

SOFT, KIND and GENTLE

A. 1. **Soft** money
   2. A **soft** option
   3. **Soft** as shit
   4. A **gentle** giant
   5. In **kind**
   6. Kill <u>someone</u> with **kindness**

B. Place the idioms correctly in the sentences below

1. Although Kumar is as big as an ox, he's still _____.

2. Mr. Smith takes the _____ every year, and passes every student, because he doesn't like to deal with complaints from parents.

3. Farmer Bill does not like to accept cash payments for his crop. Instead, he likes to be paid _____.

4. It is not wise to become dependent on _____ because it is not always easy to make money without working hard for it.

5. Sid's _____ when it comes to his girlfriend. She can get him to do whatever she wants him to do.

6. Samantha has a problem with her father because he always _____ her _____. He even tests the bath water to make sure it is not too hot before she takes a bath.

C. Discussion

1. Do you know anyone that's a gentle giant? Talk about this person.
2. Do you feel it is such a bad thing to be killed with kindness?

D. Meanings

1. Money that is obtained without the use of much effort
2. The easiest or least painful option or choice available to a person
3. Refers to someone with a weak character, who can be easily pushed around
4. Refers to a person who is very big or large, but who is kind or gentle
5. To be paid for goods or a service, in goods or services, rather than money
6. To treat someone with too much kindness, especially when they do not want, or do not need, to be treated with this much kindness

TIRED, ASHAMED or WORN OUT

A. 1. Under a **cloud**
    2. **Down** in the **dumps**
    3. Wear <u>yourself</u> to a **frazzle**
    4. On the **fritz**
    5. **Hang** <u>your</u> **head**
    6. The **pits**

B. Place the idioms correctly in the sentences below

1. I'm _____ at work because my boss suspects me of stealing. It feels terrible to work under those conditions.

2. Many men in Japan or Korea _____ <u>themselves</u> _____ _____, because their employers always expect them to work overtime.

3. Dan is _____ <u>his</u> _____ these days because lost his job.

4. My workplace is _____. There's a lot back biting going on, and the boss is always mean to us.

5. I was _____ for years after my divorce, but I recently met someone who has perked me up.

6. My TV and DVD player have been _____, so I have nothing to watch at night when I'm at home.

C. Discussion

1. Have you ever worked or studied at a place where you were under a cloud?
2. Discuss the similarities or the differences in meaning between the idioms "Down in the dumps", and "Hang your head".

D. Meanings

1. Refers to someone who is not trusted because of recent behaviour
2. To feel very depressed
3. To become exhausted and tired through overwork
4. Refers to something that does not work well anymore
5. To feel ashamed or embarrassed for something you have done, or after a recent failure
6. Refers to something that is in low working order, or that is extremely bad

TREATED BADLY

A. 1. **Back-handed** compliment
   2. **Eat** someone alive
   3. Put the **knife** in
   4. Move in for the **kill**
   5. **Stab** someone in the back
   6. A **thorn** in your side

B. Place the idioms correctly in the sentences below

1. Tom will _____ Jim _____ tonight at the bar, when he confronts him over his affair with Sarah.

2. The coyote _____ when it saw the rodent was injured.

3. Sid's _____ my _____ in class. He likes to annoy me.

4. Ed pretends to be my friend, but when I met with the boss, I was told Ed always criticizes my effort and _____ me _____.

5. Sue was very rude at the party. She gave me false compliments, but I saw through her, and noticed they were _____.

6. I thought Sonia was my friend, but other people say she always says bad things about me. I now know that she has been _____ me _____.

C. Discussion

1. Does any family member always try to be a thorn in your side?
2. Have you ever received what you at first thought were compliments, but later realized that the compliments were just back-handed compliments?

D. Meanings

1. A comment which is critical, even though it at first seems complimentary
2. (a) To purposely say bad things, or do bad things, to another person, in order to cause them grief, pain or suffering
   (b) To decisively defeat an opponent
3. To deliberately say bad things to upset another person
4. To make a decisive, final move, in order to defeat an opponent
5. To betray someone, in a secret, non-overt way
6. Someone who continuously annoys or causes trouble for another person

SECTION 7 – FOOD

APPLES

A. 1. **Apple** of someone's eye
2. How do you like them **apples?**
3. As sure as God made little green **apples**
4. Upset the **apple** cart
5. Polish someone's **apples**
6. **Apple**-pie order

B. Place the idioms correctly in the sentences below

1. Tony loves Meg so very much. She's the _____ his _____.

2. It will only _____ if we let Tony help us plan the party. Its very difficult to agree with him on anything.

3. Jim blamed me for the loss of the money, but the boss knew it was Jim. When the boss fired Jim, I said to him, "_____".

4. _____, there's no way that I'll let Johnny drive my car when after he drinks.

5. Its obvious that Terry really likes Denise. Every time he sees her, he _____ her _____.

6. I was surprised when I visited Tom's apartment because everything was in _____.

C. Discussion

1. Is there someone you know who often upsets the apple-cart?
2. Does someone you know try to polish your apples?

D. Meanings

1. Refers to someone who is treasured and loved by someone else
2. A taunting comment, made to someone as a retort
3. Something that is 100% certain
4. To ruin someone's plans
5. To flatter someone else
6. Something that is very tidy and in proper order

BANANAS

A. 1. Go **bananas**
   2. Slip on a **banana** peel
   3. Second **banana**
   4. Go **bananas** over something
   5. **Banana** oil
   6. **Banana** republic

B. Place the idioms correctly in the sentences below

1. Leaders of _____ are corrupt, and are often the ones who keep their country in poverty.

2. Everyone's _____ the Gangnam Style dance. Everyone I know wants to learn how to do it.

3. Her speech was _____. She only said those things because she wants to get reelected. She has no intention on keeping her promises.

4. Tom _____ after he was benched by the coach. He's the star player and has never been benched before.

5. I don't like being _____ to Ethel. She always bosses me around and never respects my work.

6. The star soccer player _____ and was totally embarrassed when he accidentally scored on his own goal.

C. Discussion

1. Talk about a famous person who has slipped on a banana peel.
2. When was the last time you heard banana oil come from someone's mouth.

D. Meanings

1. Refers to a person who becomes very upset or angry
2. Refers to an important person who does something that makes them look foolish and which leads to problems for them
3. The next most important person in a group or organization
4. To become very enthusiastic about a particular thing
5. An insincere thing that is said in order to gain an advantage
6. A small, poor country with a corrupt government

EGGS

A. 1. Have **egg** on <u>one's</u> face
   2. **Egg** on
   3. Put all of <u>your</u> **eggs** in one basket
   4. Lay an **egg**
   5. Walk on **eggshells**
   6. A good **egg**

B. <u>Place the idioms correctly in the sentences below</u>

1. John is _____. We can always rely on him.

2. I _____ <u>my</u> _____ when I put all my money in one investment. I then lost everything when that investment went bad.

3. Its so easy to offend Samantha. I I always feel like I'm _____ _____ when I talk with her. Even the smallest things upset her.

4. I _____ in my presentation. I didn't persuade any of the other buyers to buy my product.

5. I _____ <u>my</u> _____ last night. The speech I gave to the guests was the worst speech I ever gave.

6. You shouldn't have _____ Jane at the party. She would never have taken drugs if you hadn't pushed her to do so.

C. Discussion

1. Describe the worst time that you laid an egg.
2. Why would it be a good strategy to put all of your eggs in one basket?

D. Meanings

1. Te become ashamed or embarrassed because of something you have done
2. To encourage someone to do something, which is a thing this person would not normally do
3. To put all of your efforts or all of your resources in one thing or place, so that you will not be able to do anything else if this one thing is not successful
4. To complete and utterly fail in an endeavor
5. A situation where someone has to be very, very careful in what they say or do, because that person does not want to offend or upset someone else
6. A kind, gentile, trustworthy or reliable person

FRUIT

A. 1. Bear **fruit**
   2. The **fruit** of <u>your</u> loin
   3. Forbidden **fruit**
   4. **Fruit** of <u>one's</u> labor
   5. Low-hanging **fruit**
   6. Stolen **fruit** is the sweetest

B. Place the idioms correctly in the sentences below

1. I want to go to the party, but there will be drinking, so my dad won't let me go. Drinking for me is _____ until I turn 19.

2. I didn't want to betray Todd and steal his girlfriend, but _____ _____, so I couldn't help stealing her from him.

3. My hard work is _____, because I aced the test.

4. I finally got to the see _____ my _____ when Sue entered college. I've worked hard to save money for Sue's education.

5. I could never abandon my children if they need help. It's very difficult to do anything but totally support _____ my _____.

6. Math has always been like _____ to me. I've always been able to ace any Math course I've ever taken.

C. Discussion

1. What thing has been like low-hanging fruit for you?
2. Do you agree that stolen fruit is the sweetest?

D. Meanings

1. Hard work, or some type of action that produces successful results
2. Your children
3. Something that a person wants very badly, but is forbidden to have
4. The successful results that come from hard work
5. Refers to things that are the easiest to get
6. This idiom implies that people particularly enjoy illicit things

FRUITS and VEGETABLES

A. 1. A bad **apple**
   2. A bowl of **cherries**
   3. Sour **grapes**
   4. Offer <u>someone</u> a **carrot**
   5. Meat and **potatoes**
   6. Two **peas** in a pod

B. Place the idioms correctly in the sentences below

1. My mom _____ <u>me</u> _____ to get me to do more homework. She said she will increase my allowance if I study more.

2. Its good that Sid got kicked out of school. Sid was _____, as he was starting to negatively influence other students.

3. Sue and Jim have the same interests. They're like _____.

4. Life's been _____ for Don after he won the lottery.

5. The _____ of all school curriculums is Math and English.

6. Jane's criticisms of Patricia are just _____. Jane would love to be as successful and glamorous as Patricia is.

C. Discussion

1. If you were a teacher, how would you deal with a bad apple in your class?
2. Is there anyone that you can say that you are two peas in a pod with?

D. Meanings

1. A dishonest, unpleasant person who has a bad influence on other people
2. Refers to a life or a lifestyle that is enjoyable and pleasant
3. Refers to a person who is bitter and jealous over other people's success, and who criticizes these other successful people
4. Offer an inducement, incentive or reward to others so as to influence them to make them do what you want them to do
5. The basic or important part of something
6. Refers to two people who have similar appearances or characteristics

IN THE KITCHEN

A. 1. The **cupboard** is bare
   2. Too many **cooks** spoil the **broth**
   3. Separate the **wheat** from the chaff
   4. Have someone for **breakfast**
   5. Know which side your **bread** is buttered
   6. **Bread** and **butter**

B. Place the idioms correctly in the sentences below

1. Tim _____ his _____, so he's respectable to his boss. He knows his status at work depends on his boss's approval.

2. I don't want my sons arguing, because John is much stronger and fiercer than Ted. John can _____ Ted _____.

3. The star players demonstrate their talents very early on in training camp. It then becomes easy to _____.

4. There were too many people working on the Engineering project, so it was bound to fail. _____.

5. The step and stutter move is the _____ move of the Lion's running back. Most of his success depends on that move.

6. I told Stuart that _____, but he still wants me to buy him that bike. I told him I have no money to buy it, though.

C. Discussion

1. Are there situations where too many cooks do not spoil the broth?
2. Talk about a style or fashion which is not your cup of tea.

D. Meanings

1. There is nothing more available because everything has been used up, whether this be money, or some other material thing
2. If too many people work on one thing together, then it will be hard to be successful, because all of the ideas of the different people can conflict
3. Decide what things are good or useful and which are not good or useful
4. Refers to someone who is much stronger or more aggressive than another person, meaning that the 1st person can dominate the 2nd person
5. To know who or what the best possible situation is for yourself, and then to know who to please in order to arrive at this situation
6. A person's most important source or income, or most important talent

Marco Antonio Bussanich

KITCHEN UTENSILS

A. 1. Twist the **knife**
   2. You could cut the atmosphere with a **knife**
   3. The **knives** are out
   4. A greasy **spoon**
   5. The wooden **spoon**
   6. Stick a **fork** in it

B. Place the idioms correctly in the sentences below

1. Pam _____ further into me when she kept talking about my ex-boyfriend at the party last night.

2. Brad gets _____ for coming in last in the race.

3. Fran is overweight because she always eats at _____.

4. We all went vey quiet when Jill and Tom were arguing at the party. It was so tense, you _____.

5. I told Mike to _____ when he wouldn't stop talking about my financial problems at dinner.

6. _____ for me at work. Everyone feels I should be held responsible for the loss of the account.

C. Discussion

1. Have the knives ever been out for you, or for a close friend of yours?
2. Have you ever told anyone to stick a fork in it?

D. Meanings

1. A saying that people use to inflict more pain on a person who is already experiencing difficulties
2. Implies that the atmosphere in a particular place or situation is very tense
3. A situation where people are trying to criticize and/or cause further problems for a person
4. A type of diner that specializes in fried food
5. A prize people get when they are worst or last in a particular activity
6. Advice given to someone who should cease doing a particular thing

56

MEALS AND COOKING

A.
1. Done like **dinner**
2. **Food** for thought
3. **Fried**
4. **Steamed**
5. There's no such thing as a free **lunch**
6. Out of the **frying pan** and into the fire

B. Place the idioms correctly in the sentences below

1. I was really _____ at the party when I saw Ted make a pass at my wife.

2. When Edna broke off with Ted and started dating Bill, she went _____
_____, because Bill is even worse than Ted.

3. Tom was _____ when he tried to take on the boss.
He should have known that he'd get fired for doing that.

4. If the city builds the bridge, then our taxes will go up. You should know
that _____.

5. Watching the travel video gave me _____ for my next trip.

6. Sid was totally _____ at the party. It was obvious that he took a lot
of drugs.

C. Discussion

1. Talk about something that you recently heard that gave you food for thought about
some important issue.
2. Do you believe that there's no such thing as a free lunch?

D. Meanings

1. To be defeated by an opponent, in a way that may be unfair
2. If something is food for thought, it makes you think very deeply about it
3. To be stoned on drugs, or to get very drunk by drinking alcohol
4. To be in a very angry state
5. A person cannot expect to get things for free
6. To go from a bad situation to an even worse situation

TEA and COFFEE

A. 1. **Coffee**-table book
   2. Wake up and smell the **coffee**
   3. **Tea** and sympathy
   4. Not for all the **tea** in China
   5. Tempest in a **teapot**
   6. Not my cup of **tea**

B. Place the idioms correctly in the sentences below

1. Sue should _____. She can't expect Tom to do all of her homework for her, because she will never learn anything.

2. Tim has a lot of books, but they all seem to be _____. I think he just puts them on display so that other will think he reads a lot.

3. Jim and Bob argue a lot, but the things they argue about are very trivial. The issues in their arguments are _____.

4. Horror films are _____. I prefer fantasy movies.

5. All I could offer Jim was _____ after he failed the year, but it seemed that talking his problems out with him helped a lot.

6. I'd never betray my best friend, _____.

C. Discussion

1. Is it sometimes difficult to find someone to offer you tea and sympathy, especially when you need someone to talk to?
2. Talk about a school subject which is not your cup of tea.

D. Meanings

1. A book that is more suited for display rather than for being read
2. To tell someone to be become more realistic and/or aware of the realities about themselves
3. The kindness and sympathy you show to someone who is upset
4. To let it be known that you will not do a certain thing, no matter what
5. Something that is blown out of proportions, as it is not important
6. Something that is not a person's preference

VEGETABLES

A. 1. Red as a **beet**
2. As cool as a **cucumber**
3. Know <u>your</u> **onions**
4. Couch **potato**
5. Hot **potato**
6. **Veg** out

B. Place the idioms correctly in the sentences below

1. Our quarterback is _____, even in the biggest games.

2. If you want to know the answer, go and ask Tammy. When it comes to Math, she really _____ her _____.

3. I've worked very hard lately, so on the weekend, I'm going to do nothing but _____.

4. The reason that Dan is out of shape is that he's a _____. All he does in his spare time is watch TV.

5. Will's face turned as _____ when he was caught stealing.

6. Passing laws to protect the environment has been a _____ issue for most politicians because jobs will be lost with these laws.

C. Discussion

1. Are you as cold as a cucumber when you are under pressure?
2. Is there a subject or issue in which you really know your onions?

D. Meanings

1. To blush because you have been embarrassed
2. To be calm and relaxed, especially under pressure
3. To know a lot about a particular thing
4. A lazy person who watches TV a lot
5. A delicate issue that people cannot agree upon
6. To take it easy, and to relax

WATER

A. 1. Blown out of the **water**
   2. Dead in the **water**
   3. In deep **water**
   4. In hot **water**
   5. Like **water** off a duck's back
   6. Not hold **water**

B. Place the idioms correctly in the sentences below

1. Your theory does _____. It's been proven by many scientists that second hand smoke can still cause lung cancer.

2. Carl is _____ now, because he crashed his dad's car.

3. My chances of attending law school have been _____ _____ after I scored a low mark on the LSAT.

4. Media criticism doesn't bother me, because what they are saying is false. Their criticisms are _____ to me.

5. The politician's chances of getting reelected are _____ _____ after it was found he misused the party's re-election funds.

6. Joel is _____ with his mortgage. He could barely make payments before, but he is in worse shape now that he lost his job.

C. Discussion

1. Discuss a time when you were in hot water with your parents.
2. Does criticism from your friends bother you, or is it like water off a duck's back for you when you receive such criticism?

D. Meanings

1. Refers to something that is destroyed or defeated completely
2. Refers to someone or something that failed and no longer works
3. To be in trouble, or to be in a difficult or dangerous situation
4. To have done something wrong, with the result that others are angry at you
5. A reference to criticism that does not have any effect on the person that is being criticized
6. A theory or argument that is incorrect, or can be proven to be incorrect

SECTION 8 – HEAVEN, HELL and THE SUPERNATURAL

DEATH

A. 1. At **death's** door
2. **Death** and taxes
3. Fight to the **death**
4. Come back from **death's** door
5. A living **death**
6. Sign someone's (or your own) **death** warrant

B. Place the idioms correctly in the sentences below

1. I feel like I'm in a _____ with James over the plan to pave the streets. He just doesn't want to give in on his position.

2. I thought for sure that my grandfather was going to die, but he has miraculously recovered. He has _____.

3. Our mayor _____ his _____ when he had affairs with women at work. Someone was bound to find out about them.

4. When my wife left me, it was _____. I didn't want to go on after that.

5. Your daughter will eventually get a boyfriend, there is no way to avoid that. It's just like _____.

6. My grandfather is _____ now. He doesn't have much time to live.

C. Discussion

1. Were you ever in a fight to the death over something?
2. Did you ever feel at one time you were signing your own death warrant?

D. Meanings

1. Refers to a person that is very ill, and that will soon die
2. When something is compared to death and taxes, this mean this thing is impossible to avoid
3. Refers to something in which a person has to fight extremely hard in order to avoid losing something
4. Refers to someone who has recovered from a very, very serious illness
5. Refers to someone whose quality of life is very low
6. To cause someone else's ruin, or to cause your own ruin

61

THE DEVIL

A. 1. A **devil** of a job
   2. Better the **devil** you know
   3. Play **devils** advocate
   4. The **devil** take the hindmost
   5. Speak of the **devil**
   6. Between the **devil** and the deep blue sea

B. Place the idioms correctly in the sentences below

1. I _____ in the debate today because I thought it was important to provide counterargument to Sarah's ideas.

2. Well, _____. We were just talking about you John.

3. I am caught _____. If I support my son, I will hurt my daughter's feelings. If I support my daughter, I will hurt my son's feelings.

4. Renovating my house is going to be _____. The house is quite old, so it will take a lot of money and effort to do the job.

5. I am keeping my doctor, even though I am not totally happy with him. If I go to a new one, that doctor may be even worse. _____.

6. Don't worry about the other employees Jen. You should do what is best for you, and discuss these issues with the boss. _____.

C. Discussion

1. Discuss something you were required to do, that was a devil of a job.
2. Have you ever had to play devil's advocate with a friend?

D. Meanings

1. A job that is very difficult to do
2. You would rather deal with a person that you already know, rather than someone you don't know, because the other person may be worse
3. To purposely disagree with someone to make people think deeply about a topic, or to make a discussion more interesting
4. To do what is best for yourself, without considering anyone else's interests
5. Used when someone you have been talking about suddenly appears
6. Used when a person is in a difficult situation, and where 2 equally difficult courses of action are either difficult or bad

DREAM

A. 1. The American **Dream**
   2. A **dream** ticket
   3. Like a **dream**
   4. Work like a **dream**
   5. Beyond <u>your</u> wildest **dreams**
   6. In <u>your</u> **dreams**

B. <u>Place the idioms correctly in the sentences below</u>

1. I'm receiving a very high salary now, something that I thought would be _____ my _____.

2. I was hoping _____ would happen to me and it has. I started my business with little money, and now it's booming.

3. This new blender _____. It can puree anything I put in it.

4. Pam's dance lessons really paid off. She dances _____ now.

5. Adam wants to date me, but I never will date him. I told him that the only place that this can happen is _____ his _____.

6. The president and vice president of the company are _____ _____. I've never seen two people work so well together

C. Discussion

1. Has anything happened to you that was beyond your wildest dreams?
2. Does anything you own not work like a dream?

D. Meanings

1. An idea from America that states that anybody can achieve success, no matter how poor they are or were in the beginning
2. A pair who it is thought will be very successful working together, especially in the field of politics
3. To do something very well, or a reference to something that works very well
4. Something that works very well or is done very well
5. Something that is much better than can ever be hoped for
6. A saying that implies that some thing will never happen, or, that it will happen only in their dreams

GHOSTS and SCARY THINGS

A. 1. Give up the **ghost**
   2. A **ghost** of a chance
   3. White as a **ghost**
   4. Afraid of <u>your</u> own **shadow**
   5. A **skeleton** in <u>your</u> closet
   6. Like a **bat** out of hell

B. Place the idioms correctly in the sentences below

1. I _____ and stopped trying to impress Tanya. I finally realized that she had no feelings for me.

2. Figo is _____ his _____. There's no chance he'll approach Dorothy, and ask her to dance.

3. May became _____ when she hit the deer with her car. She didn't mean to, so it really frightened her.

4. There's only _____ that I'll finish my essay on time. I started researching it too late, so I didn't leave myself enough time.

5. Sarah is not as perfect as everyone thinks. If I dig deep enough, I know I will be able to find _____ her _____.

6. I ran _____ when the farmer saw me picking his fruit. There was no way I was going to let him catch me.

C. Discussion

1. Do you think that everyone has the same type of skeleton in their closet?
2. Talk about something that you gave up the ghost in doing.

D. Meanings

1. To stop doing something because you can no longer succeed
2. Something that you have very little chance in completing, or succeeding in
3. To look pale and white, because you are very, very frightened
4. Refers to a person who is very nervous or anxious, and very, very shy
5. A secret that a person would like to keep secret, because it would cause a great deal of embarrassment if it were revealed
6. Refers to a place that someone goes to very quickly, or to something that happens, or that is done, very, very quickly

BUT FOR THE GRACE OF GOD

A. 1. On the side of the **angels**
   2. Play **God**
   3. **God's** gift to <u>something</u>
   4. Take <u>something</u> as **gospel**
   5. Saving **grace**
   6. Not have a **prayer**

B. <u>Place the idioms correctly in the sentences below</u>

1. I do _____ to make the basketball. All players from last year are returning, and they won our province's championship.

2. His _____ is that he does go to church. He therefore still has a chance to redeem himself for all his bad behaviour.

3. I _____ Paula's promise _____, that she'd stop drinking, but now I've found that she's still drinking.

4. Jake thinks he's _____ <u>to women</u>, but the women that I talked to think Jake's too conceited.

5. Doctors believe they have the right _____, but I believe it's ultimately the family's decision to end a terminally ill relative's life.

6. I'm _____ when it comes to protecting the homeless and offering them shelter.

C. <u>Discussion</u>

1. Why do you think that some men think they are God's gift to women, when in fact, they are actually not?
2. Do you take everything your best friend tells you as gospel?

D. <u>Meanings</u>

1. To do, or to support, the morally correct course of action
2. To believe that you have the ultimate say in saving or taking a person's life
3. Refers to someone who thinks they are the best in doing something, or are very skilled in it
4. To believe that something is 100% true, when in actuality, it is not
5. A redeemable quality in a person that prevents them from being totally bad
6. Refers to the fact that someone has no chance to complete or accomplish a certain task

HEAVEN 1

A. 1. In seventh **heaven**
2. Move **heaven** and earth
3. The **heavens** open
4. Like manna from **heaven**
5. Stink to high **heaven**
6. A marriage made in **heaven**

B. Place the idioms correctly in the sentences below

1. I want the students to take the attitude that they will _____ _____ to make sure that they all pass this test.

2. I didn't have an umbrella when _____, so I got soaked.

3. I've never seen a couple get along as well as Bob and Terra do. There's is _____.

4. This pig farm _____. Let's get out of here!

5. The extra money for the X-mas bonus was _____. I didn't expect to get this money, especially at a time that I really needed it.

6. I'm _____ now that I'm dating Michelle.

C. Discussion

1. Name a time when the heavens opened unexpectedly.
2. When have you moved heaven and earth to make something happen?

D. Meanings

1. Refers to someone who is extremely happy or content
2. Do everything possible to make sure something happens
3. When it begins to rain very heavily
4. Refers to a situation where a person gets something that they really need, but when they are not expecting to get it
5. To smell horribly bad
6. A very happy and harmonious marriage

HEAVEN 2

A. 1. Stink to high **heaven**
   2. **Heaven** forbid
   3. **Heavens** to Betsy!
   4. In **heaven's** name
   5. **Heaven** help us
   6. A match made in **heaven**

B. Place the idioms correctly in the sentences below

1. The city's deal with the coal company _____.
   I'm sure the coal company bribed politicians to get their smelter built.

2. _____! What was that loud noise?

3. The merger between the steel company and the automobile company is
   _____. They can work much better together now.

4. _____if my daughter tries to date the quarterback!
   I won't allow it, because he already has so many girlfriends.

5. _____ if the oil pipeline gets approval. One oil spill will
   destroy most of the sea creatures in the sea.

6. _____, who chose to watch this movie? Its terrible!

C. Discussion

1. Have you ever thought that a specific situation stunk to high heaven, and then
   had your suspicions confirmed when you found that you were right?
2. Talk about a specific match that you thought was made in heaven.

D. Meanings

1. A suspicious situation where someone feels that something is very wrong
2. A strong statement regarding a person's feelings that they will do anything
   possible to prevent some particular thing from happening
3. A proclamation of extreme surprise
4. A statement used to question why people are doing a particular thing
5. A statement where a person feels that a situation is hopeless, so that
   intervention from heaven is the only thing that can remedy the problem
6. Refers to the very happy and harmonious union between two entities

HELL

A. 1. All **hell** breaks loose
2. Go to **hell** and back
3. A living **hell**
4. Raise **hell**
5. There'll be **hell** to pay
6. Until/when **hell** freezes over

B. Place the idioms correctly in the sentences below

1. My life's been _____ since my spouse passed away.

2. _____ if Sarah isn't home by 10 PM.

3. We've _____ working on this new proposal, because if it fails, then our company could go bankrupt.

4. _____ at the game when the other team hurt Tom. He's our best player, and there was no way we'd let them get away with that.

5. The only time that I'll admit that Roger is a better athlete than me is _____.

6. Soccer fans sometimes _____ before their team plays.

C. Discussion

1. Have you ever witnessed a situation where all hell broke loose?
2. What is the difference between the idioms "Go to hell and back", and "A living hell"?

D. Meanings

1. A situation that is uncontrollable, often with a lot of fighting and/or arguing
2. To have a terrible experience
3. An extremely unpleasant place or situation
4. To cause trouble, especially when a person gets drunk, with the person destroying things or causing property damage
5. A warning issued to someone if they don't do something, or, if they do something that is essentially forbidden
6. (a) Refers to something that a person thinks will not happen
   (b) Refers to something that a person thinks will happen for a very, very long time, or that will happen forever

POSITIVE ENERGY

A. 1. Pleased as **punch**
   2. In the **groove**
   3. The land of **milk** and **honey**
   4. **Nice** as pie
   5. **Reach** for the **sky**
   6. The **sky's** the limit

B. Place the idioms correctly in the sentences below

1. I've been _____ at work ever since I took the self-help course. It really helped me to define my goals and to be more positive.

2. Tamara is as _____. I never expected her to be so nice.

3. I love working with Sonia, because for her, _____. We always accomplish a lot because her positive energy rubs off on me.

4. The United States has always been _____, but at the moment, other countries in Asia are doing better economically.

5. Claudia is _____ about her daughter's high exam scores. That's why Claudia is taking her to Disneyland.

6. My mother told me to _____ and go after my dreams. It was her encouragement that helped me get through law school.

C. Discussion

1. Is there someone you know who is the bee's knees and is as nice as pie?
2. Discuss the difference in meaning between the idioms "Reach for the sky", and "The sky's the limit".

D. Meanings

1. To be very pleased about something
2. To perform well at something
3. A prosperous land with abundant resources, and a lot of jobs
4. Refers to someone who is friendly, pleasant and gracious
5. To be ambitious, and give a lot effort in accomplishing a difficult thing
6. A motto that states that anyone can be very successful at what they do

SECTION 9 – IMPLEMENTS

BOX

A. 1. The first out of the **box**
   2. Black **box**
   3. A **box** of birds   ***   **British Idiom**
   4. Come out of the **box**
   5. Out of your **box**   ***   **British Idiom**
   6. Think outside of the **box**

B. Place the idioms correctly in the sentences below

1. I wish I was as in good shape as Joanie is. She's _____.

2. The grade ones are _____ in a slow, measured way this year. The new teacher is not doing a very good job.

3. The most successful companies _____ _____. They always come up with new and innovative ideas.

4. The workings of the company are virtually a _____. No one knows who makes the decisions, or how the company operates.

5. Microsoft is usually _____ when it comes to inventing new computer software.

6. The killer was definitely _____ his _____ when he committed his crimes. A normal person wouldn't have done what he did.

C. Discussion

1. Describe someone you know who is good at thinking outside of the box.
2. Is it always necessary to know how something operates in order to know how to use it? (Hint: do people have to know how computers operate in order to successfully use them? Try to think of other examples as well).

D. Meanings

1. To be the first person to do something
2. A reference to something that produces an output or a result, but without knowing how the output or result is obtained
3. A reference to someone who is very healthy
4. A reference to how someone or something starts an activity or process
5. A reference to someone who is very drunk, stupid, or who acts foolishly
6. To have new or revolutionary ideas

FLAGS

A. 1. A red **flag**
   2. Fly the **flag**
   3. Keep the **flag** flying
   4. Wrap yourself in the **flag**
   5. Run something up the **flagpole**
   6. Is like waving a red **flag** before a bull

B. Place the idioms correctly in the sentences below

1. I'm going to _____ this new idea _____ in the meeting and see what others in the firm think about it.

2. Very often, talking about history in a social situation _____ _____. Historical issues are often very sensitive.

3. I'm going to _____ and support our troops over-seas. I'll continue to support the troops until their mission is over.

4. We should all _____ for our country on July 4th, to show support for the President.

5. Joe's poor performance in the first exam should have been _____ _____. We should've taken it as a sign that he'd do poorly later on.

6. I don't trust the senator when he says he supports our troop's mission. He is just _____ himself _____ to gain political support.

C. Discussion

1. In which situations is it useful to run things up the flagpole?
2. What red flags are you good at predicting or forecasting?

D. Meanings

1. A warning about an impending bad situation
2. When someone flies their flag, they are showing support for their country, or for a group they belong to
3. To do something to show continued support for your country, or support for something else you believe strongly in
4. A person who tries to make others believe he is doing something good for the country, when he is really just doing it for his own political benefit
5. To make a suggestion about something, to find out people's opinions on it
6. To stalk about sensitive issues, or do an offensive thing, so as to make a person, or group of people, angry

ROPE

A. 1. Give <u>someone</u> enough **rope** to hang <u>themselves</u>
   2. At the end of <u>one's</u> **rope**
   3. Money of/for old **rope**
   4. Learn the **ropes**
   5. On the **ropes**
   6. Show <u>someone</u> the **ropes**

B. Place the idioms correctly in the sentences below

1. Elsa's usually _____ her _____ by dinner time. The twins are very active all day, so its very stressful caring for them.

2. Mark was _____ for most of the basketball game. He had to guard the other team's best player, so it was a difficult assignment.

3. The interviewer wanted to see how I'd do under pressure. He _____ <u>me</u> _____ <u>myself</u>, so I didn't do very well.

4. I had an easy time learning the new job because Todd _____ <u>me</u> _____ before I had to handle any difficult tasks by myself.

5. My job as a security guard is _____ most of the time, because all I do is sit in a chair most nights.

6. Don't worry if you had a tough first day on your new job. It always takes time to _____.

C. Discussion

1. Do you often find yourself at the end of your rope when dealing with a particular person?
2. What are the benefits of learning the ropes on your own, rather than having someone else show you the ropes?

D. Meanings

1. To give someone the freedom they want, because you know they are likely to fail in their endeavor
2. To be no longer able to handle or deal with a difficult situation
3. An easy way to earn money
4. To learn how to do something
5. Refers to someone who is very close to failing or being defeated
6. To show someone how to do a particular job or task

STICK

A. 1. Carry a big **stick**
   2. Get the short end of the **stick**
   3. Make something **stick**
   4. Get a lot of **stick**
   5. More things than you can shake a **stick** at
   6. **Stick** in your throat

B. Place the idioms correctly in the sentences below

1. The policeman was able to _____ the charges _____ in court, which meant that the criminal was found guilty.

2. She's always a _____, because she knows how to push my buttons and make me angry.

3. I usually _____ from the boss, even if I'm not at fault for what goes wrong in the office. I should complain to head office.

4. The US president _____ whenever he goes into negotiations with anyone else.

5. I always _____ when Renaldo hands out our assignments. He always gives me the most difficult ones to do.

6. My car has _____ features _____ _____ in this car. I can't believe how many features are included in this model.

C. Discussion

1. Talk about someone who is a stick in your throat.
2. Why do certain people always seem to get the short end of the stick?

D. Meanings

1. To have a lot of power, and to be able to use that power to get what you want
2. To be in an inferior or worse position than others around you
3. To continue to make something successful or effective
4. To be blamed a lot for something, even if you are not at fault
5. Have an inordinately large number of things
6. Refers to someone that is annoying you

STONES AND ROCKS

A. 1. Leave no **stone** unturned
2. Kill 2 birds with 1 **stone**
3. Hit **rock** bottom
4. **Rock** the boat
5. **Rock**, **rocks**, **rocked**
6. Set in **stone**

B. Place the correct idioms in the sentences below

1. Joe _____ when he bought his wife a TV for Christmas. His wife loves the TV, and Joe can also watch sports on it.

2. I don't think we should _____ now. We've had a lot of success lately. We don't need to make any changes now.

3. Sarah: How was the concert last night, Jane?
Jane: The concert was awesome. It really _____!

4. My mother's ideas are completely _____. There's no way that she'll change her mind and allow me to go to the party.

5. The police claim that they will _____ in their efforts to find the thief.

6. Jeremy has _____. He lost his job, he is bankrupt, and now he's in jail.

C. Discussion

1. Discuss a situation where you have killed 2 birds with 1 stone.
2. Is it advantageous to occasionally rock the boat?

D. Meanings

1. Use every possible method, or spare no efforts, in solving a problem
2. To solve 2 problems, with one solution
3. To reach such a low level in either your personal life, or in a particular situation, so that the person can go no lower
4. To try to bring tumultuous change to a stable situation
5. Refers to something or someone that is totally awesome
6. Something that has been decided upon and that is now unchangeable

STRAW

A. 1. The **straw** that breaks the camel's back
2. A **straw** in the wind
3. The last **straw**
4. Draw the short **straw**
5. Draw **straws**
6. Grasp at **straws**

B. Place the idioms correctly in the sentences below

1. The senator's poor handling of the budget was _____
_____. That's the reason he didn't get re-elected.

2. We can't decide which of us will pay for the broken plates. Lets _____
_____, because that's the only way we're going to settle this.

3. Cam is _____ if he thinks he can beat me at
tennis. He's never won a game against me yet.

4. Elmer _____, so he had to take out the garbage.

5. When Pam came home late last night, that was _____
_____. I had to ground her because of all of the bad things she's done.

6. The flowers are starting to bloom now. This is but the latest _____
_____ that spring is finally here.

C. Discussion

1. Name a time when you had to straws to decide something.
2. Are the idioms "the straw that breaks the camel's back", and "the last straw",
almost identical in meaning?

D. Meanings

1. The last event, in a series of events, that makes something untenable, or that
makes something fail
2. A sign, or an omen, which signifies the way that things will go
3. The latest event, in a series of events, that makes a person unable to deal with
a particular situation any longer
4. To be the person that is chosen to do something, from amongst a group of
people, that nobody else in the group wants to do
5. To which person, from a group of people, will do a particular thing
6. Try to desperately do something a person has little chance to succeed in

75

STRING

A. 1. Add another **string** to your bow
   2. Have someone on a **string**
   3. Pull **strings**
   4. Pull the **strings**
   5. With no **strings** attached
   6. With **strings** attached

B. Place the idioms correctly in the sentences below

1. I didn't realize that my girlfriend _____ me _____ until my best friend talked it over with me.

2. Tom's help usually comes _____. If he does you a favor, he'll expect something in return.

3. Audrey _____ her _____ when she studied photography. This will supplement her main skill, which is drawing.

4. Sid _____to get me a membership to the yacht club.

5. My mother's help came _____ before, but now she helps less because she wants me to be more independent.

6. The senator's assistant worked behind the scene and _____ _____, which helped the senator get his legislation passed.

C. Discussion

1. Talk about another string you added to your bow recently.
2. Has anyone ever pulled strings to help you get what you wanted?

D. Meanings

1. To add an extra skill that a person can use if their primary skill is unsuccessful
2. To have the ability to make someone do whatever you want them to do
3. To use connections or friendships that a person has with powerful people, to get what they want
4. To control someone, without other people noticing what you are doing
5. An offer that **DOES NOT** require a reciprocal favor or act in return
6. An offer that **DOES** require a reciprocal favor or act in return

SECTION 10 – LIFE AND LIVING

ALERT, ALIVE and KICKING

A. 1. **Alive and kicking**
   2. An eager **beaver**
   3. **Fresh** as a daisy
   4. In a **blaze** of **glory**
   5. **Loaded** for **bear**
   6. **Riding high**

B. Place the idioms correctly in the sentences below

1. Jim's _____ now that he's back from vacation. He's working a lot of overtime, so he can get time off and go another vacation.

2. Tom's _____ now that he's living on campus. The girls really like him, and he's doing very well in school.

3. Loretta is _____ now that she works less hours. She looks refreshed and lively all the time, and is not tired anymore.

4. Samantha's really _____. She finished all her homework, and now she's doing the dishes.

5. My dad's 92 and is still _____. He still exercises everyday, and goes out dancing twice a week.

6. Dick wants to go out _____ and win the championship in his last year as coach of the hockey team.

C. Discussion

1. Have you ever been loaded for bear with regard to an important event?
2. Do you like to do things in a blaze of glory in front of friends?

D. Meanings

1. To still be active, alive, and well
2. A person that is an eager worker, and who wants to please others
3. Awake, alert, and full of energy
4. To do something successfully, and in a very impressive way
5. Refers to someone who is eager to start an argument, or who is eager to take on a difficult task
6. To presently be very successful and/or popular

LIFE

A. 1. Cannot for the **life** of me
   2. Get a **life**
   3. **Life** in the fast lane
   4. **Life** is a bowl of cherries
   5. You bet your **life**
   6. Take your **life** into your hands

B. Place the idioms correctly in the sentences below

1. Tom should _____. He doesn't seem to care about anything.

2. I _____ me remember what I had to do tonight. My memory is getting very bad.

3. For Steven, _____ now. He did very well in his investments, so he retired early and travels a lot.

4. Jane's _____ her _____ her _____ when she skis on the out of bounds area of the ski hill. She knows that's dangerous.

5. You _____ your _____ that I'll compete in the marathon tomorrow. Having the flu will not stop me from running.

6. Tammy lives _____. She travels a lot and has a very active nightlife.

C. Discussion

1. How dangerous is it to live life in the fast lane?
2. Are there some things you cannot do, for the life of you?

D. Meanings

1. Refers to something a person cannot do, no matter how hard they try
2. A reference to someone who's life is boring, or who cares about what seems (to other people) to be unimportant things
3. Refers to a person whose life is exciting, active and highly pressured
4. Life is enjoyable and pleasant
5. To say yes, in a very forceful way
6. To take a lot of risks by doing something

LIVE, LIFE and LIVING

A. 1. **Live** and let live
   2. Nine **lives**
   3. **Live** and breathe <u>something</u>
   4. Larger than **life**
   5. **Live** the **life** of Riley
   6. Think <u>someone</u> owes <u>you</u> a **living**

B. <u>Place the idioms correctly in the sentences below</u>

1. I was _____ when I was living in Asia. I was making a lot of money, travelling a lot, and not worrying about raising a family.

2. In our multi-cultural and diverse society, people have to accept the adage of _____.

3. Fred _____ everyone _____ him _____.
   He's usually unemployed, and often borrows money from others.

4. Pete _____ engineering. He works so hard, so I know he'll be a successful Engineer once he graduates.

5. Bob has certainly been lucky enough to survived up to this point in business, even though he takes lots of risks. He seems to have _____.

6. Muhammad Ali is _____. He has such strong charisma, and a magnetic personality.

C. Discussion

1. Talk about someone who you think is larger than life. Why is this so?
2. Do you sometimes live on the edge? Why or why not?

D. Meanings

1. To be accepting of the different lifestyles and opinions of other people
2. A situation when someone survives, and even prospers, after managing to get out of many difficult circumstances
3. To spend a lot of time on something that you are very enthusiastic about
4. Someone who has a strong personality and who stands out in a crowd
5. Someone whose life is very enjoyable, problem free, and who seems to have a lot of money
6. The thought that government, or that parents, should furnish you the money to allow you to continue to live, without you working

LIVING DANGEROUSLY

A. 1. Up the **ante**
   2. **Cheat death**
   3. **Dice** with **death**
   4. Live life in the **fast lane**
   5. Its <u>your</u> **funeral**
   6. Play **Russian Roulette**

B. Place the idioms correctly in the sentences below

1. I refuse to go para-gliding with Tom. It's a dangerous pastime, so I just tell Tom, "_____ <u>your</u> _____", every time he goes para-gliding.

2. I _____ in the car accident, because my car rolled over many times, and I was not injured badly.

3. Bill _____ with his life when he speeds in his car.

4. Sarah travels, skis, and goes partying every night. She certainly _____ _____.

5. Sam has _____ in our competition. He has ruled there will now be no net beneath us when we attempt to cross the gorge.

6. Fire fighters and police officers often _____ in their jobs.

C. Discussion

1. Have you ever played a type of Russian Roulette?
2. Talk about someone you know who has cheated death.

D. Meanings

1. Take greater risks, or make greater demands on someone or on yourself
2. To escape serious injury, or even death, in a dangerous situation
3. Take risks that will put your life in danger
4. Live life vigorously, and to the fullest, by doing exciting things
5. A warning issued to someone who does dangerous and even life threatening things
6. To take great risk by doing something dangerous

SECTION 11 – MONEY

GAMBLING

A. 1. The **dice** is loaded against <u>you</u>
   2. No **dice**
   3. Have an **ace** in the hole
   4. Play <u>your</u> **ace**
   5. The **joker** in the pack
   6. All **bets** are off

B. Place the idioms correctly in the sentences below

1. The teacher doesn't know that I _____, in that I have copies of all the previous exams.

2. Ethel is _____ when comes to her food preferences. I don't what she likes so I'm not sure what to cook at the dinner tonight.

3. I _____ my _____ already, when I showed the boss my proposals. If he doesn't like them, I have nothing else to fall back on.

4. I am not the smartest person in the class, so even though _____ _____ me, I still scored the highest in the test.

5. "_____ Karl, you cannot persuade me to lend you my car".

6. _____ with regards to tonight's football game. Both teams are equally matched, and no one knows who will win.

C. Discussion

1. Talk about a situation when the dice were loaded against you, but you still persevered and were successful in the end.
2. Talk about a friend who is the joker in the pack in regards to their fashion.

D. Meanings

1. A situation where things are purposely arranged to your disadvantage
2. To refuse to do what is asked of you
3. To have something which can be used to your advantage, when needed
4. To do an unexpected thing, giving you an advantage over others
5. Refers to a person who is different from others, which means that no one will know how they will act or behave
6. A situation where it is impossible to know the outcome

MONEY 1

A. 1. **Buck** the trend
   2. The **buck** stops here
   3. Pass the **buck**
   4. Bet your bottom **dollar**
   5. **Dollars** to doughnuts
   6. The $64,000 **dollar** question

B. Place the idioms correctly in the sentences below

1. Its _____ that the economy will keep getting worse. We have too much debt, and not enough investment.

2. I'll _____ my _____ that John was the culprit. I'm sure it was him that told the boss I came in late today.

3. I'm going to _____ and get a different haircut. I don't want the same hairstyle that everyone else does.

4. My dad always _____ and lets our mom discipline us.

5. _____ is, when will economy get better?

6. I'm going to take responsibility for this mess. I was the one who recommended that we invest in silver. _____.

C. Discussion

1. Talk about someone you know who always passes the buck, instead of living by the motto, the buck stops here.
2. Why do people wear the same styles and not buck the trend?

D. Meanings

1. Someone who "Bucks the trend", takes an alternative path to what is popular
2. When someone says, "The buck stops here", they mean that they are taking total responsibility for an issue or a matter
3. If someone "Passes the buck", then they are not taking responsibility for an issue, and that they are expecting someone else to deal with it
4. You are saying that you are absolutely certain that something will definitely happen, or that something is definitely true
5. A saying used to convey the impression that if you think that something will happen, then you are certain that it will happen
6. A question that is very, very important, but that is difficult to answer

MONEY 2

A. 1. Hit the **jackpot**
   2. Break the **bank**
   3. Laughing all the way to the **bank**
   4. A **cash** cow
   5. Made of **money**
   6. Even **money**

B. Place the idioms correctly in the sentences below

1. Elsie seems to be _____. She bought an expensive car, and then she's going on that long, expensive vacation.

2. Ethan _____ when he bought his new house. Now he has no money left for anything else.

3. Bob _____ when he opened his pizza parlor. His place is very popular, so he's making a lot of money from it.

4. Its _____ whether my son goes to Yale or Harvard. He his not sure which school he is going to attend.

5. This lottery is _____ for our charity. We wouldn't survive without the money we get from it.

6. I'm _____ with this investment. It's made me a lot of money.

C. Discussion

1. Have you ever broke the bank when you spent too much for something?
2. Talk about a game or sporting event when you thought it was even money with regard to which team would win.

D. Meanings

1. To earn a lot of money by being successful at something, or to unexpectedly come across a good fortune, or have some good luck
2. To have something cost too much money
3. To make a lot of money very easily
4. Something that makes a lot of money
5. If a person is made of money, then they have a virtual unlimited ability to spend money for anything
6. Refers to two possible outcomes, which are equally likely

PENNY

A. 1. The **penny** drops
   2. A pretty **penny**
   3. A **penny** for your thoughts
   4. **Penny** wise and **pound** foolish
   5. In for a **penny**, in for a **pound**
   6. Not have a **penny** to your name

B. Place the idioms correctly in the sentences below

1. I'm _____ on the construction of the ski lodge. Even though it's costing more than we thought, I still believe in the plan.

2. John realized that _____ when his wife asked for a divorce.

3. Thomas is in much worse shape than we thought. He's so broke, that he does _____ his _____.

4. Martha said "_____ your _____", when I finally told her what I was thinking. She really wanted to know what was on my mind.

5. Tim's car must have cost _____. I bet you it cost over $100,000.

6. John is _____. He spends very little on clothing, but then gambles a lot of his money away.

C. Discussion

1. Describe a situation where the penny has finally dropped on you.
2. Describe someone you know who is penny wise and pound foolish.

D. Meanings

1. A situation that is attained when someone finally realizes the truth about something
2. Something that costs a lot of money
3. A thing that is said when someone really wants to know what you are thinking
4. Refers to a situation where someone is very frugal about small amounts of money, but then is careless when spending large amounts of money
5. To demonstrate that you will definitely continue on with some endeavor, even if it will require more money or more effort
6. To be totally and utterly broke

SECTION 12 – MOTHER NATURE

AIR 1

A. 1. A breath of fresh **air**
    2. Left hanging in the **air** OR Leave <u>someone</u> hanging in the **air**
    3. Full of hot **air**
    4. Out of thin **air**
    5. Be walking on **air**
    6. Up in the **air**

B. Place the idioms correctly in the sentences below

1. Our new supervisor is _____. Unlike our old supervisor, she treats us with respect and makes us feel appreciated.

2. Sue has _____ ever since Time proposed to her.

3. The new teacher _____ us _____ because she did not explain the Math problem very clearly.

4. Jamie is _____. He brags to women that he played football in college, but he never even went to college.

5. The new boss expects us to work magic with the budget, but I just can't pull money _____ to balance the budget.

6. The status of my transfer is now _____, because the company lost a lot of money last year. I might not be able to go now.

C. Discussion

1. Have you ever been left hanging in the air when someone failed to deliver on something they promised you?
2. Talk about the last time you were walking on air.

D. Meanings

1. Refers to a person whose sincerity and honesty is welcomed or appreciated
2. Refers to an issue or question which is not discussed or answered
3. Refers to a person who is insincere and cannot be believed
4. Something that appears suddenly or unexpectedly
5. To feel very happy or very excited
6. Something whose outcome is uncertain

85

AIR 2

A. 1. Clear the **air**
2. Free as the **air**
3. Hot **air**
4. Into thin **air**
5. Pluck <u>something</u> from the **air**
6. Put on **airs**

B. Place the idioms correctly in the sentences below

1. After I paid all my debts off, I felt as _____.

2. I'm happy that I talked to Billy and Jim. They hadn't talked to each other for weeks, so getting them talking _____.

3. Cliff thinks he's the best worker around here, but I'm the one that's getting the promotion. Cliff _____, thinking he's better than everyone else, but he's in for a surprise when I get promoted instead.

4. After Bob won the lottery, he vanished _____. No one knows where he is now.

5. The Smith family is full of _____, trying to make everyone think that they're wealthy, but we all know that they're not.

6. When the teacher asked Tim to answer the question, he didn't have a clue how to answer it so he just _____ <u>a number</u> _____.

C. Discussion

1. Talk about someone you know that seems to always put on airs.
2. Why do you feel that it is sometimes difficult to get two arguing parties together, when getting them together, and making them talk will solve their dispute, and allow them to clear the air?

D. Meanings

1. To discuss something that has caused divisions or problems, so as to make the divisions or problems go away
2. To be completely free and/or to have no problems or worries
3. Something that is not sincere or truthful
4. Something or someone that vanishes completely, so that no one knows where that thing or person is
5. To say something spontaneously without considering if it is actually factual
6. To behave like you think you're better or more important than others

BURN AND FIRE

A. 1. A slow **burn**
   2. **Burn** your bridges
   3. **Burnt** out
   4. **Fired** up
   5. **Light/relight** my fire
   6. **Fire** sale

B. Use the idioms correctly in the sentences below

1. It was _____, but Tommy finally caught on to Math.

2. My life is quite boring these days. I need something new and exciting in my life to _____ my _____.

3. I needed money very badly, so I held a _____ and sold some of my dearest possessions at very low prices.

4. The coach doesn't have to encourage us to play with more spirit. The next game is against our biggest rival, so we're already _____.

5. Tom _____ his _____ when he quit his job after getting into an argument with the boss. The boss will never hire him back now.

6. Most students are _____ just before summer vacation, because they have studied a lot for their final exams.

C. Discussion

1. Can a person find good quality items in a fire sale?
2. What thing in particular gets you fired up easily?

D. Meanings

1. Refers to something that develops slowly or gradually
2. To destroy all previous business or personal contacts
3. To be extremely and totally fatigued, and in need of rest
4. To be extremely excited, sometimes to a point of over-agitation
5. To excite, or re-ignite someone's interest in something, because their life has become very boring
6. To sell things at extremely low prices because the person or business is desperately in need of money

COLD, ICY AND CHILLING

A. 1. **Chill** out
   2. **Chill**
   3. On **ice**
   4. **Cold** turkey
   5. **Cold** as ice
   6. **Cold** comfort

B. Use the idioms correctly in the sentences below

1. _____ Bob. Why are you so angry?

2. I was going to paint the house, but I put that idea _____. I don't have enough time to do that now.

3. I wanted to stop smoking right away, so I went _____.

4. Bob: "What do you want to do today Sue?"
   Sue: "I'm very tired, so I'm just going to _____ and stay home."

5. Bob's _____. He showed no emotion after he left Pam.

6. It was _____ to her that other students also failed the exam, because it didn't make her feel any better.

C. Discussion

1. Do you often just chill out on weekends?
2. When is the last time you put something on ice?

D. Meanings

1. To relax and take it easy
2. Something said to someone to make them calm down, when they are angry, irate or frustrated
3. To delay something
4. To quit smoking suddenly
5. Refers to someone who shows little feelings or emotions
6. A statement that when said to someone, does not make them feel any better

DAY

A. 1. Carry the **day**
   2. The **day** of reckoning
   3. Don't give up your **day** job
   4. Have had your **day**
   5. Late in the **day**
   6. Seize the **day**

B. Place the idioms correctly in the sentences below

1. You always wait until _____ to start studying for your tests. You should've started studying weeks ago.

2. Number 30 on the basketball team _____ his _____. He was a star once, but he can no longer perform how he used to be able to.

3. I feel that to be successful in the stock market, you have to _____ _____, and take risks, or you will never make money.

4. Tanya's ideas _____ with the boss. Everyone will now work on the guidelines set out by Tanya.

5. _____ finally came for Elias when he had to give up his credit cards. He couldn't pay his debt, so the cards were taken away.

6. I heard Kate sing at the karaoke bar last night, and then I advised her, _____ her _____. She's a terrible singer.

C. Discussion

1. When was the last time your ideas ever carried the day in a discussion?
2. Has the day of reckoning ever come for you or anyone you know?

D. Meanings

1. To win an argument or a competition
2. To face the time when a person has to deal with an unpleasant thing, because the person has delayed facing it in the past
3. A negative comment, implying to someone that they are not very good at doing something
4. Refers to when a person's best achievements are in the past, and the person can no longer live up to the same type of achievements
5. To do something in the final stages of a situation
6. To do something at the very instant that you want to do it, and then not worry about the future consequences of the action

Marco Antonio Bussanich

FIRE

A. 1. **Fire** on all cylinders
   2. Play with **fire**
   3. Draw **fire** from someone
   4. Fight **fire** with **fire**
   5. Breath **fire**
   6. Light a **fire** under someone

B. Place the idioms correctly in the sentences below

1. Simon is _____ by taking drugs. He could easily get into trouble by overdosing, or by being arrested.

2. Joe was _____ when he saw Sam make a pass at his girlfriend.

3. The coach had to _____ his players during the last game, because most of them were not playing with any type of emotion.

4. The teacher's plan to add extra lessons at the end of the day has _____ _____ parents. They don't want their children coming home late.

5. I was _____ today. I aced my exam, scored the most points in the basketball game and Jen agreed to be my date for the prom.

6. I decided to _____, so I hired a lawyer. My wife's lawyer was becoming very difficult, so I had no option but to fight back.

C. Discussion

1. Discuss a situation where you had to fight fire with fire.
2. Has anyone ever lit a fire under you?

D. Meanings

1. To utilize all of your capabilities or capacities, to the fullest
2. Doing something that is very risky, and that may lead to further problems
3. To be criticized strongly by someone else
4. To attack someone or something forcefully, after you have been attacked
5. To be very angry about something
6. To motivate someone, to try to force them to do something with more energy or vigor

90

HILLS and MOUNTAINS

A. 1. A **hill** of beans
2. Over the **hill**
3. Make a **mountain** out of a **molehill**
4. A **mountain** to climb
5. If Mohammed will not come to the **mountain**
6. Move **mountains**

B. Place the idioms correctly in the sentences below

1. Bob will have to _____ in order to finish the report on time. There'll be a lot of effort and hard work needed to do this.

2. We have _____ if we want to complete the negotiations for the new park on time.

3. I'm _____ now, son. I can't run the marathon anymore.

4. Our raise won't amount to _____. It's very little money.

5. I made the long trip to go see our client, because he had no time to come to see us. _____.

6. That kind of rash behaviour is typical for Gladys. She _____ _____ on all matters that are unimportant.

C. Discussion

1. Discuss what the difference in meaning is between the idioms "A mountain to climb", and "Move mountains".
2. Do you or any of your friends make mountains out of molehills when it comes to discussing their love life?

D. Meanings

1. Refers to something that is very small in quantity, or that is insignificant
2. Refers to someone or something that is very, very old, and that does not perform as it once did
3. To complain about something that is unimportant, in a way that makes it seem that you think it is important
4. The great effort that will be needed in order to complete a big task
5. If someone does not come to you, then you have no choice but to go to them
6. To succeed in doing something difficult through much hard work

HOT AND COLD

A. 1. **Cold** shoulder
   2. Sell like **hot** cakes
   3. In the **hot** seat
   4. **Cold** feet
   5. Leave <u>someone</u> out in the **cold** OR Left out in the **cold**
   6. Blow **hot** and **cold**

B. Use the idioms correctly in the sentences below

1. Workers in the accounting department were _____.
   They were the only ones that were not invited to the party.

2. This new phone model is selling very fast. Its _____.

3. Michael gave me the _____ at work today. He totally
   ignored me all day.

4. Jimmy _____ over Lisa. He sometimes seems to like her a
   lot, but at other times, he totally ignores her.

5. I sometimes hate being the boss, because I have so many important decisions
   to make. It is very stressful to be _____.

6. Rob, John and Rick went bungy jumping, but Rick got _____ and
   was the only one who didn't jump.

C. Discussion

1. Discuss some things that you know may blow hot and cold over.
2. Why do some phone models sell like hot cakes, while others don't?

D. Meanings

1. A situation where a person does not feel any better, even after learning that others
   share the same fate as that person
2. Refers to something that is bought by many people in a short time
3. A situation where a person has to make important decisions
4. Become nervous or anxious about something you may want to do, and then do
   not do it
5. Ignore someone, and do not include them in your plans
6. Describe an occurrence when someone is sometimes very enthusiastic about
   doing something, but then suddenly become very uninterested in it

LATE AT NIGHT

A.
1. **Burn** the midnight oil
2. A **night** owl
3. A **night** on the tiles   ***   **A British Idiom**
4. In the **dark**
5. **Late** in the **day**
6. Like **night** and **day**

B. Place the idioms correctly in the sentences below

1. Jack has been _____ lately. He's working 2 jobs, because he wants to earn enough money to purchase a new car.

2. Jenny and Brad have been married for twenty years, even though they're _____. Its surprising how well they get along.

3. The doctor finally diagnosed dad's illness, but it came too _____ _____. Dad will be cured, but he won't walk properly anymore.

4. Its easy going out with Teddy. He's such _____, so he goes out a lot and knows which are the good places to party at.

5. Tony has no choice but to have _____ most nights. He finishes work at 10 PM, so he can't go out earlier.

6. I was kept _____ about Tom's low marks. The teacher never contacted me, and the school stopped issuing report cards last year.

C. Discussion

1. Did you often burn the midnight oil during your university studies?
2. Is it unhealthy to be a night owl and stay up late all the time?

D. Meanings

1. To stay up late, to either study, or to work
2. A person who does things late at night or who likes to stay up late
3. To go out late, to a night club or bar, and to also come home late
4. To be denied knowledge about something, so that the person knows very little about the thing
5. Refers to something that is done at the last possible moment
6. Refers to two or more things that are completely different

LEAVES, TREES AND BRANCHES

A. 1. Hold out an olive **branch**
   2. Fig **leaf**
   3. Turn over a new **leaf**
   4. Take a **leaf** out of someone's book
   5. Bark up the wrong **tree**
   6. Up a **tree**

B. Place the idioms correctly in the sentences below

1. I _____ to Thomas, in the hopes that we would end our disagreements and become friends again.

2. I've been _____ when I suspected that Julie was seeing another man. She was being secretive lately because she was spending a lot of time organizing my surprise birthday party.

3. Whenever my wife leaves town to visit her mother, our family is _____. None of us know how to cook, and the house is disorganized without mom.

4. I've been trying to _____ Frank's _____ lately, because he is a very successful person. I thought it would be good to imitate his methods, so I could also have similar success.

5. Cathy had to _____ because all the things she was doing lately were making her very unhappy.

6. Thomas was using his raise as a _____, in order to cover up the fact that he was still very much in debt.

C. Discussion

1. Have you ever barked up the wrong tree?
2. Have you had success when holding out olive branches to others?

D. Meanings

1. Do or say something in an attempt to end a disagreement with someone
2. Something that is used to hide an awkward or embarrassing situation
3. To try to improve to make yourself better than before
4. Copy or mimic someone's behaviour, in order to become successful as they are
5. To follow the wrong actions, usually because your beliefs are erroneous
6. To be in a difficult situation

SLEEP

A. 1. **Saw logs**
   2. **Sleep** like a log
   3. **Sleep** on <u>something</u>
   4. **Sleep** off <u>something</u>
   5. Not **sleep** a wink
   6. 40 **winks**

B. Place the idioms correctly in the sentences below

1. Bill _____. I've never seen anyone sleep so soundly.

2. I usually catch _____ late in the afternoon after coming home from work, because I'm quite tired from my busy and hectic days.

3. The boss asked if I'd be interested in moving to our other branch office, but I told him I'd _____ <u>it</u> and make the decision by tomorrow.

4. I did _____ last night. The noise from the storm kept me awake all night.

5. I didn't sleep well last night, because my husband was making too much noise. He was _____ all night long.

6. I didn't wake up until noon on Saturday because I had a hangover from the previous night. I had to _____ <u>the hangover</u>.

C. Discussion

1. Do you find it difficult to sleep like a log the night before an exam?
2. Was there something that you had to sleep on recently, because it was such a big decision for you to make?

D. Meanings

1. To snore
2. To sleep very soundly
3. To give yourself time to think something over
4. To use sleep to recover from something
5. To not sleep at all
6. A quick nap

SMOKE

A. 1. **Smoke** signals
   2. The big **smoke**
   3. Blow **smoke**
   4. Where there's **smoke**, there's fire
   5. **Smoke** and mirrors
   6. Go up in **smoke**

B. Place the idioms correctly in the sentences below

1. I really mean what I'm saying. I'm not _____.

2. Do you live in _____? That must be extremely exciting!

3. The plan to have a barbeque last Saturday _____ because it rained heavily all day.

4. Our boss has been sending us _____, so its pretty obvious that something important is going to happen soon.

5. I knew that Jim was cheating on his wife. After I saw him have lunch with Jane, I suspected something, because _____.

6. The government budget is all _____. They're promising many things, but after they get elected, they'll break their promises.

C. Discussion

1. Do you know someone that often blows smoke?
2. Have any of your plans ever gone up in smoke?

D. Meanings

1. A sign or a hint that is sent by someone to suggest that something is about to happen
2. Refers to the biggest city in a particular country
3. To deliberately confuse or deceive someone
4. Refers to a rumor that has to be true, or partially true, because the rumor would not have happened if it wasn't true or partially true
5. Something that is said that is meant to confuse or deceive people
6. Refers to an important thing that does not happen or come to fruition

TIME

A. 1. Ahead of <u>its/one's</u> **time**
    2. Living on borrowed **time**
    3. In <u>your</u> own **time**
    4. Make **time**
    5. Play for **time**
    6. **Time** will tell

B. Place the idioms correctly in the sentences below

1. I had to _____ in the meeting today, because when the boss asked me a question, I had no answer at the top of my head.

2. Some people feel that Pam's clothes are old-fashioned, but I think she's _____ her _____, as those old fashions have come back into style.

3. I had no time to see the boss, but then I had to _____, because he was adamant that I had to see him before the end of the day.

4. Cam's _____. The bank will foreclose on his house any day.

5. _____ if Mary made the right decision in studying music. I wanted her to study Law, but she said she wouldn't be happy as a lawyer.

6. I did the Math homework _____ my _____. If I tried to do it faster, like my teacher wanted me to, then I never would've understood it.

C. Discussion

1. Discuss an idea of yours that you thought was ahead of its time.
2. If the teacher asked you to give a brief talk about yourself in front of the class, would you have to play for time in order to rehearse your speech

D. Meanings

1. Something that's so new and modern, or someone whose ideas are so new and modern, that its hard for others people to accept these things
2. Refers to someone or something that is not expected to survive very long
3. To not be hurried into doing something, but doing it at your own pace
4. To create time to do a specific activity or thing, even though you may have thought that you had no time to do this activity or thing in the first place
5. To create a delay, in order to have more time to prepare for something
6. Only the passage of time will reveal if a choice made was the right one

WEATHER 1

A. 1. On **cloud** nine
   2. Take a **rain** check
   3. Chase **rainbows**
   4. The calm before the **storm**
   5. Fair **weather** friend
   6. Under the **weather**

B. Place the idioms correctly in the sentences below

1. I was _____ today, so I phoned in sick to work.

2. I found out that Greg's just a _____. When I was in trouble and needed his advice and support, he abandoned me.

3. I asked Jill to lunch today but she replied that she'd _____ _____ for our lunch date. She already had another engagement planned.

4. The quiet today is just _____. When the game is on tomorrow, there will be a lot of commotion all around.

5. Tim's been _____ ever since he started dating Faith.

6. Elmer should be more realistic. He should stop _____ because he's not talented enough to be a pro athlete.

C. Discussion

1. Was it surprising for you to find out that a person that you thought was a good friend turned out to be only a fair weather friend in the end?
2. Do you find that you too often chase rainbows, instead of having more realistic expectations?

D. Meanings

1. To be very happy, because of something that has happened lately
2. To decline an offer, and then put it off to a later day
3. To waste one's time, in an effort to chase something that is unattainable
4. A period of quite, preceding a difficult, tumultuous or intense situation
5. A person who is friendly in good times, but unsupportive when his or her friend or relative faces difficult situations
6. To be ill

WEATHER 2

A.
1. **Lightning** doesn't/does strike twice
2. Like greased **lightning**
3. The end of the **rainbow**
4. A snow **job**
5. Weather the **storm**
6. Take <u>something</u> by **storm**
7. Steal <u>someone's</u> **thunder**

B. Place the idioms correctly in the sentences below

1. Bret _____ my _____ by asking Pam out before I did.

2. Everyone was amazed that the worst team defeated the best team two times in a row. I suppose that _____.

3. The new song is _____ <u>the music scene</u> _____.

4. Tommy fixes cars faster than anyone else. When Tommy is under an engine, he's _____.

5. I _____ during the last exam period and passed, but in the upcoming exams, I will fail for sure.

6. I didn't get to _____. I wasn't accepted in law school.

7. Bob gave us _____. He lied to us that he would study hard.

C. Discussion

1. Talk about a friend who does things as fast as greased lightning.
2. Do you feel that you will ever get to the end of your rainbow?

D. Meanings

1. To imply a person has either been very lucky, or very unlucky, because the same good thing, or bad thing, will not happen again
2. To do something very quickly
3. Something that a person would like to achieve, or a place that a person would like to get to, but, it is very difficult to do either
4. An attempt to deceive someone by telling them lies about something
5. To survive a difficult situation, without being harmed by it
6. To be incredibly popular, or amazingly successful at something
7. To do something before someone else does it, so that you can steal the praise, or the reward, that they were hoping to get

Marco Antonio Bussanich

WIND

A.
 1. Blowing in the **wind**
 2. Get **wind** of
 3. Gone with the **wind**
 4. In the **wind**
 5. Spitting in the **wind**
 6. Twist in the **wind**

B. Place the idioms correctly in the sentences below

1. I wasn't surprised when Toni was made the new boss. Rumors circulated about our old boss, so I knew that change was _____.

2. The police _____ the planned protests, and stepped in before any rioting broke out.

3. The politicians left too much legislation _____ at the end of the session. They haven't been very productive this year.

4. The old ways of our fathers have _____.

5. The townsfolk are _____. The rumors of the mill's closing will result in all of them losing their jobs.

6. You're _____ if you think Danielle will go with you as your date to the prom.

C. Discussion

1. Have your parent's idea's gone with the wind, or do they still have value?
2. Has anyone ever left you twisting in the wind on an important matter?

D. Meanings

1. Something which is being thought about or considered, but which no decision has been made on
2. To find out information, even if that was not the person's original intention
3. Something that has gone and disappeared forever, never to return
4. Something that will most likely happen very soon
5. Doing a thing that is waste of time, because it has no chance for success
6. Refers to someone who puts another person in a difficult situation by controlling them, or the outcome of the situation

100

SECTION 13 – MUSIC

HIP-HOP

A. 1. **Hood**
   2. **PHAT** (Pretty, hot and tempting)
   3. **Dog**
   4. **Crib**
   5. **Hater**
   6. **Dis** OR **Dissed**

B. Place the idioms correctly in the sentences below

1. I didn't like the way Larry tried to _____ you in front of all of your friends, but you did a good job of answering him back.

2. Come to my _____ tonight, there's a party going on.

3. Pam's just a _____. She says bad things about successful people all the time.

4. Wassup, _____, what's cooking today?

5. As soon as I buy the new furniture, my _____ will look awesome.

6. Every guy thinks Sheila's the hottest girl in town. We all think she's so _____.

C. Discussion

1. Is the idiom "PHAT" an appropriate word to use?
2. Is there someone you know that's a hater, and that always disses others?

D. Meanings

1. A person's neighborhood
2. Refers to a female who is extremely beautiful
3. A reference to someone's good, male friend
4. A person's home
5. A person who constantly says negative things about other people
6. To disrespect someone else

101

Marco Antonio Bussanich

MUSIC and MUSICAL INSTRUMENTS

A. 1. Bang the **drum**
 2. Fit as a **fiddle**
 3. On the **fiddle**   ***   **A British Idiom**
 4. Face the **music**
 5. **Music** to <u>my</u> ears
 6. Lower the **tone**

B. Place the idioms correctly in the sentences below

1. It was admirable for Max to _____ and accept responsibility for the errors in the proposal.

2. Nadia has _____ for our political party for years. Its time she got rewarded, so let's promote her to the president of the party.

3. Frank _____ of the party. He was drinking beer while everyone else was drinking champagne.

4. Some politicians obtain their wealth by being _____. They obtain their wealth by being bribed.

5. I'm not surprised that Agnes is as _____. She's exercised for years, and has always eaten a healthy diet.

6. It was _____ <u>my</u> _____ when the doctors finally discovered the cause of Wendy's illness. Now she can be cured and get better.

C. Discussion

1. Have you banged the drum for a good cause?
2. Talk about a situation you witnessed where someone lowered the tone with their inappropriate behavior.

D. Meanings

1. To support someone or something publicly, in a very forceful and open way
2. To be very fit and healthy
3. To obtain something by doing illegal or dishonest things
4. To accept responsibility for something you have done wrong, and to prepare yourself to accept punishment for the wrongdoing
5. To be very happy when you hear a piece of good news
6. To make a place seem less respectable

SING and SONG

A.
1. **Sing** a different tune
2. **Sing** from the same song sheet
3. **Sing**
4. For a **song**
5. Make a **song** and dance
6. On **song**

B. Place the idioms correctly in the sentences below

1. The cop made the suspect _____, and reveal where the stolen money was hidden.

2. The striker is _____. He's scored some tremendous goals lately.

3. Jeff is _____, now that I caught him with the stolen money. He finally confessed to taking money from me all along.

4. We have to _____, and tell the boss we are united in opposition to his plan. That is the only way we can change his mind.

5. Terra _____ every time we ask her to do the dishes. She does this all the time because she hates washing dishes.

6. I picked up this bike _____. Elmer needed money and was desperate to sell, so that is why I got it at such a good price.

C. Discussion

1. Who do you know that makes a song and dance over a lot of small things?
2. Talk about something that you were adamant that you would not do, but then suddenly you started to sing a different song about.

D. Meanings

1. Refers to someone who changes their mind, and now expresses an opinion than the previous opinion they expressed only quite recently
2. To publicly express an opinion that is the same as someone else's
3. Refers to a criminal who finally reveals information to the police, when in the beginning, the criminal tried to withhold the information
4. To buy something for very little money
5. To react excitedly or nervously to something that is not important
6. Refers to an athlete who is playing very well

TUNE

A. 1. Call the **tune**
   2. Carry a **tune**
   3. Change <u>your</u> **tune**
   4. To the **tune** of
   5. Dance to <u>someone's</u> **tune**
   6. March to a different **tune**

B. <u>Place the idioms correctly in the sentences below</u>

1. I was embarrassed at the karaoke when I sang because a few people laughed at me when I was singing. I just cannot _____.

2. The boss has most people _____ his _____, but he can't bully me around.

3. My mother _____ in our family. She's always in charge.

4. Al _____ his _____ when he was questioned by Ms. Lake. He originally told us he didn't cheat on the test, but he couldn't deny it when Ms. Lake presented the proof.

5. Elsie and Bob both _____, but they get along as well as any couple we know.

6. He paid _____ $100,000 for his new car.

C. <u>Discussion</u>

1. Have you ever changed your tune when a parent or a teacher questioned you about something that you originally denied doing?
2. Talk about someone you know who marches to a totally different tune.

D. <u>Meanings</u>

1. To be in control of a situation, and to have the ability to make all the important decisions
2. To have the ability to sing a song with the right note
3. To express a different opinion than one that was previously expressed
4. A saying that is used before quoting a sum of money, especially when the amount of money is large
5. To do whatever someone else tells you to do
6. To behave differently than most people, or to have different morals or beliefs than most other people

SECTION 14 – PEOPLE

FAMOUS NAMES 1

A. 1. In like **Flynn**
   2. **Hobson's** choice
   3. Keeping up with the **Joneses**
   4. Happy as **Larry**   ***   **A British Idiom**
   5. If **Mohammed** will not come to the mountain
   6. Living the life of **Riley**

B. Place the idioms correctly in the sentences below

1. When I lived in Asia, I was _____,
   because my pay was excellent, and I loved my job.

2. Jim's as _____ now that he's married and has children.

3. _____, then I must make the
   long trip to see our client, because he had no time to come to see us.

4. He was left with a _____ of giving up drinking, or dying.

5. Lydia spends so much money, time and effort _____
   _____. She should realize that this will not bring her happiness.

6. I was _____ when Jennifer announced that she was
   having a barbeque. I really want to get to know her better.

C. Discussion

1. Is it difficult in some situations to avoid keeping up with the Joneses?
2. Were you ever presented with a Hobson's choice.

D. Meanings

1. To do something quickly, and with a lot of enthusiasm
2. A decision that must be made, when in reality, there is no other choice
3. To deliberately, buy, do or act like the successful people around you, so that
   you also appear successful as well
4. Refers to a person that is very, very happy
5. If someone does not come to see you, then you have no choice but to go to see
   them
6. Someone who is living a very enjoyable life, because they have very few
   problems, and have a lot of money

FAMOUS NAMES 2

A. 1. **Achilles** heel
   2. **Bob's** your uncle
   3. Before you can say **Jack Robinson**
   4. **Joe** public
   5. Typhoid **Mary**
   6. Robbing **Peter** to Pay **Paul**

B. Place the idioms correctly in the sentences below

1. The teacher thought my _____ was world history, but when I took the history test, I aced it.

2. If the children get too hot when they're playing, then just bring them to the swimming pool and _____ your _____, they'll cool down.

3. When Sid used his lunch money to play video games, it was like he was _____.

4. After Harry left Scarlett, she became a type of _____, trying to ruin any relationship Harry had with other people.

5. I put my wallet on the table and turned around for a few seconds, and _____ you _____, it was gone.

6. When the mayor was implicated, _____ became very angry, because it was revealed the mayor pilfered a lot of tax dollars.

C. Discussion

1. Discuss how you once robbed Peter to pay Paul.
2. Do you have an Achilles heel? What can you do to improve on this?

D. Meanings

1. A thing that causes a person problems, because it is a weakness, giving others the chance to criticize or attack it
2. This saying implies that a certain thing is easy to achieve, once a suitable remedy is employed
3. Refers to something that happens very quickly or suddenly
4. A saying used to describe ordinary people
5. Refers to a person who tries to bring bad luck or harm to people
6. To use money for one thing, that was meant to be used for another thing

QUEENS AND KING

A. 1. **Queen** bee
   2. **Queen** for a day
   3. Given the **royal** treatment
   4. Fit for a **king**
   5. **King** of the hill
   6. Pay a **king's** ransom

B. Place the idioms correctly in the sentences below

1. Pam is the _____ in our organization. Everyone does what they're told when the orders come from Pam.

2. The top athletes in any sport are _____ these days.

3. The meals in this restaurant are _____. They're all delicious.

4. Its Sarah birthday, so she's _____, today. I will treat her to dinner, and do whatever she asks me to do.

5. We were _____ at the big hotel in the Bahamas. The food was excellent and the service was superb.

6. Alfred thinks he's the _____, but he only won one tennis tournament. I don't think he should be as boastful as he is.

C. Discussion

1. Have you had to pay a king's ransom for something you really wanted?
2. Should famous people always expect to get the royal treatment?

D. Meanings

1. The top person or leader, who is a female, in a group
2. Refers to a situation where a female gets to be pampered, or is the top person in her group, for a short period
3. To be treated extremely well, as if one were royalty
4. Something that is of the best quality
5. The top or number one person in a group
6. To have to, or to be willing to, pay a lot for something, or, to overpay for something

RELATIVES

A. 1. Not <u>your</u> **brother's** keeper
    2. **Father** time
    3. **Mom** and **pop** store
    4. Be tied to <u>your</u> **mother's** apron strings
    5. Teach <u>your</u> **granny** to suck eggs
    6. A monkey's **uncle**

B. Place the idioms correctly in the sentences below

1. Telling Jenny how to do the accounting is like _____ <u>your</u> _____. She's the best accountant in our firm.

2. Jim is still _____ his _____. She washes and irons his clothes, and still cooks his meals for him.

3. Why do you keep asking me about my brother Elmer? I don't know where he is or what he's doing. I'm _____ <u>your</u> _____.

4. _____ has finally caught up with me. I'm no longer able to concentrate long enough to read the paper.

5. I don't like the fact that big supermarket chains are opening stores in our neighborhood, and then driving the _____ out of business.

6. I really am _____. I should have started my shopping much earlier because Christmas is almost here.

C. Discussion

1. Do you still like shopping at mom and pop stores?
2. At what age should people stop being tied to their mother's apron strings?

D. Meanings

1. A saying used to express the fact that you do not know where someone is, and that you should not have to know where that person is
2. Refers to the passage of time, which makes a person older, and therefore less able to do things they once used to do
3. A small, corner side grocery store, that is run as a small family business
4. Refers to a person who is still dependent on their mother, when they should, in fact, be independent
5. To give advice to someone about a thing they know more about than you
6. An expression used by someone to express surprise at something they should have known about, but did not know about

SECTION 15 – PLACES

CORNER

A. 1. In a **corner**
2. In your **corner**
3. Just round the **corner**
4. Paint yourself into a **corner**
5. Turn the **corner**
6. Cut **corners**

B. Place the idioms correctly in the sentences below

1. Our team is starting to _____ now that we have a new coach. The players now have a good game-plan to follow.

2. Erica _____ herself _____ by using credit cards all the time, and then she complains she doesn't have money to pay them off.

3. I tried to _____ by not applying undercoat before painting, so the paint job turned out terrible.

4. Elmer put himself _____ when he started overdrinking. Now he's an alcoholic. He also lost his job, so he can't pay his rent.

5. Brighter days are _____. The government's stimulus package will help improve the economy.

6. My mother's always ___ my _____. She supports me in everything.

C. Discussion

1. Talk about a time when you painted yourself into a corner.
2. Name a situation when it may be preferable to cut corners.

D. Meanings

1. To be in a difficult predicament, which is difficult to escape from
2. To be supportive of someone
3. Something that is going to happen very, very soon
4. To do something that will ultimately create difficulties for you
5. To start to recover from a troubling situation or an illness
6. To not follow the correct rules or procedures to get something done, in an attempt to save time, effort or money

EDGE

A. 1. On the **edge** of your seat
    2. At (on) the cutting **edge**
    3. Lose your **edge**
    4. On **edge**
    5. Rough around the **edges**
    6. Take the **edge** off something

B. Place the idioms correctly in the sentences below

1. Jane has been _____ a lot lately. She's expecting a baby, and is worried about the extra expenses this will incur.

2. I was happy that Samantha _____ her speech. The initial version of her speech would have offended too many people.

3. The movie that I watched last night kept me _____ my _____. It was so exciting, so it kept my attention for the whole 2 hours.

4. Microsoft's products are always _____. The company continually produces the newest and best products.

5. I'm afraid that that athlete has _____ his _____. He can no longer dominate the way he used to.

6. Tommy was _____ when he was a teenager, but now that he has graduated, he's a much more polite and gracious individual.

C. Discussion

1. What is the best way to avoid losing your edge in something?
2. What things are you still rough around the edges in?

D. Meanings

1. To be excited about something, to the point that you are eager to know what will happen next
2. Something that is the most developed or advanced development in its field
3. To lose a skill or ability that once made a person successful in their field
4. To be anxious or nervous
5. Something or someone that is good, but not perfect
6. To weaken an unpleasant feeling or situation, to the point that it is not as bad as it once was

END

A. 1. The **end** of the rainbow
   2. Make **ends** meet
   3. Keep <u>your</u> **end** of the deal (bargain)
   4. Dead **end**
   5. Do an **end** run
   6. Go off the deep **end**

B. Place the idioms correctly in the sentences below

1. I don't think I'll ever get to _____, because I want to retire at age 50.

2. Phil _____ when his wife left him.

3. Its so difficult to _____ these days. I barely have enough money to survive, let alone having enough money to golf or travel.

4. I _____ and avoided military service by enrolling in some university classes.

5. I _____ my _____ and delivered the good players. Now you have to _____ your _____ and deliver a championship.

6. I've reached a _____ at work, so I'm looking for another position. There's no way that I can advance further in this company.

C. Discussion

1. Talk about a situation where you reached a dead end, and had to make a change.
2. Do you think you can ever reach the end of your rainbow?

D. Meanings

1. A desired place where people may want to get to, but that is hard to reach
2. To find it difficult to have enough money to pay for life's necessities, due to a lack of money
3. To do what you have either promised, or are expected, to do
4. A place from where a person can go no further
5. Something that you do in order to avoid something else
6. To behave like a crazy person

FAMOUS PLACES 1

A. 1. Be/being sent to **Coventry**
   2. Not whistling **Dixie**
   3. Go **Dutch** treat
   4. A **Trojan** horse
   5. When in **Rome**
   6. **Rome** wasn't built in a day

B. Place the idioms correctly in the sentences below

1. I've always felt that _____, a person should do as the Romans do. That's why I studied French when I moved to France.

2. It felt as if I were _____ when my uncle stopped talking to me, after he caught me drinking his alcohol.

3. The small tax increase was just _____, because the mayor really wanted to raise taxes even higher in the future.

4. It will take a lot of hard work to bring your grades up in Math, Johnny.
   _____.

5. Tom is _____ when he says it will rain tomorrow. I suggest you take an umbrella with you to work tomorrow.

6. Sue and I _____ today. She wouldn't let me pay for the meal.

C. Discussion

1. Did it ever feel like you were being sent to Coventry by a relative?
2. Do you feel that men and women should always go Dutch treat?

D. Meanings

1. To be ignored by others because they disapprove of what you have done
2. If someone is not whistling Dixie, they are being honest and should be listened to
3. To share the cost equally between two people when they have a meal or share an evening out together
4. A situation where something appears useful, but is really intended to harm you in the long run
5. People should adopt the customs and behaviour of the place they are in
6. An expression used to convey the idea that it often takes a long period of time to complete a task, and that all things cannot be done quickly

FAMOUS PLACES 2

A. 1. Fiddle when **Rome** burns
   2. **Dutch** courage
   3. In **Dutch**
   4. Pardon my **French**
   5. Its all **Greek** to me
   6. As **American** as apple pie

B. Place the idioms correctly in the sentences below

1. I apologized to the host, and said _____ my _____, when I inadvertently used an improper word at the luncheon.

2. Sarah can read Chinese, but when I look at a menu written in Chinese, _____ me.

3. Cliff shows a lot of _____ and has no trouble asking women to dance, but only when he has had a lot to drink.

4. The senator _____ because he ignores important issues and only focuses on minor issues that'll get him re-elected.

5. Eating hot dogs at baseball games is _____.

6. Ed's _____ with his debts. The collectors won't stop calling him.

C. Discussion

1. Do any of your friends play Russian Roulette by taking great risks?
2. Do you gain Dutch courage by having a few drinks at the bar?

D. Meanings

1. To spend all of your time on unimportant things, when important issues need to be taken care of
2. To feel brave or confident because you have consumed a lot of alcohol
3. To be in trouble
4. A humorous apology made when a person swears or uses a rude word
5. Refers to something that is totally unintelligible, or not understandable
6. Something that is typical of the American way of life

HOUSE

A. 1. Bring the **house** down
   2. Eat <u>someone</u> out of **house** and home
   3. Get on like a **house** on fire
   4. A **house** of cards
   5. Put <u>your</u> **house** in order
   6. A **household** name

B. Place the idioms correctly in the sentences below

1. His financial affairs were like _____ and were about to collapse, even if he didn't lose his job.

2. The leading actress _____ last night. She was magnificent in her role as the Princess.

3. Sue and I _____ as soon as we met. I knew right away that she was the right girl for me.

4. The senator's name is like _____ now. I'm surprised that you didn't know about him.

5. Tom is _____ me _____. He should get a job and start paying for his own food, because I can no longer afford to feed him.

6. I told Barb to _____ her _____ because her partying would eventually catch up with her, and she'd lose her job.

C. Discussion

1. Talk about someone who gets on like a house on fire with everyone.
2. Why do so many people have a hard time putting their house in order financially?

D. Meanings

1. Refers to an audience that cheers and claps loudly, for a long time, because the audience has enjoyed the performance
2. Refers to a person that eats so much, so that it costs a lot to feed them
3. Refers to two people who become good friends very quickly
4. Describes something that is about to fail or collapse
5. To makes sure that all of your affairs and problems are dealt with and taken care of
6. If someone has a household name, then they are famous and well known

MIDEVAL and ANCIENT WORLD

A. 1. Out of the **ark**
    2. A chink in someone's **armor**
    3. **Castles** in the air
    4. A **knight** in **shining armor**
    5. Hold down the **fort**
    6. The **sword** of **Damocles** hangs over someone

B. Place the idioms correctly in the sentences below

1. _____ Tom. He refuses to give up boxing, even though doctors say the next punch could really injure him.

2. The mayor's plans are like _____. Citizens will not allow him to go on with his planned highway.

3. The only _____ Bob's _____ is that he gambles a little too much. Other than that, he's very good at saving money.

4. Can you _____ and watch my house while I'm on vacation?

5. Tim's car seems like its _____. I've never seen a more beat up and old fashioned vehicle.

6. Gordon thinks he's _____, and can ride to anyone's rescue, but he needs rescuing from his addiction.

C. Discussion

1. Does the sword of Damocles hang over a person you know, in some way?
2. Is it still appropriate to use idioms such as "A knight in shining armor"?

D. Meanings

1. Something that is very old, or very old-fashioned
2. A weakness that someone has that can be taken advantage of
3. Refers to someone who is unrealistic and has no chance of success
4. A person that bravely rescues someone from a dangerous situation
5. Refers to something you ask someone to look after while you are away
6. A situation where something bad can happen to a person at any time

ROAD and STREET

A. 1. Hit the **road**
   2. Take the high **road**
   3. The **road** less travelled
   4. Easy **street**
   5. Man in the **street**
   6. Right up your **street/alley**

B. Place the idioms correctly in the sentences below

1. It was honorable for Max to _____ and not criticize Jim, after finding out that Jim spread rumors about him.

2. Joe's just your average _____. There's nothing complicated about him.

3. I told Victor to _____ after he tried to make a pass at me.

4. I usually like to take _____ when I'm travelling. I don't like only hitting the popular tourist attractions.

5. The boss gave me the Baker account because he said this work is _____ _____my _____, but to tell you the truth, I know nothing about mutual funds.

6. Working with Tanya is like being on _____. She does her duties so well, that it makes it easier for others to do their jobs well.

C. Discussion

1. Is it difficult to take the high road when someone else criticizes you?
2. Name a situation that put you on easy street.

D. Meanings

1. To tell someone to get lost
2. To behave in a moral or acceptable way, especially when others criticize you, or do something that harms you
3. To chose a path or option that is not the one primarily used before
4. A comfortable way to do things, or a comfortable situation
5. An ordinary, average person
6. A thing you are comfortable with, know how to do well, or like

SCHOOL

A. 1. To **school** someone   **OR**   **School** someone
   2. Old **school** ways
   3. Old **school** ties
   4. The **school** of hard knocks
   5. A **school** of thought
   6. Ole **skool**

B. Place the idioms correctly in the sentences below

1. _____ says that parents should be as positive as they can be with their children in regards to their school work.

2. My dad listens to older music, and now that I listened with him, I can say that I also like _____ tunes.

3. When grandpa was a miner, no one taught him how to do his job. Grandpa learned things at _____.

4. Jim _____ Ted in the basketball game. Now Ted can't brag that he's the best basketball player.

5. Our math teacher is not very current in his methods. He always relies on _____ to teach his subject.

6. Lots of people in our firm used _____ to get their job.

C. Discussion

1. Why do you think ole skool tunes are becoming popular again?
2. Have you ever been to the school of hard knocks? When and how?

D. Meanings

1. To beat someone in something by a large margin, thereby teaching this person a lesson in how to do this particular thing
2. Refers to the old traditional values or ways of doing things
3. Refers to people who use their previous personal ties with friends from their old school, to enhance each other's personal positions
4. Refers to instances where lessons are learned the hard way
5. A particular point of view on a subject or topic
6. Refers to things that were popular in the past, like older music

WORLD

A. 1. Come down in the **world**
2. It's a small **world**
3. Not the end of the **world**
4. On top of the **world**
5. Out of this **world**
6. The **world** is your oyster

B. Place the idioms correctly in the sentences below

1. I bumped into June in France last week. _____.

2. Tom travels a lot and seems to meet the most exciting people. I can truly say that _____ his _____.

3. The newly elected President feels like he's _____.
   He came from a long way back in the polls to defeat the incumbent.

4. Jim _____ when his company went bankrupt.
   Now he has a lot less money, and very few influential friends.

5. Its _____ that you're not dating Pamela now. If you give it time, she'll probably come back to you soon.

6. My vacation was _____. I had a terrific time travelling through Western Europe.

C. Discussion

1. Has anything happened to you to make you think that it is a small world?
2. Do you know anyone for whom the world is her or his oyster?

D. Meanings

1. Refers to a person that is not as rich as they used to be, or that does not have the same social status as they once had
2. A comment made when someone bumps into someone in an unexpected place, or when they both know someone that they thought they didn't
3. This means that a person should not take too seriously anything bad that happens
4. To feel very, very happy, or to have achieved a great feat
5. To feel a sense of excitement over something that is truly incredible
6. A comment made to anyone who can do whatever they want, or go to any place that they want

SECTION 16 – SCIENCE, ATOMS, ELEMENTS and NUMBERS

ASTRONOMY

A. 1. Ask for the **moon**
   2. Men are from **Mars** and women are from **Venus**
   3. What/which **planet** are you on/from?
   4. Reach for the **stars**
   5. Have **stars** in your eyes
   6. The **Sun** is over the yardarm

B. Place the idioms correctly in the sentences below

1. Its now 7 PM and we can finally have a beer because _____
   _____.

2. Ken _____ his _____. He's trying to become an actor.

3. Mike's dad pushed him hard and made him _____
   when he was a boy playing hockey. That's why Mike made it to the NHL.

4. When Tom asked to borrow $5,000, I asked him _____
   _____ you _____. Tom should know I don't have that kind of money.

5. I don't understand women and women don't understand men. Its obvious
   that _____.

6. Tanya is _____ when she asks me to stand up to
   the boss. If I do that, she knows I'll get fired.

C. Discussion

1. Do you agree that men are from Mars and women are from Venus?
2. Have ever dated anyone that seemed to ask you for the Moon?

D. Meanings

1. To ask for something that is unattainable
2. This implies that men and women have completely different mind frames
3. A reference to someone who has unrealistic expectations, or who is not aware
   about certain simple issues or facts
4. To try to achieve a very difficult thing, or to have high expectations
5. To be excited and enthusiastic about what your future expectations are
6. To be late enough to have an alcoholic beverage

119

ATOMS AND ELEMENTS

A. 1. **Lead** foot
   2. Get the **lead** out
   3. Go down like a **lead** balloon
   4. **Carbon** copy
   5. Take <u>something</u> with a grain of **salt**
   6. Have a **tin** ear

B. Place the idioms correctly in the sentences below

1. I _____ because I've never been able to really appreciate classical music, or even play a musical instrument.

2. I don't like being in the car with Samuel because he has a _____ _____. He drives too fast so I'm afraid for my safety when he drives.

3. You should nearly always _____ what Pat says _____ _____. She always stretches the truth.

4. Bill and Joe aren't _____ of each other, even though they're identical twins. They have totally different values and interests.

5. The ideas I presented at the meeting _____ _____. The president rejected all my proposals.

6. Boss: "_____ Alf, you're not producing enough at work!"

C. Discussion

1. Does anyone in your family have a lead foot?
2. Is there anyone you know that is practically a carbon copy of yourself?

D. Meanings

1. Refers to someone who drives too fast
2. To tell someone to start working faster or moving faster
3. An idea or a concept that is very unpopular and that people do not like
4. Two things that are very similar or almost identical
5. If you take something (like information) with a grain so salt, this means that you should not totally believe this information
6. To not be able to understand or hear music well

BRASS

A. 1. The **brass** ring
   2. Cold enough to freeze the balls off a **brass** monkey
   3. Get down to **brass** tacks
   4. A **brass** farthing   ***   **an old-fashioned British Idiom**
   5. The **brass**
   6. Bold as **brass**

B. Place the idioms correctly in the sentences below

1. Negotiations will _____ now that the minor items have been agreed to. Now we have to agree on the important items.

2. Even though the new boarder has been in the dormitory for 2 months, he still hasn't paid even _____ in rent.

3. I lived up north for 1 year, so I wouldn't recommend living there. Its _____ _____ where I lived.

4. Our football team wants to win the championship every year. Our players and coaches will do anything to grab _____.

5. Jack's attitude is as _____. He showed up at Emily's party, and he wasn't even invited. She doesn't like him at all.

6. We'll put on a big parade in the center of town when _____ from the nearby military base visits the town square next week.

C. Discussion

1. Is it more important to always try to grab the brass ring, or to play with good sportsmanship?
2. Has any family member paid a lot for something, where you would not even pay a brass farthing for the same thing?

D. Meanings

1. A very successful or profitable thing or venture
2. A reference to extremely cold weather
3. To discuss the most important or fundamental points of an issue
4. To do with the paying of money, but used negatively. If you don't want to pay for something, then you won't pay a brass farthing for that thing.
5. High-ranking military or civilian officials
6. Bold, impudent or shameless

GOLD

A. 1. All that glitters is not **gold**
2. As good as **gold**
3. Pot of **gold**
4. Strike **gold**
5. There's **gold** in them thar hills
6. Worth its weight in **gold**

B. Place the idioms correctly in the sentences below

1. I _____ when I bought those stocks last year. They have increased in value almost ten times since I bought them.

2. My mother's advice is _____. She's the one who advised me to buy my house, and it has doubled in price now.

3. Ted's _____. He offered all of his support when I was going through tough times last year.

4. John's quite handsome, and seems to have a good personality, but when he double-crossed me, I realized _____.

5. I hope to get my _____ the old-fashioned way: by working hard and saving my money. Then I'll be able to retire comfortably.

6. _____. I invested in some local companies, and have done very well financially in these investments.

C. Discussion

1. Talk about advice that your received that was worth its weight in gold.
2. Discuss something that made you realize, all that glitters is not gold.

D. Meanings

1. Refers to something, or someone, that may not be as good as first thought
2. Refers to someone, or something, who does something very well, is very good at something, or that behaves very well
3. A large amount of money that a person hopes to get in the future
4. To become rich either by being doing something, or by being successful at something
5. Refers to the possibility of making money in a particular place, or by doing a particular activity in that place
6. Something that is very, very valuable, given its size

IRON

A. 1. **Iron** fist
   2. Have a lot of **irons** in the fire
   3. Cast **iron**
   4. Strike while the **iron** is hot
   5. An **iron** fist in a velvet glove
   6. Pump **iron**

B. Place the idioms correctly in the sentences below

1. His word is of the _____ variety. I totally believe in what he says.

2. Tom's muscles are so big because he has been _____ a lot.

3. It looked as if that small, gentle looking guy would lose the fight to the bigger guy, but he had _____, because he beat up the bigger guy quite badly.

4. Russian Tsars and Soviet leaders ruled with _____ before Gorbachev changed Russia for the better. Russians now have more freedom.

5. I _____ with my numerous investments. Some of them have done very well, so I have made quite a bit of money

6. I didn't buy gold when it was at a very low price so I didn't _____ _____ was _____. Now the price has gone very high, so I missed out on making a big profit.

C. Discussion

1. Do you often have many irons in the fire?
2. What is the disadvantage to striking too quickly when the iron is hot?

D. Meanings

1. Do something with great force
2. To have a number of different plans or opportunities, so that some of them will likely succeed, even if others fail
3. Something that can be believed in and that is totally and absolutely certain
4. To act quickly and absolutely when the right opportunity presents itself, and when the best chance to succeed is offered
5. Something that looks gentile or benign, but which has a lot of force
6. To lift weights

NUMBERS

A. 1. A **zero** sum game
   2. **One** love
   3. Put **two** and **two** together
   4. Give me **five**
   5. At **sixes** and **sevens**
   6. Talk **nineteen** to the **dozen**

B. Place the idioms correctly in the sentences below

1. Todd was _____ during his fight at the bar. He was very drunk, so he was making no sense.

2. After I scored the winning basket, everyone _____ me _____.

3. I believe in the motto of _____, where all people are equal.

4. Things were _____ when the boss was on holidays. Everything became very disorganized without her here.

5. Even though the evidence was scant, the policeman put _____ _____ and solved the crime.

6. Ted views nearly everything as _____. He feels he can only win if someone else loses.

C. Discussion

1. Do believe that you can avoid making anything a zero-sum game?
2. Are you good at putting two and two together when reading other people's thoughts?

D. Meanings

1. A scenario where there can only be a loser and a winner, and where an advantage to one person comes at a disadvantage to another person
2. All humanity is the same and everyone should love everyone else
3. To make a correct guess on something, based on available information
4. To slap hands together without someone else because you are both pleased that some thing just happened
5. Refers to someone who is confused and disorganized
6. To talk very quickly, without pausing

OIL and GAS

A. 1. He's/she's a **gas**
   2. Run out of **gas**
   3. I'm **gassed**
   4. The good **oil**
   5. No **oil** painting   ***   **mainly a British Idiom**
   6. Strike **oil**

B. Place the idioms correctly in the sentences below

1. Make sure to invite Tom to the party because he always knows how to make people laugh. He's _____.

2. Barb _____ with her new invention. Now that's its patented, she stands to make a fortune.

3. The information Alf gave me is _____. It's very reliable.

4. I was winning the race until it came to the last stretch. The other runner from Nigeria passed me because I _____.

5. I can't go out to the dinner meeting tonight. I did too many things today so I'm _____. I need to have a good rest instead.

6. If you ask me, that model is _____. I wonder how she became a model.

C. Discussion

1. What's the difference between the idioms "I'm gassed", and "Run out of gas"?
2. Did you ever receive information that turned out to be the good oil?

D. Meanings

1. To be a very funny person
2. To run out of energy or to lose interest in something
3. To be very, very tired
4. Good or reliable information
5. To comment on somebody that is not attractive
6. To become suddenly successful in something, or, to suddenly come into a lot of money

ORIDNAL NUMBERS

A. 1. Draw **1st** blood
   2. Play **2nd** fiddle
   3. The **3rd** degree
   4. A **3rd** wheel
   5. **6th** sense
   6. The **11th** hour

B. Place the idioms correctly in the sentences below

1. The deal between the union and the owners came at the last possible moment, narrowly averting a strike. It came at _____.

2. The other team won the 1st game and _____ in the volleyball tournament, but they still have to win 2 more games to beat us.

3. I felt like _____ when I went to dinner with Pete and Sonia. They hardly paid attention to me the whole night.

4. The boss hassles me and gives me _____ whenever I'm late.

5. I don't mind _____ to Jim for now, because he knows I'll be promoted first and have a better job than him in the future.

6. Mary has a _____ about my feelings towards love. She's the only one that can read my mind when it comes to this.

C. Discussion

1. What things do you think you have a 6th sense about?
2. Have you felt like a 3rd wheel when you went out with another couple?

D. Meanings

1. To be the first to score or win in a competition
2. A person that is less important, or has a lesser role, than someone else
3. To be grilled, questioned, harassed or interrogated by someone else, over something you did, whether that thing is good or bad
4. Someone who is not wanted, or not needed, when a couple will suffice
5. To have an intuitive feeling about a particular event or occurrence, without using or relying on any of the 5 primary senses
6. Usually refers to something that is accomplished or completed at the absolutely last possible second

SCIENCE

A. 1. The **acid** test
   2. Have **chemistry**
   3. In a **vacuum**
   4. Its not **rocket science**
   5. Blind someone with **science**
   6. On the same **wavelength**

B. Place the idioms correctly in the sentences below

1. Why can't Will understand grade 7 Math? _____.

2. Sid seems to think that his personal life exists _____.
   He doesn't realize his constant partying is affecting his work.

3. Jim and Pam are usually _____. They seem to
   agree on almost everything.

4. _____ for the new teaching methods will be in how well
   the students do in the final exams.

5. Sal and Tanya _____. They're a match made in
   heaven.

6. The boss _____ us _____ whenever he explains how
   to work office machinery. He should use simpler ways to teach us.

C. Discussion

1. Do your personal life and educational life exist in separate vacuums?
2. Talk about someone that you had an immediate feeling of chemistry with.

D. Meanings

1. A test that determines how effective or valid something is
2. Where two people are a perfect match for each other
3. Something that exists or happens separately from what it would be expected to
   happen with
4. Refers to something that should not be difficult to do
5. To tell someone about something in a very difficult or technical way, making it
   very hard for them to understand you
6. To have the same line of thought or method of thinking as someone else

127

SILVER and GOLD

A. 1. **Gold** digger
   2. **Gold** mine of information
   3. **Golden** handshake
   4. On a **silver** platter
   5. A **silver** lining
   6. Born with a **silver** spoon in your mouth

B. Place the idioms correctly in the sentences below

1. Bob is fortunate that Tammy found another man. Tammy isn't motivated by love, she's only interested in money, that _____.

2. _____ in being fired is you won't have to work with Sid anymore.

3. Ann's extremely knowledgeable in all aspects of the stock market. I count on her advice because she's a _____.

4. Sam's always had things given to him. He hasn't work hard for anything because he was _____ his _____.

5. Jamie retired early because of the incentives his company gave him. He got the _____, so now he has a lot of money.

6. Mike's dad owns the company, so he didn't have to work hard to get his job. Mike gets everything handed to him _____.

C. Discussion

1. Have you ever had anything handed to you on a silver platter?
2. Who do you know that is a gold mine of information?

D. Meanings

1. Refers to someone who is only interested in another person's money
2. Refers to someone or some thing that is a great source of information
3. Refers to a person who receives a large sum of money to leave a job years before they are scheduled to retire
4. Refers to something that is given to someone, without that person having to work hard for it
5. A good or positive thing, in an otherwise bad situation
6. A child who has very rich parents, and who is usually very spoiled

SECTION 17 – SPORTS AND GAMES

BALL 1

A. 1. **Ball** and chain
   2. A crystal **ball**
   3. Drop the **ball**
   4. Have a **ball**
   5. Keep the **ball** rolling
   6. On the **ball**

B. Place the idioms correctly in the sentences below

1. I don't have _____, Becky, so I don't know if the price of houses will drop in the future, or whether prices will rise.

2. Kyle's always _____ at work, as he seems to be able to anticipate changing market conditions.

3. Debt is now the _____ that is bringing down Greece.

4. My family wants me to _____ and join the army, like my father and grandfather before me, but I want to be a chef, not a soldier.

5. The lawyer _____ when he failed to produce evidence that would have gotten his client acquitted.

6. I _____ in Europe this summer. I especially enjoyed staying with our relatives in France.

C. Discussion

1. If you had a crystal ball, what kind of future would you predict for yourself?
2. Have you ever been asked to continue a process, and keep the ball rolling?

D. Meanings

1. Something that limits a person's, or a thing's, freedom
2. Something that is used to predict the future
3. To make a mistake or do something that is considered foolish
4. To have a great time
5. To make sure that some thing that you are involved in keeps on going
6. To deal with something in an quick, intelligent and alert manner

129

Marco Antonio Bussanich

BALL 2

A. 1. Pick up the **ball** and run with it
   2. Play **hardball**
   3. Start the **ball** rolling
   4. A whole new **ball** game
   5. Break someone's **balls**
   6. Keep **balls** in the air

B. Place the idioms correctly in the sentences below

1. I couldn't _____ (all my) _____ this semester.
   I was trying to work at 2 part-time jobs while taking a full load of courses.

2. I _____ in our neighborhood last year when I was the
   first person to rollerblade. Now everyone's doing it.

3. Amanda's _____ my _____ about the date I cancelled.
   She won't let me forget it, and now I'm depressed over the matter.

4. I _____ with Mike's blueprints of the building.
   Now I'm continuing on with the process of building it.

5. Its _____ now that we have a new teacher.
   She's very strict, and disciplines anyone for the smallest transgressions.

6. My mom's _____ with me now. She won't give me
   my allowance until I start studying hard for Math.

C. Discussion

1. Have you ever had to play hardball with someone? In particular, did you have to
   threaten to take drastic actions against them?
2. As a student, do you feel you have to keep many balls in the air?

D. Meanings

1. Use a plan or idea that someone else started, and then develop it further
2. Try to force someone into doing what you want them to do
3. To be the person that starts a process which other people join in on later
4. Something that is totally different than the thing that preceded it
5. Create problems for a person to make him lose his confidence
6. Deal with a number of different matters at the same time

GAME

A. 1. The **game** is up
   2. Ahead of the **game**
   3. New to the **game**
   4. Beat <u>someone</u> at <u>their</u> own **game**
   5. Play a waiting **game**
   6. Give the **game** away

B. Place the idioms correctly in the sentences below

1. Khloe's _____ when it comes to her fashion sense.

2. I _____ Terrence _____ his _____ by going to the same tennis school as him. Now I've learned all of his tricks, and I can beat him.

3. Sally _____ when she told the other team's cheerleader about our team's secret plays. That's why their team beat us last week.

4. I can't ask anyone else to the prom. I have to _____ _____ because Sabrina hasn't told me if she'll go to the prom with me.

5. Bob sensed that _____ when the teacher pressured him, so he finally admitted that he cheated on the Math test.

6. I'm _____ when it comes to dating, so I'm not sure how to ask a girl out on a date.

C. Discussion

1. Is it difficult to keep ahead of the game when it comes to fashion?
2. Talk about a situation when someone gave the game away, when you did not want them to.

D. Meanings

1. Refers to a situation where a person can no longer continue to do things illegally, because it has now been revealed what this person is doing
2. To know about all recent developments with respect to something, and then to use this knowledge to keep ahead of others
3. To have no experience in a certain area or activity you are now involved in
4. To defeat someone, or do something better than them, in an activity that they were thought to have an advantage in
5. To wait out a situation, for the purpose of seeing how it will develop
6. To reveal something which others have been trying to keep secret

GOLF

A. 1. **Par** for the course
   2. On **par** with
   3. Under **par**
   4. To a **tee**
   5. Down to a **tee**
   6. In full **swing**

B. Place the idioms correctly in the sentences below

1. Emma's singing ability is _____ some of the greatest opera singers. I believe she'll be a star one day.

2. I've got linear algebra _____ now. I know I'll ace the exam.

3. Jane's results in the Math test are just _____ for her. She didn't fail, but she didn't do all that well.

4. The celebrations for Halloween are now _____. There's so many people, both children and adults, dressed in Halloween costumes.

5. This suit fits me _____. I won't have to pay extra for any alterations.

6. Your results in the test were _____ Joel. We both know that you can do much better than that.

C. Discussion

1. Describe a piece of clothing you once bought that fit you to a tee.
2. Talk about a movie you saw recently where the acting was under par.

D. Meanings

1. Something which is not very good, but as good as can be expected
2. Something that is of the same standard as something else
3. A thing that is not on as high as a level as it could be
4. Something that is perfect or 100% right
5. A thing that has practiced so many times, so that the person can do it perfectly now
6. Something that has been operating fully for some time, rather than it just beginning, or just starting up

SPORTS 1

A. 1. Out of **bounds**
   2. For a **kick-off**
   3. **Offside**
   4. **Play by play** description
   5. Monday morning **quarterback**
   6. **Three strikes** against someone (and now you're out)

B. Place the idioms correctly in the sentences below

1. I didn't like it when Al gave a _____ of my personal life in front of everyone at the party. That was very rude.

2. Kevin was _____ making those rude comments at the social.

3. That area of the ski hill is _____ because there have been a few avalanches there.

4. Its easy to be a _____ and criticize my performance, but Jim would not have done any better at the time.

5. _____, you've been late to school a number of times: and that's just one of the many things you've done wrong at school.

6. Willie, that's _____ you now. You know if you commit three crimes, then you have to go to jail for a very long time.

C. Discussion

1. How many times have you been a Monday morning quarterback, especially when it comes to analyzing the mistakes your friends make?
2. What's your opinion of the three strikes you're out law? Is it fair?

D. Meanings

1. A place where people are not allowed to go to
2. Refers to just the first thing in a long list of things that can be mentioned about a particular occurrence
3. Refers to a particularly rude comment or gesture
4. To give a detailed analysis or description of something
5. A person who criticizes something from a distance, after having the benefit of hindsight to analyze the situation
6. A law in America that punishes a person very severely if they commit three separate crimes

SPORTS 2

A. 1. A **ballpark** figure
   2. **Jockey** for position
   3. A level **playing field**
   4. A **ringside** seat
   5. Settle an old **score**
   6. On the **sidelines**

B. Place the idioms correctly in the sentences below

1. There's not _____ for the students in our class. The teacher favors the students who suck up to her.

2. I had _____ to the feud between Joe and Pete because my desk is right in between theirs.

3. I stayed _____ when John and Stan had an argument. I didn't want to get involved because I'm friends with both of them.

4. I knew that Joe would want to _____ with Andy at the class re-union. I wasn't surprised, then, when they started fighting.

5. _____ for the renovation of our home is about $10,000.

6. People in the crowd with cameras _____ when the royal couple came out of the hotel. Everyone wanted to get a good picture.

C. Discussion

1. Have you ever tried to settle an old score with someone?
2. Give a ballpark figure on how much it will cost for your post-secondary school education.

D. Meanings

1. A rough estimate
2. To try to get in a better position than your competitors
3. Where no one has an unfair advantage over anyone else
4. To have a clear view of what is happening
5. To get revenge for something done to you in the past
6. To watch something happen without being involved in it

SPORTS 3

A.
1. Get to **1st base**
2. The **ball** is in <u>your</u> court
3. Play **ball**
4. Throw <u>someone</u> a **curve ball**
5. Move the **goalposts**
6. Hit a **home run**

B. Place the idioms correctly in the sentences below

1. Tammy _____ me _____ when she said that we couldn't get married yet. She now wants to attend university first.

2. The boss _____ after I agreed to cater the company picnic. He originally told me twelve people were coming, but that's now been changed to 25 people.

3. Tony wouldn't _____ with me when I asked him to date Beth's cousin. Now Beth won't go out with me.

4. I can't even _____ with Tanya. I'd like to date her long term, but she won't even go out on a first date with me.

5. The _____ Vicky's _____ now. I asked her to marry me, so now its her decision to say yes or no.

6. I _____ when I bought my apartment. The prices in the area suddenly doubled right after I purchased it.

C. Discussion

1. Has the ball ever been in your court regarding an important decision?
2. What thing have you hit a home-run in?

D. Meanings

1. To begin to see progress in the carrying out of a plan
2. It is now a person's responsibility to make the next decision or to make the next move
3. Refers to someone who makes you do what they want you to do
4. Refers to something that is done unexpectedly, which causes problems
5. To change the rules or something about a situation, which suddenly makes it more difficult for other people to compete as effectively
6. To do something successfully, or to have an unexpected gain

SECTION 18 – THE HUMAN BODY

BLOOD

A. 1. Bad **blood**
   2. Be after **blood**
   3. Get **blood** out of a stone
   4. New **blood**
   5. Have **blood** on your hands
   6. **Blood** on the carpet

B. Place the idioms correctly in the sentences below

1. I can't get Adam to tell us who broke the window. Getting Adam to rat on his friends is like _____.

2. There's been a lot of _____ between Jack and Bob ever since Jack stole Bob's girlfriend from him.

3. Harry wants retribution and has _____ ever since Norm wrongly blamed him for the car accident.

4. The only way stop to our losing streak is to bring in _____.

5. The feud between the two vice presidents of our company has hurt our company a lot. The fighting left a lot of _____.

6. No one believed that bad weather was the cause of the accident. We all know the driver of the van _____ his _____.

C. Discussion

1. Why is it difficult for some people to forgive others, and instead, allow bad blood to continue to exist?
2. Why do some people continue to try to get blood out of a stone?

D. Meanings

1. The bad feelings that exist between people because of past arguments
2. A desire to punish someone for something they have done to you
3. A situation where it is almost impossible to get someone to give you something
4. New people who are brought into a group, to add some needed energy
5. A person who's responsible for a death, or for a bad thing happening
6. Refers to the trouble within a group that is a result of a struggle between members of a group

BODY PARTS

A. 1. Cover your **back**
   2. **Elbow** grease
   3. **Heart** of the matter
   4. **Knee** jerk reaction
   5. Stick your **neck** out
   6. Vent your **spleen**

B. Place the idioms correctly in the sentences below

1. I think its okay to _____ every once in a while. A person can release a lot of tension in that way.

2. I _____ my _____ for James when he was last in trouble, but he didn't appreciate my efforts. I won't be doing that anymore.

3. Brad's _____ to the teacher's comments brought him a lot of trouble. The teacher is upset at him now because of this.

4. I always _____ my _____ by recounting the money at the end of the day.

5. It took a lot of _____ to restore my old car.

6. Sid never gets to the _____ in conversations. He always talks about issues that have nothing to do with what we're discussing.

C. Discussion

1. Talk about a time when you stuck your neck out for someone.
2. How often do you vent your spleen, either in public or private.

D. Meanings

1. To take measures to protect yourself, against things like criticism, or accusations of wrongdoing
2. To expend great effort to work hard at something
3. The most important part of an issue
4. A quick, senseless reaction to something
5. To do something for someone, even though this may cause you harm, pain or misfortune
6. To express your anger about some thing

Marco Antonio Bussanich

FEET

A. 1. Find your **feet**
   2. Get cold **feet**
   3. Get one's **feet** wet
   4. Have two left **feet**
   5. Stand on your own two **feet**
   6. Vote with your **feet**

B. Place the idioms correctly in the sentences below

1. My son has to _____ his _____ and stop relying on me for assistance. He still doesn't make enough money to support himself.

2. It was embarrassing for me to dance with my wife at my wedding because I _____. I'm not a good dancer.

3. I still don't know the new neighborhood very well. I've only been here one month, so I'm still _____ my _____.

4. The burger joint closed down a few weeks after it opened. The food was quite bad, so people _____ their _____ and stopped going.

5. I thought I'd start the new employee on some easy things, just so she could _____ her _____.

6. Elsa _____ at the last minute and backed out of the wedding.

C. Discussion

1. What is the most recent thing that you have gotten your feet wet on?
2. At what age should a son or daughter be able to stand on their own two feet?

D. Meanings

1. To learn what to do in a new situation and become more confident doing it
2. To become nervous or anxious over a planned endeavor, and to either not do it anymore, or begin to have doubts about not doing it
3. To begin a new endeavor, and try it for the first time
4. Do not have the talent or ability to dance
5. To be independent, without relying on anyone else for help or support
6. To show displeasure over a place, a situation, or an event, by leaving it

FINGER

A. 1. Point your **finger** at someone
   2. Put your **finger** on something
   3. Get your **fingers** burned
   4. Have your **finger** on the pulse
   5. Wrap someone around your **finger**
   6. Have a **finger** in every pie

B. Place the idioms correctly in the sentences below

1. I _____ my _____ the last time I got turned down after asking Becky out, so I won't be asking her out again.

2. Sue _____ Jon _____ her _____ as soon as they started dating.

3. Samantha has a good knack of _____ her _____ _____ of things around the office. That's why she got promoted.

4. John is good at _____ his _____ at other people when things go wrong, but he's usually the one who makes the mistake.

5. Its hard to _____, in the same way that Jan does. I don't know where she finds the time to do all those things.

6. I can't _____ my _____ on the reason, but for some unknown reason, I haven't been on a date in months.

C. Discussion

1. What problem in your life went unsolved for a long time because you were unable to put your finger on what was the cause of the problem?
2. Is it realistic to assume that a person can have a finger in every pie?

D. Meanings

1. To blame someone for something
2. To be able to determine the root cause of something
3. To face unpleasant consequences for something a person has done
4. To understand something very well, or to have thorough knowledge about something
5. To be able to make someone do anything that you want them to do
6. To be involved in a lot of activities or things

Marco Antonio Bussanich

FOOT

A. 1. Get a **foot** in the door
   2. Get off on the wrong **foot**
   3. One **foot** in the grave
   4. Put your best **foot** forward
   5. Put your **foot** down
   6. Shoot yourself in the **foot**

B. Place the idioms correctly in the sentences below

1. My dad's very ill and won't recover. He has _____.

2. Terra's not really content with her new position, but she took it to _____ _____ in the hopes of being promoted in the future.

3. I'm going to _____ my _____ for the interview, by dressing as well as I can, and by being on my best behavior.

4. Dan _____ himself _____ when he insults his clients, but the still hopes they'll do business with him.

5. Its too bad Tim and Sid _____ when they first met. They have lots in common so they'll eventually become good friends.

6. Mom's going to _____ her _____, and ground us the next time we act up. We should start behaving, because mom's quite angry.

C. Discussion

1. Talk about a time when you shot yourself in the foot in front of others.
2. Have you ever gotten off on the wrong foot with someone, only to become extremely good friends with them at a later time?

D. Meanings

1. To start in a lower position than desired in a company you want to work for, for the purpose of eventually moving up and getting your coveted position
2. To start a relationship in a negative or bad way
3. To be gravely ill, and near to death
4. To show your best quality or to work as hard as you can
5. To act with force, telling someone they must stop a certain activity
6. To say something, which harms your future chances of success, or which causes you problems in the future

140

GUTS

A. 1. Spill <u>your</u> **guts**
   2. **Gut** feeling
   3. Work <u>your</u> **guts** out
   4. Hate <u>someone's</u> **guts**
   5. **Gut** reaction
   6. **Guts**

B. <u>Place the idioms correctly in the sentences below</u>

1. I _____ my _____ preparing for that presentation, and all of my hard work paid off, because the manager loved my ideas.

2. Bob has a lot of _____. He criticized the teacher in front of the class.

3. I _____ <u>Wilma's</u> _____. She gossiped about my personal life, and told everyone that I love Johnny. I will never speak to her again!

4. My initial _____ about Andy were correct. I knew that he wouldn't keep his promises.

5. My _____ were wrong. I prejudged Billy, and thought that he was a bad kid, when he really wasn't.

6. I _____ my _____ to the police and told them everything. I'm safe now, but the other students will be in trouble because I ratted on them.

C. Discussion

1. Have you ever had a gut reaction about something before, only to find out that your intuitions were true?
2. What is the difference in meaning between the idioms "Have a gut reaction", and "Gut feeling"?

D. Meanings

1. Confess to something, OR, talk about things that are secret or private
2. To know that you are right about something, without having proof to justify your feelings
3. Work very hard at something
4. To dislike or hate someone very much
5. To have an immediate and strong reaction to something or someone, without thinking it through, or without knowing the reasons for your reaction
6. Refers to a person who has a lot of courage

HAIR

A. 1. Split **hairs**
   2. Tear <u>your</u> **hair** out
   3. In <u>your</u> **hair**
   4. Let <u>your</u> **hair** down
   5. A **hair's** breadth
   6. Make <u>your</u> **hair** curl

B. <u>Place the idioms correctly in the sentences below</u>

1. Seeing Sarah's son drive the way he does _____ <u>my</u> _____ _____. I'm so worried that he'll get into a serious accident one day.

2. Tom's always _____ <u>my</u> _____ at work. I can never get him to stop giving me advice.

3. I came within _____ of failing the exam. I only scored 50%.

4. Stop _____ Agnes. You always seem to cause the greatest amount of commotion over the smallest details!

5. I'm extremely happy this hectic day is over. Now that the boss of the company is gone, I can finally _____ <u>my</u> _____ and relax.

6. I'm _____ <u>my</u> _____ over losing my phone. I had all of my important phone numbers stored in it.

C. <u>Discussion</u>

1. What things make your hair curl when you see them?
2. Describe the actions of a person who always seemed to get in your hair.

D. <u>Meanings</u>

1. To emphasize or argue about very, very small details, even when they are not important enough to argue about
2. Refers to someone who is very upset or anxious about something
3. Refers to someone or something that is either annoying you, or is interfering with what you are trying to do
4. To relax, usually after something hectic or stressful has happened
5. Something that is within the smallest of margins
6. Refers to something that causes you great worry, or that shocks you

HAND 1

A. 1. Bite the **hand** that feeds <u>you</u>
    2. Force <u>someone's</u> **hand**
    3. Get out of **hand**
    4. Give with one **hand** and take with the other
    5. **Hand** in glove
    6. **Hand** over fist

B. Place the idioms correctly in the sentences below

1. We can _____ the government's _____ by threatening them with a boycott of the vote.

2. Tony _____ because he helps with my homework, but then he demands that I carry his books at school.

3. Gangs in some cities actually work _____ with the police.

4. The new restaurant is making money _____ because its the only Italian restaurant in the area.

5. The protest _____ after a policeman was shoved.

6. Pam coddles her son, Jack, but Jack gets angry when he doesn't get what he wants: talk about _____ <u>you</u>.

C. Discussion

1. Has anyone tried to force your hand with regard to something?
2. Talk about a situation you were in when someone gave something to you with one hand, but then took with the other hand.

D. Meanings

1. To betray or do something bad to a person who helps or supports you
2. To force someone to do something they do not want to do
3. Refers to a situation that has gotten out of control
4. To help someone in one way, but then to do something else that hurts or hinders them
5. To work very closely with someone or some thing
6. To make or lose a lot of money very quickly

HAND 2

A. 1. Have to **hand** it to <u>someone</u>
   2. Have <u>someone</u> eating out of the palm of <u>your</u> **hand**
   3. Have a **hand** in <u>something</u>
   4. **Hand** in the till **OR** Have <u>your</u> **hand** in the till
   5. In the palm of <u>your</u> **hand**
   6. Know <u>something</u> like the back of <u>your</u> **hand**

B. <u>Place the idioms correctly in the sentences below</u>

1. The performance tonight was terrific. All the teachers worked hard at it, so everyone _____ <u>producing it.</u>

2. I _____ these mountain trails _____ <u>my</u> _____. I've been hiking them since I was a kid.

3. I _____ <u>Bill.</u> He beat Sid in golf today, and Bill only started playing last year. Sid is a seasoned pro.

4. The camp staffer <u>has the children</u> _____ <u>his</u> _____. The children have never had someone that treats them so well.

5. I caught Sam with his _____ at work, so I had to let him go.

6. Sue thinks she has me _____ <u>her</u> _____, but I'm not influenced by her as much as she thinks.

C. <u>Discussion</u>

1. Have you ever thought that you had someone in the palm of your hand, only to realize that they somehow slipped away?
2. What thing do you know like the back of your hand?

D. <u>Meanings</u>

1. Implies that someone admires something that someone else has done
2. Refers to a situation where someone will do anything you want them to do, because they either like or admire you a lot
3. To be one of the people involved in doing or creating something
4. To steal from an employer, or a group you belong to
5. To keep someone under control, by using your wits or personality
6. To know something very, very well

HAND 3

A. 1. Old **hand**
   2. The right **hand** doesn't know what the left hand is doing
   3. Show your **hand**
   4. Take someone in **hand**
   5. Throw in your **hand**
   6. The upper **hand**

B. Place the idioms correctly in the sentences below

1. You can trust Bill. He's an _____ in dealing with horses.

2. Western countries used to have _____ over Eastern countries, but this is changing with the economic development of the East.

3. Our department does not coordinate well with accounting. There is too much confusion and we're not working well together. In our situation,

   _____.

4. I _____ my _____ in trying to pass Math because I can never understand it.

5. The other coach hasn't _____ his _____ in how he'll deal with our top player. I know he has some good plans on how to try to stop him.

6. The teacher _____ Johnny _____, because it was clear that Johnny would fail if he were left to try to pass on his own.

C. Discussion

1. Has anyone ever taken you in hand to help you with a problem of yours?
2. Does someone you know always try to get the upper hand on you?

D. Meanings

1. Someone that has a lot of experience in something
2. The people in one part or section of something do not know what the people in the other part are doing, leading to a confusing situation
3. To reveal to other people what your intentions are
4. To take control of someone, in order to help them with their situation
5. To give up on something because you realize you will not succeed
6. To be in a dominant or superior position over someone else

HEAD 1

A. 1. Have <u>your</u> **head** in the clouds
   2. In over <u>your</u> **head**
   3. Have <u>your</u> **head** screwed on backwards
   4. Go over <u>someone's</u> **head**
   5. Keep <u>your</u> **head** down
   6. Lose <u>your</u> **head**

B. Place the idioms correctly in the sentences below

1. I _____ my _____ when I noticed that I had lost my wallet because I had all of my savings in the wallet.

2. I _____ Stanley's _____ when I went to his boss for the authorization for this project. This made Stanley very unhappy.

3. I _____ my _____ when I heard the other gang was coming into our turf, because I wanted to avoid a confrontation with them.

4. We realized Justin was getting _____ <u>his</u> _____ when he bought that expensive apartment and car. Now he's unable to pay his bills.

5. It seems to me that May _____ her _____. She doesn't seem to possess the intelligence to understand simple directions.

6. Bret _____ his _____ because he doesn't accept the fact that this overdrinking is affecting everything in his life.

C. Discussion

1. Do you think it is proper to go over your boss' head at work?
2. Describe a situation where you have lost your head in public.

D. Meanings

1. Refers to a person who does not know what is happening around them, and who is not realistic about things
2. To be in situation that is too difficult to deal with
3. To be unsensible and unrealistic
4. To open a line of communication with someone that is in a superior position to the person in authority whose directives you are trying to override
5. To avoid being noticed
6. To lose your calm and cool, and to panic in a difficult situation

HEAD 2

A. 1. Off the top of your **head**
   2. Bang your **head** against a wall
   3. Laugh your **head** off
   4. Scratch your **head**
   5. Keep your **head**
   6. Put your **head** in a noose

B. Place the idioms correctly in the sentences below

1. Zack _____ his _____ too often. He provoke the teacher too much, so this will almost assure that he'll fail the class.

2. I was able to _____ my _____ when the robbery happened, because I didn't panic. I therefore got a very good look at the robber.

3. _____ my _____, I can't tell you whether all the students will pass. I haven't looked at their grades lately.

4. I felt like _____ my _____ yesterday in class. My students were very disobedient and wouldn't listen to my directions.

5. We were all _____ our _____ at the club last night when Jim got up to dance. His dancing was just horrible.

6. We were all left _____ our _____ when we saw Sue out on a date with Ralph. We never thought Ralph could date such a beautiful woman.

C. Discussion

1. Discuss a situation where you have felt like banging your head against a wall.
2. How often do you think people talk off the top of their heads?

D. Meanings

1. To say something spontaneously without knowing much about it, or without checking the facts in regard to this thing
2. To feel frustrated, because it seems that you are not making progress in the thing that you are trying to do
3. To laugh a lot
4. To be puzzled and uncertain about something
5. To remain cool and calm in a tense or difficult situation
6. Do something deliberately that will put you in a difficult or dangerous situation

HEAD 3

A. 1. Bury your **head** in the sand
   2. Get your **head** around something
   3. Fall **head** over **heals**
   4. Get into someone's **head**
   5. Go to your **head**
   6. Keep your **head** above water

B. Place the idioms correctly in the sentences below

1. I'm just _____ my _____ these days. Most steel companies have collapsed, but I have managed to avoid bankruptcy.

2. It's very disturbing that I'm letting Angelo _____ my _____. He seems to almost always know what I am thinking.

3. I think that being elected class valedictorian _____ Billy's _____. He's too conceited these days.

4. Tim and Patty _____ in love with each other as soon as they met. They make a great couple.

5. My mother _____ her _____ when I tell her I'm not going to university. She won't accept this.

6. It was difficult for me to _____ my _____ the idea that my daughter is dating boys now. She's 17, but to me, she's still my little baby.

C. Discussion

1. Name a situation where you have continually buried your head in the sand.
2. Has someone else ever gotten into your head? How has this happened?

D. Meanings

1. To refuse to accept the truth about an unpleasant thing
2. To try to succeed in accepting or understanding something
3. To fall suddenly and completely in love with someone
4. To be able to know or understand what someone is really thinking
5. A situation where someone starts to believe that they are more intelligent or better than other people
6. To have just enough money to survive, either in a personal sense, or for a business

HEART

A. 1. Bleeding **heart**
  2. Cross <u>my</u> **heart**
  3. Lose **heart**
  4. Take <u>something</u> to **heart**
  5. Have <u>your</u> **heart** set on <u>something</u>
  6. Wear <u>your</u> **heart** on <u>your</u> <u>sleeve</u>

B. Place the idioms correctly in the sentences below

1. Jan _____ everything _____ in the worst way. She becomes too emotional over even the smallest issues.

2. When I asked Pam to marry me, I _____ my _____, and promised that my days of partying were over.

3. This government has too many _____ in it. They spend too much money and time on social issues.

4. John doesn't _____ his _____, so I wasn't sure about his reaction to Jennifer dating other guys.

5. I _____ when I got fired. Its difficult finding work these days.

6. I _____ my _____ going on vacation, but then there were too many things to do at work, so I had to cancel my vacation.

C. Discussion

1. Is it a difficult thing to do, to not wear your heart on your sleeve in front of friends?
2. What is your opinion of bleeding heart politicians?

D. Meanings

1. A person who has sympathy for poor or disadvantaged people
2. To make a very solemn promise that can be believed
3. To feel that you will be unsuccessful in doing something
4. To be greatly influenced and/or upset by a particular thing
5. To want or desire something very much, and then to put a great amount of effort into achieving this thing
6. To openly display your feelings about an issue to other people

LIP

A. 1. Button your **lip**
   2. Pay **lip** service to
   3. A stiff upper **lip**
   4. Licking your **lips**
   5. Read my **lips**
   6. My **lips** are sealed

B. Place the idioms correctly in the sentences below

1. Tom _____ our ideas about protecting the environment, but then he makes no effort to recycle his trash.

2. I _____ my _____ when the teacher talked about me in class. I completely disagreed with her, but I didn't speak and cause trouble.

3. Bob kept _____ when he went in for the operation. He was very afraid, but he didn't show his emotions to anyone.

4. _____ my _____, there's no way I'll let Tom use my car.

5. Although Jamie wanted me to tell him how the movie ended, I just replied, "My _____". I didn't want to ruin the movie for him.

6. Joan is _____ her _____ in anticipation of the concert.

C. Discussion

1. Talk about a time when you had to button your lip in front of friends.
2. Are you usually a "my lips are sealed" type of person when someone tells you a secret?

D. Meanings

1. To keep silent, although there is a great urge to say something
2. To be in favor of something, without saying anything to support it
3. To hide one's emotions, not letting other people see the person is upset
4. To look eagerly forward to something that is coming up
5. Refers to an issue that a lot of people are talking about
6. To state that you will keep a secret that has been told to you

MOUTH

A. 1. Foam at the **mouth**
   2. Shoot <u>your</u> **mouth** off
   3. Speak out of both sides of <u>your</u> **mouth**
   4. Put <u>one's</u> foot in <u>one's</u> **mouth** **OR** put <u>my</u> foot in <u>my</u> **mouth**
   5. All **mouth** and no trousers
   6. Live hand to **mouth**

B. <u>Place the correct idioms in the sentences below</u>

1. I got embarrassed during my speech last night. I tried to be funny, but all I did was _____ my _____ my _____ several times.

2. Pat is in a difficult situation every month. She spends her paycheck very quickly, so she _____ for most of the month.

3. Jim was _____ at the party when he saw another person flirt with his girlfriend.

4. Samuel is going to get into trouble one day. He always _____ his _____ in a social situation.

5. Jane _____ her _____ too often. She told me not to smoke, but then I saw her smoking at the party.

6. Eric is _____. He says that he'll one day dive off the cliff, but then he can't summon the nerve up to do it.

C. Discussion

1. Describe a person you know who shoots his or her mouth off.
2. Discuss a time when you put your foot in your mouth.

D. Meanings

1. To be very angry
2. To brag or boast about yourself.
3. To give different or conflicting advice on the same topic, but in different situations
4. To inadvertently say something embarrassing about someone else, when the person can hear it. This embarrasses both yourself, and the other person
5. Refers to someone who continuously says he will do something dangerous and exciting, but then never does it
6. A situation where a person can barely afford the necessities of life

Marco Antonio Bussanich

NOSE 1

A. 1. Follow your **nose**
   2. Get up someone's **nose**
   3. Keep your **nose** clean
   4. Keep your **nose** out of something
   5. Keep your **nose** to the grindstone
   6. Lead someone around by the **nose**

B. Place the idioms correctly in the sentences below

1. I told Jake to _____ his _____ my business. He was asking too many questions about my personal life.

2. Tom's girlfriend _____ him _____ all the time. He won't do anything unless she tells him to do it.

3. I _____ my _____ in college by studying Science. I would've made more money in business, but I love my career in Science.

4. While studying in university, I had to _____ my _____ _____ and study a lot, so I had little time to do anything else.

5. Sid had to _____ his _____ in his senior year of high school, because he got into too much trouble during his junior year.

6. I don't like Samantha very much, because she knows how to irritate me. It seems she enjoys _____ my _____.

C. Discussion

1. Talk about someone who seems to get up your nose.
2. Do you find it difficult to keep your nose out of your friend's life?

D. Meanings

1. To seek something by using intuition, and not by following a plan
2. Refers to someone who irritates you greatly
3. To behave properly and avoid getting into trouble
4. To tell someone, in an abrupt way, not interfere in your personal business
5. To keep working hard on something, while at the same time not devoting any time to anything else
6. Refers to someone who controls another person, and makes them do whatever they want the other person to do

NOSE 2

A. 1. Cut off <u>your</u> **nose** to spite <u>your</u> face
   2. Give <u>someone</u> a bloody **nose**
   3. Look down <u>your</u> **nose** at <u>something</u>
   4. A **nose** for <u>something</u>
   5. Cannot see beyond <u>your</u> **nose**
   6. On the **nose**

B. <u>Place the idioms correctly in the sentences below</u>

1. Jack was _____ when he predicted that investing in coffee companies would lead to the biggest gains.

2. Tara _____ her _____ and figure out that being dishonest with her husband only hurts her family.

3. Jane sure has _____ <u>being a reporter</u>. She was incredibly intuitive to have realized the mayor was the culprit in the political scandal.

4. Tim's _____ his _____ his _____. He thinks that by punishing me, he'll win in the end, but he's just hurting himself more.

5. I don't like how Samantha _____ her _____ at everyone else. She's very beautiful, but she shouldn't carry herself in that way.

6. Our team _____ <u>the other team</u> _____ in the soccer match. We defeated them quite badly.

C. <u>Discussion</u>

1. Talk about something you have a nose for.
2. Why do you think other people sometimes look down their nose at other people, or other things?

D. <u>Meanings</u>

1. Refers to a situation where someone does something to punish another person, but in doing so, actually hurts themselves more
2. To defeat or harm someone when engaging in a competition
3. To look down upon someone or something with disrespect
4. Refers to a person who has a good ability to recognize or find something
5. Refers to a person who is concerned only with their own personal satisfaction, rather than other people, or other future possible outcomes
6. Refers to a person who is exactly on time, or exactly correct in a prediction

NOSE 3

A. 1. Plain as the **nose** on <u>your</u> face
   2. Put <u>someone's</u> **nose** out of joint
   3. Rub <u>someone's</u> **nose** in it
   4. Thumb <u>your</u> **nose** at <u>someone</u>
   5. Turn <u>your</u> **nose** up at <u>something</u>
   6. Under <u>your</u> **nose**

B. <u>Place the idioms correctly in the sentences below</u>

1. Joe _____ his _____ <u>at the teacher.</u> She cannot control him.

2. I _____ <u>Peter's</u> _____ when Sally agreed to go to the prom with me instead of him.

3. Rita _____ <u>her</u> _____ <u>other girls</u> because she thinks she's the most beautiful of all.

4. The absence of the workers was happening right _____ <u>the boss'</u> _____, but he did nothing about it. That's why he was fired.

5. I didn't like it when John _____ <u>my</u> _____ after he won the tennis match. His excessive celebration was quite insulting.

6. It's as _____ <u>your</u> _____, Tommy. Jill no longer wants to see you. Leave her alone and stop pursuing her.

C. <u>Discussion</u>

1. Did you fail to see something that was as plain as the nose on your face?
2. Has someone else put your nose out of joint in public before?

D. <u>Meanings</u>

1. Something that is very obvious, and is easy to see or understand
2. To offend someone by treating them with disrespect
3. To embarrass someone by talking about something they'd rather forget
4. To show lack of respect for someone
5. To reject someone or something, and show disrespect towards it, because you believe it is not good enough for you
6. (a) refers to something which happens right in front of you, but you can do nothing to stop it, even though it is quite obvious that it is happening
   (b) refers to something which happens right in front of you, but you do not notice it, even though it is quite obvious that it is happening

PARTS OF THE FACE 1

A. 1. **Cheek** by jowl
    2. Turn the other **cheek**
    3. Keep <u>your</u> **chin** up
    4. Tug <u>someone's</u> **forelock**   ***   **British Idiom**
    5. **Eyeball** to **eyeball**
    6. Up to <u>your</u> **eyeballs**

B. Place the idioms correctly in the sentences below

1. I hate some parts of my job, because I have to _____ the client's
    _____ before they come in to talk to the boss.

2. I fell behind at school, so I'm _____ my _____ in homework.

3. A fight almost broke out between Bob and Sid when they came _____
    _____ today. We had to separate them.

4. _____ your _____ Jan, you'll do better on the next test.

5. It was very strange to see Peter and Ted standing _____
    _____ the other night, because they really don't get along very well.

6. It thought it was noble of Kyle to _____ and
    ignore Sam's bullying. Sam is always trying to pick fights.

C. Discussion

1. Have you stood cheek by jowl with someone you didn't get along with?
2. Discuss a situation where you turned the other cheek.

D. Meanings

1. Refers to a situation where two people are very close to each other, but in a very
    strange situation
2. To not take action when someone hurts or harms you, or to not take action
    when someone tries to hurt or harm you
3. To try to stay cheerful in a difficult situation
4. To show a lot of respect to a person who has a high position or a high standing
    in society
5. Refers to a situation where two people are very close to each other, and
    arguing, while staring into each other's eyes
6. When you are very deeply involved in an unpleasant situation

PARTS OF THE FACE 2

A. 1. Pay through the **nose**
   2. Raise **eyebrows**
   3. Not bat an **eyelid**
   4. Find <u>your</u> **tongue**
   5. Fight **tooth** and nail
   6. By a **whisker**

B. Place the idioms correctly in the sentences below

1. After Sarah took the public speaking course, she _____ her _____, and is no longer afraid to speak in public.

2. Even though I failed the test _____, I still have to take the course all over again.

3. I didn't _____ when the city revealed it was deeply in debt. Everyone knew that city council consistently overspends.

4. Oscar _____ for his house. The price was way too high.

5. We _____ against the developer's plan to build a high rise in our neighborhood, but in the end, we won the battle.

6. I did _____ when Frank told us he wasn't going on vacation with us. I know that he's deeply in debt.

C. Discussion

1. Discuss the difference in meaning between the idioms, "not bat an eyelid", and, "raise eyebrows".
2. What thing have you had to fight tooth and nail over?

D. Meanings

1. To pay too much for something
2. Refers to something that shocks or surprises people
3. To not appear shocked or surprised when potentially startling news is told
4. To gain the courage to finally be able to talk, after being too afraid or shy to do so
5. To fight particularly hard for something
6. To fail or succeed by only the smallest margin

SHOULDERS

A. 1. Rub **shoulders** with someone
   2. Look over your **shoulder**
   3. Give someone the cold **shoulder**
   4. Straight from the **shoulder**
   5. A **shoulder** to cry on
   6. Stand **shoulder** to **shoulder**

B. Place the idioms correctly in the sentences below

1. The Los Angeles Lakers held an open practice today, so I got to talk with and shoot hoops with some of their star players. This was the first time that I got to _____ star basketball players.

2. The most prosperous time in the history of company was last year, when we all _____ and worked together.

3. I didn't like it when my father gave me a lecture and talked _____ _____ about my problems, but now, after some contemplation, I can see that he gave me good advice.

4. Francine is a wonderful friend. She always listens to my problems and gives me _____.

5. We were all _____ our _____ at work today. The boss was extremely upset we lost the account, so he watched us all like a hawk.

6. I couldn't believe how rude Erica was at work today. She totally ignored me and _____ me _____ the whole day.

C. Discussion

1. Have you ever rubbed shoulders with an important person?
2. In what situations would you or would you not offer a shoulder to cry on?

D. Meanings

1. Spend time with someone important
2. Refers to someone who is anxious because he or she thinks that others are trying to harm them or do bad things to them
3. Ignore someone deliberately
4. To say something directly and with complete honesty
5. Refers to someone who is sympathetic to your problems, and offers you support
6. To work together with others in a cooperative way, to achieve the same goal

SKIN AND FLESH

A. 1. In the **flesh**
   2. Press the **flesh**
   3. Put more **flesh** on <u>something</u>
   4. By the **skin** of <u>your</u> teeth
   5. Get under <u>your</u> **skin**
   6. Have a thick **skin**

B. <u>Place the idioms correctly in the sentences below</u>

1. Tom's proposal was lacking in many respects, but Sonia added a lot more detail and _____ on it.

2. Debbie _____. Nothing I say bothers her.

3. I've seen celebrities TV but I've never met one _____.

4. Jason knows how to _____ my _____. All he has to do is talk about my ex-girlfriend in front of others, and I go crazy.

5. The mayor likes to mingle with people and _____ but he does little else. His administration has accomplished very little.

6. The deadline to submit the essays was 12 noon, and I just handed it in _____ my _____. I handed it in at 11:59 AM.

C. <u>Discussion</u>

1. Have you ever met or seen a famous person in the flesh? When?
2. What do you think the idiom "have a thin skin" means?

D. <u>Meanings</u>

1. If a person sees or meets a person in the flesh, then they actually see or meet a famous person
2. To be in a crowd and talk with people, or shake their hands
3. Add detailed information to a particular thing
4. To accomplish or do something by the barest of margins
5. Refers to someone that has the ability to annoy you
6. To be unbothered in any way by any type of criticism

SWEETH TOOTH

A. 1. **Flavor** of the month
   2. Have your **cake** and eat it too
   3. Take the **cake**
   4. Like taking **candy** from a baby
   5. Catch someone with their hand in the **cookie** jar
   6. That's the way the **cookie** crumbles

B. Place the idioms correctly in the sentences below

1. Pete has done some stupid things before, but when he hit the teacher, well, that _____.

2. Jen is the _____. A lot of guys want to date her.

3. I _____ Tony _____ his _____ _____ today. I saw him stealing money from the safe at work.

4. Tom wants to _____ his _____. He's dating Pam, but he thinks he also has the freedom to date other women as well.

5. I didn't get into Law school, so I have to accept this. That's _____ _____.

6. Its too easy to win in this video game. When I play it, it feels _____ _____.

C. Discussion

1. Talk about a time when you had to accept the way the cookie crumbled.
2. Can you have your cake and eat it too? Give an example.

D. Meanings

1. To be very popular, at the present time
2. It is not possible to enjoy the benefit of two conflicting situations: a person can only have one of these things, but not both at the same time
3. A person or a form of behavior that is the most extreme example of a bad thing
4. Something that is very easy to do
5. To catch someone doing something wrong or illegal
6. A saying that implies that a person must accept the way something turns out, even if the end result is not what the person wants

TEETH

A. 1. Gnash your **teeth**
    2. Grind your **teeth**
    3. Grit your **teeth**
    4. Have **teeth**
    5. Lie through your **teeth**
    6. Show your **teeth**

B. Place the idioms correctly in the sentences below

1. Tim _____ his _____ when his boss kept ordering him around. He wasn't afraid to show his displeasure to his boss.

2. I fended off the bully at school when he tried to intimidate me. I pushed him back when he pushed me, showing him I also _____.

3. When Abner heard about the oil spill, he _____ his _____ because he was worried what this would do to the dolphins in the cove.

4. Sometimes you have to _____ your _____ and accept your fate, just like Tom, who remained stoic when he didn't make the team.

5. The teacher knew Thomas was _____ his _____ about cheating on the test. She had the evidence so she still punished him.

6. I had to _____ my _____ in the meeting and not show that I was upset when the boss criticized our department for our poor efforts.

C. Discussion

1. When was the last time you had to grit your teeth, and not show any emotions, over something that upset you?
2. Which people do you know that lie through their teeth a lot?

D. Meanings

1. To show your annoyance or anger at something or someone
2. To be angry, but to hold your anger back and not show it
3. To accept a fate or to continue doing something, even if it is painful to do so
4. To have the necessary authority to be able to enforce a law, or to force people to do something
5. To tell an obvious lie without feeling embarrassed about doing so
6. To show others that you have the will and the power to enforce something, or the will and power to defend yourself

THUMB

A. 1. Have a green **thumb**
   2. Stick out like a sore **thumb**
   3. Under a person's **thumb**
   4. All **thumbs**
   5. Give something the **thumbs** down
   6. Twiddling your **thumbs**

B. Place the idioms correctly in the sentences below

1. I _____ at the costume ball. I didn't have a costume on, so I looked really ridiculous.

2. The teacher _____ my essay proposal _____.
   Now I have to start over and do it again.

3. Jim tried to open a can, but he couldn't even do that. He's _____.

4. Jack was _____ his _____ in class today, and didn't hear one thing the teacher said.

5. I have a talent for gardening. I've always _____.

6. Sue's _____ Ed's _____. She can't do anything without his approval.

C. Discussion

1. Do you know a couple where one of them is under the other person's thumb?
2. In which activity are you all thumbs?

D. Meanings

1. To be good at gardening
2. To be different and noticeable, especially in comparison to other things
3. To be under the control of another person
4. To be a very clumsy person
5. To give or show disapproval towards something
6. To be idly wasting time, with nothing to occupy you

TOOTH and TEETH

A. 1. Fight **tooth** and nail
   2. Long in the **tooth**
   3. Sweet **tooth**
   4. Armed to the **teeth**
   5. Cut your **teeth**
   6. Sink your **teeth** into something

B. Place the idioms correctly in the sentences below

1. Don't let Bob load the cargo with the forklift. He hasn't _____ his _____ on working with the forklift. He could damage a lot of the cargo.

2. Quebec students _____ to limit tuition fee increases, and they were successful because fee hikes were minimized.

3. Protesters were _____ so police couldn't stop the riot.

4. Dad's a little too _____ for skydiving. He's too old for that kind of activity.

5. Betty _____ her _____ into her new duties, so she ended up finishing the project ahead of time. She did a great job.

6. Sarah has a _____, and always has too much dessert. That's why she can't lose weight.

C. Discussion

1. Is it easy for you to sink your teeth into learning about idioms?
2. Discuss something you feel that it is worth fighting tooth and nail over.

D. Meanings

1. To fight as hard as one can to achieve a goal
2. Refers to someone or some thing that is particularly old
3. To enjoy, like or love eating sweet things
4. To have many weapons
5. To gain the experience of doing a particular thing for the first time
6. To do a particular thing with a lot of enthusiasm

SECTION 19 – THINGS

BIG AND SMALL

A. 1. Too **big** for your britches
   2. **Big** frog in a small pond
   3. **Small** fry
   4. **Small** potatoes
   5. **Big** tuna/ **big** cheese/ **big** kahuna
   6. Make someone feel **small**

B. Place the correct idioms in the sentences below

1. Sam's _____. He can't boss me around at work. I'm in management and he's not.

2. Agatha is the _____ around here. She owns the company.

3. Tom always felt like a _____ in our small town. That's why he moved to the city.

4. Hi there, _____. Where's your mother?

5. Rita was very rude today. She insulted Hank at work and _____ him _____.

6. Ever since Henry got promoted, he's become very conceited. I don't like being around him anymore. He's become _____ his _____.

C. Discussion

1. Have you ever felt like a big frog in a small pond?
2. How do you feel about a person when they make you feel small?

D. Meanings

1. A person that behaves or thinks that he is more important than he really is
2. An important person in a small group
3. A child, or in some cases, an unimportant person
4. An issue that is unimportant, or a person that is unimportant
5. An important or powerful person, or the boss
6. To insult someone for the purpose of belittling that person

163

CHIP and CHIPS

A. 1. A **chip** off the old block
   2. Have a **chip** on your shoulder
   3. Have/had had your **chips**
   4. Call in your **chips**
   5. Cash in your **chips**
   6. When the **chips** are down

B. Place the idioms correctly in the sentences below

1. Tom _____ his _____ because he thinks he's the best dancer, but I've won the dance competition 5 years in a row.

2. Sam has the exact same behavior patterns as his father. He really is _____.

3. Most of our stockholders sold their stocks and _____ their _____ when the bad news came out about our company.

4. _____, I can always count on Sarah for support. She has always been a true friend.

5. The mayor needed help in his re-election campaign, so he _____ _____ his _____ and asked his friends to campaign for him.

6. The mayor realized he _____ his _____ when he finally got news that he had lost the election.

C. Discussion

1. Has a friend ever let you down when the chips were down?
2. Are you, in a way, a chip off the old block?

D. Meanings

1. A person who is similar to their parents in character, behaviour or appearance
2. A person who is resentful or angry, and who feels like they are being treated unfairly
3. To fail completely in a person's attempt in doing something
4. To use one's influence and connections to gain an advantage over others
5. To sell something, such as an investment, in order to get money
6. A reference to how someone behaves when they are placed in a difficult or dangerous situation

HIT AND BREAK

A. 1. **Break** the ice
   2. **Hit** the books
   3. **Hit** the hay/sack
   4. **Hit** and miss
   5. **Break** the news
   6. **Break** my word

B. Use the idioms correctly in the sentences below

1. I don't often _____ my _____. I usually keep my promises.

2. She was very tired, so she _____ early last night.

3. It was difficult to _____ to my friend that his pet had died.

4. The items on the menu at this restaurant are _____.
   Some of the dishes are excellent, but some of them are really bad.

5. I can't go out tonight, because I have an exam tomorrow. I have to
   _____ and study all night.

6. The students were tense, and were unresponsive to the teacher, so the teacher
   told a joke to _____.

C. Discussion

1. Do you hit the books a lot before exam time, or do you usually study consistently throughout a school term?
2. Describe a situation you have experienced in a classroom, where someone had to break the ice, because the atmosphere was too tense.

D. Meanings

1. Do something to make people feel more relaxed, in a tense environment
2. To study hard
3. To go to sleep
4. Used to describe something whose quality varies from good to bad, or from bad to good
5. (a) To be the person to have to tell bad news to someone, because another person does not realize something that is truly obvious
   (b) To tell someone some bad news, even though this will be hurtful
6. To purposely break a promise that you originally intended to keep

LINE 1

A. 1. The bottom **line**
   2. Cross the **line**
   3. Draw the **line**
   4. Walk a fine **line** between <u>something</u>
   5. In the **line** of fire
   6. Put <u>yourself</u> (or your <u>neck</u>) on the **line**

B. <u>Place the idioms correctly in the sentences below</u>

1. The President puts himself _____ every day, especially when he makes difficult decisions regarding war and peace.

2. Ken _____ when he makes personal comments about me.

3. Although you study very hard, Max, _____ is, you'll still fail the semester.

4. Although this involves great risk for me Harold, I am going to co-sign your loan, and _____ <u>my</u> _____ for you.

5. A teacher can _____ between <u>getting too close to students</u>, or being criticized for being too distant with them.

6. I had to _____ for Steven last night, and tell him to stop drinking, because he was becoming more obnoxious after each drink.

C. <u>Discussion</u>

1. Discuss a situation where someone had to draw the line for you.
2. Have you ever put your neck on the line for someone else? When & how?

D. <u>Meanings</u>

1. The most important issue when dealing with something
2. To begin to behave in an offensive or improper manner
3. To choose a point where something begins to be unacceptable or improper
4. A situation where something is acceptable or proper, but the situation could suddenly become unacceptable or improper with the slightest change or variation of behaviour
5. Refers to person in a position such that he or she could easily come under criticism, or be subject to attack
6. To do something that is personally, very risky

LINE 2

A. 1. Come on **line**
2. Down the **line**
3. Along the **line**
4. Sign on the dotted **line**
5. Get a **line** on someone
6. Lay it on the **line**

B. Place the idioms correctly in the sentences below

1. I have to _____, Sam, I don't love you anymore.

2. When the 3rd subway system _____, their will be a lot less traffic on Highway number 1.

3. The soldier tried to get out of his military commitments after 1 year, but he couldn't, because he had _____, and had therefore agreed to serve for 2 full years.

4. _____, when you have children, you will more fully understand why I'm not letting you date that boy.

5. _____, after you graduate, you can get a driver's license.

6. I was trying to _____ Steven, by asking his old teachers about his past study habits.

C. Discussion

1. Do you always lay it on the line when discussing personal issues with your friends?
2. How do you think you will finally feel, when you sign on the dotted line when purchasing your first house?

D. Meanings

1. Refers to some thing, or some endeavor, that starts to operate, usually at its full capacity
2. Refers to something that will happen at a later time
3. Refers to something that will happen, but at a later time, that cannot be predicted or identified
4. To sign a document, signifying that you formally agree to some thing
5. To get information about a certain person
6. To say something truthfully, often in rather difficult circumstances

MARK

A. 1. Hit the **mark**
   2. A black **mark**
   3. Leave a **mark**
   4. On the **mark**
   5. Quick off the **mark**
   6. Way off the **mark**

B. Place the idioms correctly in the sentences below

1. Karl was _____ on his prediction of the auto industry. He predicted a downturn in the auto industry, and he was correct.

2. I got some great deals at the Boxing Day Sale because I was _____ _____ when the store opened. I got there early, so I was first in line.

3. The weatherman _____ on the news last night. He said it would rain heavily, and it did rain very heavily today.

4. I thought I could travel Europe on the cheap, but I was _____ _____. It cost a lot more to travel Europe than I thought.

5. Athletes that take steroids leave _____ on their sports. Fans view this type of action very negatively.

6. Michael Jordan _____ on the game of basketball. He was basketball's best player, and he changed the way the game was played.

C. Discussion

1. Which athlete has left the biggest black mark on his sport?
2. Discuss a situation where your parents have been way off the mark.

D. Meanings

1. To accomplish what you intend to accomplish, or to be accurate in your intentions or predictions
2. A situation where people form a bad opinion about something, as a result of something bad that is done by one person, or by a group of people
3. To leave an impression or to have a lasting effect
4. To be accurate or totally correct
5. To be quick in starting something, or to responding to something
6. Something that is totally wrong or inaccurate, or something that is rude or inappropriate when said

NEWS

A. 1. Bad **news**
   2. To be **news** to <u>someone</u>
   3. Break the **news**
   4. No news is good **news**
   5. No news is bad **news**
   6. Be the bearer of bad **news**

B. Place the idioms correctly in the sentences below

1. I'm worried about Cam. He's on that mountain in the that blizzard and he should've called by now. I hope that _____.

2. I hate to _____ Ted, but your relationship with Tamika is not working out well.

3. That's _____ me that my daughter has been skipping classes. The teacher hasn't contacted me all term about that.

4. I don't think the radar machine caught us speeding. It happened months ago, so since we haven't heard anything yet. I suppose then that _____ _____.

5. Sue should stay away from Clifford. He's _____.

6. I hate to _____, Anna, but I think the clothes you're trying on don't match at all.

C. Discussion

1. Discuss the difference between the idioms, "no news is good news", and "no news is bad news".
2. Have you had to be the bearer of bad news before?

D. Meanings

1. Refers to a person who is troublesome and has a bad character
2. To be surprised about something that a person did not know about before
3. To tell something to someone concerning a bad occurrence or event
4. A positive statement, meaning that if bad news has not yet come, then nothing bad has happened
5. A negative statement, meaning that if good news has not yet come, then something bad has happened
6. To be the one that reveals something someone didn't know about before

ORDER

A. 1. A tall **order**
   2. Out of **order** (1)
   3. Out of **order** (2)
   4. Marching **orders**
   5. Give <u>someone</u> their marching **orders**
   6. Pecking **order**

B. Place the idioms correctly in the sentences below

1. Tony _____ <u>Jack</u> <u>his</u> _____ today, so Jack is no longer with the company.

2. John was _____ with our new clients. He treated them quite rudely.

3. The vending machine is _____. We can buy nothing from it.

4. I'm not very high on the company's _____, so I have little chance of advancing into the new position.

5. Getting 100 % on the Math exam will be _____. Mrs. Smith gives very difficult exams.

6. Our _____ are to wait for the General to arrive before we attack. We can go no further.

C. Discussion

1. How high are you in the pecking order in your family?
2. Talk about a remark that you heard someone make in public that was out of order.

D. Meanings

1. Something that is very difficult to do, achieve, or get
2. Refers to something that is no longer working or operating
3. A reference to someone's behaviour, which is unacceptable, or rude
4. Instructions that someone is given so that they can carry out a plan
5. Tell someone to leave
6. A ranking that shows or tell where you place, or are arranged, in a hierarchy

POINT

A.
1. Labor the **point**
2. Reach a boiling **point**
3. Not put a fine **point** on it
4. A sore **point**
5. A sticking **point**
6. **Point** blank

B. Place the idioms correctly in the sentences below

1. Discussions between the union and management _____
   _____ when management refused to honor the past agreement.

2. I asked Sue _____ out on a date, but she refused.

3. I keep having to _____ with Jim about how
   important it is too do well in school, by he just doesn't seem to care.

4. I did _____ on it when I told my husband how
   neglected I feel when he goes out most nights with his friends.

5. The issue of equal pay for equal work has been _____ for
   the women at our place of work for a long time.

6. Tom's smoking is _____ with me in our relationship.
   I won't marry someone who puts their health at risk by smoking.

C. Discussion

1. Have you ever had to keep laboring the point about something important with a
   friend, but they refused to heed your advice?
2. Is often necessary to tell someone something point blank, even if it will hurt
   their feelings?

D. Meanings

1. To keep explaining something, even though people already understand it
2. Refers to anger, or an emotion, that can no longer be controlled
3. A saying used to convey that what is about to be said will not be pleasant for
   someone else to hear
4. Something that makes someone feel upset, angry or embarrassed
5. A topic, idea or subject that people cannot agree upon, thereby leading to
   absence of progress or harmony
6. To say something very directly and bluntly, without feeling apologetic

QUESTIONS AND ANSWERS

A. 1. Have a lot to **answer** for
   2. Dusty (or dirty) **answer**
   3. Won't take no for an **answer**
   4. Only a **question** of time
   5. Beg the **question**
   6. Pop the **question**

B. Place the idioms correctly in the sentences below

1. I hope John will _____ tonight at dinner at my parent's home. I'm so looking forward to marrying him.

2. Betty _____. She failed every exam, and she didn't attend many classes as well this last semester.

3. Its _____ before the coach gets fired. His team is always loosing, and they're not playing with any enthusiasm.

4. It _____, why are so many teenagers continuing to ski out of bounds, when so many of them have already died doing this?

5. I received a very _____ from Pete when I asked him about his grades. It seems he's embarrassed about his performance in class.

6. The salesman keeps asking me to buy his product, but I keep telling him I don't want to. He just _____.

C. Discussion

1. Is it now appropriate for women to pop the question?
2. Talk about some dirty or dusty answers that you have received.

D. Meanings

1. Refers to a person that is now coming under pressure to take responsibility for something bad that has happened
2. A negative or unpleasant answer
3. Will not accept the fact that someone refuses to do what you asked of them
4. Something that will eventually happen
5. Something that makes people want to ask a question about it
6. To ask someone to marry you

SHOT

A. 1. Like a **shot**
    2. A cheap **shot**
    3. A big **shot**
    4. A **shot** in the arm
    5. A **shotgun** wedding
    6. Call the **shots**

B. Place the idioms correctly in the sentences below

1. Cathy and Stuart had to have _____. Cathy didn't want others to find out she was pregnant while she wasn't married.

2. The convention in our city came at the right time. Our city's economy was stagnant, so it provided _____ for local businesses.

3. Emily _____ around here. She made that clear in the meeting last night when she disciplined Brad and Joanna.

4. Joe is acting like _____ because he received a promotion.

5. That was _____, Janice, for you to criticize what I was wearing in front of everyone else at the party last night.

6. I'd go on that ski trip _____, but my mother won't let me go.

C. Discussion

1. How do you feel when someone tries to give you a cheap shot?
2. Is it more important for one person to call the shots, or to accomplish something by using a team effort?

D. Meanings

1. To do something, or to have something done, eagerly and immediately
2. To criticize something unfairly or in an unpleasant way
3. An important person
4. Help that is given by someone, or something, when the help is direly needed
5. A wedding that takes place quickly, because the woman is pregnant
6. To make all of the important decisions

Marco Antonio Bussanich

WORD

A. 1. Eat your **words**
2. The last **word**
3. At a loss for **words**
4. Put **words** into someone's mouth
5. Take the **words** out of someone's mouth
6. Not mince your **words**

B. Place the idioms correctly in the sentences below

1. Don't _____ my _____ Harry. I do think that Angela will finish her project.

2. I'm _____, now that my team is eliminated from the competition. I thought they were going to be the new champions.

3. You _____ my _____, Cynthia. I was thinking the same thing as you were about the city's new tax plan.

4. I did _____ my _____ when I had a talk with Junior today. I told him very directly that he had to work harder at school.

5. I had to _____ my _____ at the dinner table, and admit that Sam was right all along. That was very humiliating.

6. I got _____ in today at our meeting with Toni and the boss. I made the better argument, so the boss sided with me.

C. Discussion

1. Talk about someone you know who often tries to put words in your mouth.
2. Have you ever had to eat your words in front of other people?

D. Meanings

1. To state publicly that what you once said or thought, is completely wrong
2. To be able to make the final decision, or to win an argument
3. Refers to a situation where a person is speechless, because he or she does not know what to say, because of what has just transpired
4. To tell someone what their opinion should be, instead of listening to what that person's opinion is
5. To say something that someone else is about to say
6. To state your opinion openly, even if this means offending other people

WORK

A. 1. Do <u>someone's</u> dirty **work**
   2. Make light **work** of <u>someone</u>
   3. A nasty piece of **work**
   4. Have <u>your</u> **work** cut out for <u>you</u>
   5. A piece of **work**
   6. **Work** <u>your</u> arse off

B. <u>Place the idioms correctly in the sentences below</u>

1. The Premier is popular because he always gets someone else to _____ his
   _____ for him.

2. After the arsonist was arrested and brought to trial, we all could see from the
   look on his face that he was _____.

3. We didn't realize it when Tanya was first hired, but we quickly noticed that her
   work habits were impressive. She really is _____.

4. We _____ <u>the other team</u> by beating them soundly.

5. After the storm destroyed much of the town, everybody _____ <u>their</u>
   _____ <u>them</u> in rebuilding the town.

6. Sue _____ <u>her</u> _____. That's why she gets good grades.

C. <u>Discussion</u>

1. Talk about someone you know who is either a piece of work, or a nasty piece of
   work.
2. Have you ever had to do someone else's dirty work for them?

D. <u>Meanings</u>

1. To do some difficult or unpleasant thing for someone, because they do not want
   to do it themselves
2. To defeat an opponent decisively
3. Refers to an unpleasant or nasty person
4. To have a very big and/or unpleasant task to deal with
5. Refers to a very unusual, impressive or surprising person
6. To work very, very hard

SECTION 20 – VICES AND VIRTUES

AT THE BAR 1

A. 1. **Happy** hour
    2. On the **rocks**
    3. Run a **tab**
    4. Buy a **round**
    5. On the **house**
    6. **Last call**

B. Place the idioms correctly in the sentences below

1. Sue: "How much did you pay for that drink, Betty?"
    Betty: "Nothing, it was free. The bartender said it was _____".

2. I brought my credit card tonight, so I'm going to _____.
    I don't want to pay for my drinks every single time I order them.

3. Let's go to the bar at 6 PM today. That's when they have _____
    _____, so its a night out that will fit my budget.

4. I enjoy having all of my drinks _____. I like to
    have my drinks cold.

5. Everyone else has _____ so its my turn to buy drinks.

6. What time is _____ at this bar? I want to have one more
    drink before the bar closes.

C. Discussion

1. What disadvantages are there to going to the bar during happy hour?
2. How often do you get drinks on the house?

D. Meanings

1. The period of time (6:00 – 7:00 PM, for example) that drinks are half-price.
2. Drinks that are served with ice cubes in the glass
3. To pay for your drinks at one time at the end of the night, instead of paying for
    them each time the server brings them to you.
4. To buy drinks for everyone in your circle of friends
5. Refers to a drink that is free.
6. When the server announces that it is last call, this means that no more drinks
    can be bought after this time.

AT THE BAR 2

A. 1. Get **86'ed**
   2. **Bum** a smoke
   3. Get **carded**
   4. **Cover charge**
   5. **Hit** on someone
   6. Leave a **tip**

B. Place the idioms correctly in the sentences below

1. Bob tried to _____ Rachel all night, but she wouldn't even dance with him.

2. Sid _____ at the bar last night after he got into a fight.

3. There's no _____ for ladies on Lady's Night.

4. I couldn't _____ for the bartender. I spent all of my money buying rounds for other people.

5. I don't like it how Hank always tries to _____ instead of buying his own cigarettes.

6. Tamara always _____ even though she's 29. She looks very young for her age.

C. Discussion

1. Do you know of any bars or clubs that don't charge a cover charge, or do not charge a cover charge if you get there before a certain hour?
2. Do you know someone who always get carded at the bar, even though he or she is older than 19?

D. Meanings

1. To be bounced or thrown out of a bar or club
2. Borrow a cigarette
3. To have to present your identification for age verification at the bar
4. To pay an entrance fee before entering the bar
5. To make a pass at another person in the bar
6. To leave a gratuity for the waitress, waiter or bartender

DATING and MARRIAGE

A. 1. A **blind date**
   2. Make an **honest women** out of <u>someone</u>
   3. Tie the **knot**
   4. All's fair in **love** and war
   5. **Play** the field
   6. **Puppy love**

B. Place the idioms correctly in the sentences below

1. Tom _____ and is not serious about anyone, so he may sometimes hurt a person's feelings when they fall in love with him.

2. When are you and Sid going to _____, Pam? You've been dating for quite a long time, so you should get married soon.

3. I don't believe that Tamara is serious about Greg. Its her first relationship, so I think its more of a case of _____.

4. When Frank left me, I was quite hurt, but my friends told me _____ _____, so I just had to accept what happened.

5. You should marry May, Bill, and _____ her.

6. Its odd, but some people meet their spouse on _____.

C. Discussion

1. What are the advantages or disadvantages of going on a blind date?
2. Do you really believe that all's fair in love and war? Give some examples.

D. Meanings

1. To have an arranged date with a person you've never met before
2. This happens when a man marries his girlfriend
3. To get married
4. This implies that any form of behaviour is acceptable, even in love or war. This may equate the state of relationships as being like warfare
5. Date a number of people, without having the intention of settling down
6. A love that is not considered serious, like the love between children

DRINKING

A. 1. Belt down a **drink** **OR** Belt down a few **drinks**
   2. **Drink** someone under the table
   3. **Drink** like a fish
   4. I'll **drink** to that
   5. Knock back a **drink**
   6. Drive someone to **drink**

B. Place the idioms correctly in the sentences below

1. I can _____ Sam _____. He can't hold as much liquor as I can.

2. Betty's husband _____. Betty is very worried that his constant drinking will ruin their relationship.

3. Albert _____ when he found out that he lost his job.

4. That son of ours is going to _____ me _____. He refuses to take his studies seriously.

5. We_____ after the golf tournament.

6. When Todd told us that he was paying for the drinks, I responded by saying, "_____"!

C. Discussion

1. Is it fashionable for only men to belt down their drinks?
2. Talk about someone or something that almost drove you to drink.

D. Meanings

1. To drink rapidly
2. To have the ability to drink more than someone else
3. Drink a lot
4. To agree with something
5. Swallow an alcoholic drink
6. Make another person anxious and unhappy

DUMB, STUPID or IDIOTIC

A. 1. Grab a **brain**
   2. **Out to lunch**
   3. Have a **screw loose**
   4. **Dumb** as a doornail
   5. Have a **brain** like a sieve
   6. Get your **brain** into gear

B. Place the idioms correctly in the sentences below

1. That donkey is as _____. It doesn't realize it could get hit by a car if it eats grass by the roadside.

2. _____ your _____, Manny. You know this question isn't that difficult to answer.

3. You seem to _____, Ed. You should do a better job at remembering the important things about your duties.

4. Our neighbor seems to _____. He sometimes does the craziest things.

5. _____, Sarah. You'll never become a millionaire overnight.

6. Derek is really _____. He doesn't realize that Daphne will never go out on a date with him. She's already married.

C. Discussion

1. Do you have a problem getting your brain into gear in the morning?
2. Do you feel that is insulting to use any of these idioms when talking about someone?

D. Meanings

1. A negative comment said to someone who cannot understand something, probably because they are either naïve, or stupid
2. Refers to a person who does not understand or comprehend a situation
3. A person who is not sane
4. A person who is very, very stupid
5. Refers to someone who is bad at remembering things
6. Start to think more clearly, so that you can accomplish a certain task

FALL

A. 1. **Fall** on hard times
   2. Take a/the **fall**
   3. **Fall** guy
   4. **Fall** for
   5. Heading for a **fall**
   6. **Fall** over <u>oneself</u> to impress

B. Use the idioms correctly in the sentences below

1. Many families in the town have _____ since the steel mill closed last year.

2. I thought Max was _____ last year, because of his partying. He smarted up, though, studied hard, and passed all his tests.

3. Christina is so very beautiful, so I _____ her right away.

4. When the NDP lost the last election, the part leader quit. Someone had to _____ for the party's miserable showing.

5. Horton was made the _____ for the company's failure to make money. It wasn't his fault, though, so he shouldn't have been fired.

6. Nearly every guy at school is _____ themselves _____ _____ Anne.

C. Discussion

1. Describe a situation where you fell on your face.
2. Should politicians be more honest, and begin taking a fall for their actions?

D. Meanings

1. To go through a difficult time or period, especially in a financial sense
2. To take the blame for something, so as to excuse someone else from fault
3. A person who is blamed for something, even though this person may not be at fault
4. To easily fall in love with someone (or something)
5. To be doing things that will cause problems later on
6. To be very enthusiastic about doing something

Marco Antonio Bussanich

GETTING DRUNK

A. 1. **Drunk** as a skunk
2. Dead **drunk**
3. Punch **drunk**
4. Can't hold <u>your</u> **liquor**
5. Hit the **bottle**
6. **Tie** one on

B. Place the idioms correctly in the sentences below

1. I think Frank sometimes _____ only because he faces too much pressure at work.

2. Brad _____ his _____. He gets drunk on one beer.

3. I don't usually drink a lot, but last night, I was _____.

4. The boys at work were _____ last night after work. Most of us got really drunk.

5. I studied for 12 hours straight last night, so I went to bed feeling like I was _____.

6. Rod drank too many beers last night, but he had no choice. He was taking part in the initiation ceremony, so he got _____.

C. Discussion

1. Do you think it is strange for people to brag that they can hold their liquor?
2. Is hitting the bottle too often a dangerous thing for young people?

D. Meanings

1. Very drunk
2. Extremely drunk
3. To be very tired and confused
4. Get drunk very easily
5. To drink too much
6. To drink a lot, to get drunk

GOSSIP and SILENCE

A. 1. Hear <u>something</u> through the **grapevine**
   2. Set **tongues** wagging
   3. Blow <u>your</u> own **trumpet**
   4. A conspiracy of **silence**
   5. Draw a **veil** around <u>something</u>
   6. Keep <u>something</u> under **wraps**

B. Place the idioms correctly in the sentences below

1. Its difficult for police to solve crimes when those who know about a crime refuse to talk, and engage in _____.

2. I _____ it _____ that Pam's marrying Alfred.

3. Gladys isn't well liked because she brags about herself too much. Not too many people like someone who _____ their _____.

4. It _____ when Roy danced the last dance with Sue.

5. The principal and Mrs. Jones tried to _____ the fact they were dating, but everyone found out anyways.

6. I'm happy we _____ the surprise party _____ for this long. The party's tonight, so we know its still a secret.

C. Discussion

1. Is it difficult to keep juicy gossip under wraps for a long period of time?
2. Do you often hear about news of your private life through the grapevine?

D. Meanings

1. To be told information from a second hand source
2. To have things said about you because of something you said or did
3. To tell people good or positive things about yourself
4. Refers to a group who have vowed that they will not tell anyone else about something which is common knowledge to them
5. Make a deliberate effort to keep something quite because it is private
6. To keep something secret

IN TROUBLE

A. 1. Left holding the **baby**
   2. In deep **doo-doo**
   3. In the **dog** house
   4. In over your **head**
   5. Cook your own **goose**
   6. There'll be **hell** to **pay**

B. Place the idioms correctly in the sentences below

1. Ed can't get into university because his marks are too low. He promised to study hard, but he didn't. When I see him _____.

2. Bob has been _____, ever since he came home late last week. He still has to sleep on the couch.

3. I'll be _____ when the teacher finds I wrote on the desk.

4. Tom _____ his _____ when he started doing drugs.

5. Beth realized she was _____ her _____ when she could no longer afford to pay for both her rent and her debts.

6. I was _____ when the boss came in lunchroom, and found everything in a mess. Now he's blaming me for everything.

C. Discussion

1. Have you ever been left holding the baby for something you didn't do?
2. What thing have you been in over your head over?

D. Meanings

1. To be blamed for something that was not your fault
2. To be in serious trouble for something you did
3. When someone puts you in the dog house, or in their dog house, they punish you for something you did
4. Refers to a situation that is too difficult for a person to deal with
5. To do something which spoils your chances for success
6. A warning to someone, given to inform the person that they will be in great trouble if they don't do or accomplish what they should do

LIE and LYING

A. 1. Live a **lie**
   2. Give the **lie** to something
   3. A white **lie**
   4. **Lie** low
   5. Nail a **lie**
   6. The lie of the **land**

B. Place the idioms correctly in the sentences below

1. The new poll _____ the idea that the mayor was popular.

2. When I checked _____ of our company's budget, I realized that someone had been stealing money.

3. I told Jeb _____ when I denied I saw Sue with another guy.

4. Our victory last night _____ that the other team was the best team in the league.

5. I found out about my husband's gambling problem last week. He told me he had given up gambling, but he's been _____.

6. John's been _____ and not driving his car lately. He doesn't want others to know he was the one who drove into the lamppost.

C. Discussion

1. Talk about a time you told a white lie to protect a friend's feelings.
2. Did you ever give the lie to something that a friend of yours told everyone was absolutely true?

D. Meanings

1. To live life in a dishonest or false way
2. Prove that something is not true
3. To say something that is not true, to prevent from upsetting someone, or to protect that person
4. To hide, making sure others do not notice you
5. To show that something is not true
6. The simple basic facts of an issue, or a situation

NOISE and SILENCE

A. 1. **Empty vessels** make the most **sound**
   2. **Hush** money
   3. **Quiet** as a mouse
   4. **Silence** is golden
   5. **Sound** hollow
   6. The **squeaky wheel** gets oiled

B. Place the idioms correctly in the sentences below

1. Tom's promises always _____ to me. He has promised a lot of things to me before, but he never delivers on his promises.

2. Ted talks like he knows a lot about China, but in reality, he's never been to China, nor has he been to Asia. _____.

3. When I'm in my home at night, I don't like to hear screaming kids. I work very hard in the day, so for me at night, _____.

4. The tenant upstairs is _____. He never makes noise.

5. When Tim complains at work, the boss always listens and gives Tim what he wants. I guess its true that _____.

6. The mobster was paid _____ by his mafia boss, so he's not revealing anything to the police, even if it means going to jail.

C. Discussion

1. Do you know someone who is an empty vessel, and makes a lot of noise?
2. Talk about someone you know whose promises sound hollow.

D. Meanings

1. People who talk a lot, and who think they know a lot about many things, are often the ones who know very little about a subject
2. Money paid to someone to make them keep quiet, and not reveal a secret
3. Refers to a person, or persons, who are very quiet
4. Silence and quiet are wonderful and blissful things
5. Something that does not seem to be true or sincere
6. The person who complains the most gets his or her complaints addressed

ON THE DOLE

A. 1. Get **axed**
2. Get **canned**
3. On the **dole**
4. Nice **work** if you can get it
5. A **bad workman** blames his tools
6. On the **wallaby** track   ********   **Australian Idiom**

B. Place the idioms correctly in the sentences below

1. Being a lifeguard has got to be the best job in the world. _____
_____.

2. Jim likes to be _____ in the winter. In that way, he has a lot of time to go skiing.

3. I've been _____ for 6 months now. Its tough finding a job in the forestry industry, because there are fewer and fewer jobs.

4. I _____ from work because I came in late too many times.

5. Tony thought he got fired because of his faulty computer, but in reality, he wasn't a very skilled accountant. In Tony's case, I'd have to say _____
_____.

6. The poorest sales person in our firm _____ every 3 months. Its unfair, but in that way, the boss makes sure we're productive.

C. Discussion

1. Do people on the dole take too much advantage of a good thing?
2. Is it natural for a bad workman to blame his tools, or do you think some people do get fired because they work with poor or faulty equipment?

D. Meanings

1. To be fired from a job
2. To be fired from a job
3. To be receiving government issued unemployment insurance
4. A job that you do not have, but that you would like to have, because it is either easy, or it pays well
5. A person who does a bad job, then blames the quality of the tools or or the equipment, instead of admitting that they didn't do the job well
6. To be unemployed

PREGNANT

A. 1. **Bun** in the oven
   2. You can't be half **pregnant**
   3. **Knocked** up
   4. Baby **bumps**
   5. **Pregnant**
   6. Have a **baby**

B. Place the idioms correctly in the sentences below

1. Jenny's _____. Her pregnancy wasn't planned.

2. The minds of the people at the conference were _____ with good ideas. I've never heard such varied points of view before.

3. Jessie's _____ are really showing up now. It's very obvious from looking at her that she's pregnant.

4. Tom _____ when he found out I had a date with Ethel.

5. Jessica hasn't gained weight. She's got a _____.

6. While in university, a student must be very committed. _____ _____, and think you can study and still party a lot.

C. Discussion

1. Which movie star's baby bumps have been discussed a lot lately?
2. Can anyone or anything be half-pregnant, or must everything be defined or discussed in black and white terms?

D. Meanings

1. To be pregnant
2. Refers to a situation where the outcome is clear cut. There can be no half-measures in this situation. Or, a person must have a definite point of view: there can be doubts, or no half measures.
3. To become pregnant, usually by illegitimate means, or by accident
4. The visual sight of the enlarged stomach of a pregnant woman
5. Full and plentiful
6. To react irately and/or with anger at someone or something

STEAL or CHEAT

A. 1. **Take** someone to the **cleaners**
   2. **Pull** the **wool** over someone's eyes
   3. **Under the table**
   4. **Ill gotten** gains
   5. Highway **robbery**
   6. Be **sold** a **pup**

B. Place the idioms correctly in the sentences below

1. I was _____ when I bought the used car. The car kept breaking down, and the warranty didn't cover the important things.

2. Vince doesn't make much at his regular job, but then he works _____ _____ on evenings, and makes some tax-free cash then.

3. The vendor at the flea market _____ Jill _____. She paid way too much, especially since the clothing was of low quality.

4. The gangster's car and mansion were confiscated by police because they were _____, and attained through the sale of drugs.

5. Jim had the _____ his _____ by the salesperson. Jim was so mesmerized by her beauty, so she duped him.

6. My car broke down on vacation, so the garage knew they could get away with _____ because there were no other garages for miles.

C. Discussion

1. Have you ever had the wool pulled over your eyes by a close friend?
2. Do you feel that it is immoral to make money under the table?

D. Meanings

1. To use illegal or dishonest ways to make someone lose a lot of money,
2. Deceive someone, so as to take advantage of them
3. To earn money in an illegal way, by not paying taxes on it
4. The use of illegal methods to gain a monetary advantage
5. Refers to a situation where a person is vastly overcharged for something
6. To buy something, or to be given something free, that is not of as good quality as advertised

TRICK

A. 1. A one **trick** pony
   2. Do the **trick**
   3. Up to <u>your</u> same old **tricks**
   4. Use every **trick** in the book
   5. The oldest **trick** in the book
   6. Not/never miss a **trick**

B. Place the idioms correctly in the sentences below

1. Bob is _____ his _____. He pretends he's sick when exam time comes, because he knows he'll fail if he takes the exams.

2. Sue fell for _____ when she gave money to that guy on the street. He's not really homeless, he just pretends to be.

3. Tom is _____. He's good at Math, but nothing else.

4. Susan _____. There's no way any guy can fool her.

5. I tried to _____ when I tried to sneak into the fair, but I couldn't fool the security guards.

6. I was sure that I would get well by taking the new cough medicine, but it didn't _____ because I'm still coughing.

C. Discussion

1. Name one of the oldest tricks in the book that you have fallen prey to.
2. Talk about someone you know who is a one trick pony.

D. Meanings

1. Refers to someone or something that is only good at one thing
2. Something that achieves want a person wants done
3. Refers to someone who continues to behave in the same dishonest, foolish or irrational way that they always have behaved in before
4. Refers to someone who uses every possible way to achieve their goal
5. A very common thing that most people do, so it is a very understandable or expected behaviour
6. Refers to someone who can take advantage of any situation because this person seems to always know what is going to happen

TRUTH

A. 1. Take <u>something</u> to be the gospel **truth**
   2. **Truth** will out
   3. The moment of **truth**
   4. Economical with the **truth**
   5. Stretch the **truth**
   6. A grain of **truth**

B. Place the idioms correctly in the sentences below

1. Bob's tried to hide his illness from his family, but it became quite obvious he was ill. When he was hospitalized, no one was surprised. _____ _____.

2. There isn't even _____ to Billy's story. He lied about everything.

3. When the bank repossessed Mick's car, that was _____ _____ for him because he finally realized how much in debt he was in.

4. My dad _____ a lot, especially when he goes fishing. He told us he caught a big fish last week, but it wasn't very big.

5. John _____ the fact that Sarah is loyal to him _____ _____, even though we tell him she dates other guys.

6. Jim was _____ when the principal questioned him about the fight I got into, but his deception saved me from being punished.

C. Discussion

1. Have you ever stretched the truth to get out of trouble?
2. Have you ever taken something to be the gospel truth, only to find out later that it was not true?

D. Meanings

1. To take something to be the undeniable truth, even if it is not
2. The truth will always be discovered
3. A time that comes so that a person can no longer avoid facing the truth
4. To deceive others by not telling them the whole truth
5. To purposely manipulate the facts, and present this as the truth
6. Even the smallest amount of truth

ANSWERS

SECTION 1 – ANIMALS AND LIVING THINGS   Pages 1 – 20

Amphibians and Reptiles

<u>1.</u>   6   <u>2.</u>   4   <u>3.</u>   2   <u>4.</u>   1   <u>5.</u>   5   <u>6.</u>   3

Animals 1

<u>1.</u>   1   <u>2.</u>   3   <u>3.</u>   5   <u>4.</u>   2   <u>5.</u>   3   <u>6.</u>   4

Animals 2

<u>1.</u>   6   <u>2.</u>   1   <u>3.</u>   4   <u>4.</u>   5   <u>5.</u>   2   <u>6.</u>   3

Birds

<u>1.</u>   3   <u>2.</u>   6   <u>3.</u>   5   <u>4.</u>   1   <u>5.</u>   2   <u>6.</u>   4

Bulls and Oxen

<u>1.</u>   5   <u>2.</u>   6   <u>3.</u>   1   <u>4.</u>   4   <u>5.</u>   2   <u>6.</u>   3

Cats

<u>1.</u>   3   <u>2.</u>   2   <u>3.</u>   1   <u>4.</u>   5   <u>5.</u>   6   <u>6.</u>   4

Cats, Dogs, Mice and Birds

<u>1.</u>   3   <u>2.</u>   1   <u>3.</u>   4   <u>4.</u>   2   <u>5.</u>   6   <u>6.</u>   5

Chicken

<u>1.</u>   6   <u>2.</u>   5   <u>3.</u>   1   <u>4.</u>   4   <u>5.</u>   2   <u>6.</u>   3

Dogs

<u>1.</u>   4   <u>2.</u>   6   <u>3.</u>   1   <u>4.</u>   5   <u>5.</u>   2   <u>6.</u>   3

Fish 1

<u>1.</u>   2   <u>2.</u>   6   <u>3.</u>   5   <u>4.</u>   1   <u>5.</u>   4   <u>6.</u>   3

Marco Antonio Bussanich

Fish 2

<u>1.</u> 1   <u>2.</u> 5   <u>3.</u> 6   <u>4.</u> 4   <u>5.</u> 3   <u>6.</u> 2

Flowers

<u>1.</u> 5   <u>2.</u> 1   <u>3.</u> 6   <u>4.</u> 4   <u>5.</u> 3   <u>6.</u> 2

Fowl

<u>1.</u> 3   <u>2.</u> 4   <u>3.</u> 1   <u>4.</u> 6   <u>5.</u>   <u>6.</u> 2

From the Water

<u>1.</u> 6   <u>2.</u> 1   <u>3.</u> 4   <u>4.</u> 5   <u>5.</u> 3   <u>6.</u> 2

Hogs and Pigs

<u>1.</u> 6   <u>2.</u> 2   <u>3.</u> 1   <u>4.</u> 3   <u>5.</u> 4   <u>6.</u> 5

Horses

<u>1.</u> 3   <u>2.</u> 1   <u>3.</u> 6   <u>4.</u> 4   <u>5.</u> 2   <u>6.</u> 5

Lion

<u>1.</u> 5   <u>2.</u> 2   <u>3.</u> 1   <u>4.</u> 4   <u>5.</u> 6   <u>6.</u> 3

A Monkey's Uncle

<u>1.</u> 2   <u>2.</u> 5   <u>3.</u> 6   <u>4.</u> 4   <u>5.</u> 3   <u>6.</u> 1

Sheep and Goats

<u>1.</u> 2   <u>2.</u> 5   <u>3.</u> 6   <u>4.</u> 1   <u>5.</u> 4   <u>6.</u> 3

SECTION 2 – CLOTHING   Pages 21 – 30

Boots

<u>1.</u> 1   <u>2.</u> 6   <u>3.</u> 2   <u>4.</u> 4   <u>5.</u> 3   <u>6.</u> 5

Clothing 1

1.   6   2.   1   3.   5   4.   2   5.   4   6.   3

Clothing 2

1.   1   2.   6   3.   5   4.   2   5.   3   6.   4

Hat 1

1.   3   2.   6   3.   2   4.   5   5.   1   6.   4

Hat 2

1.   6   2.   3   3.   4   4.   1   5.   2   6.   5

Pants and Shirts

1.   3   2.   1   3.   6   4.   5   5.   4   6.   1

Pockets

1.   6   2.   2   3.   1   4.   3   5.   4   6.   5

Shirt

1.   5   2.   4   3.   1   4.   2   5.   6   6.   3

Shoes

1.   5   2.   1   3.   6   4.   3   5.   2   6.   4

Socks

1.   1   2.   3   3.   5   4.   2   5.   6   6.   4

SECTION 3 – COLORS   Pages 31 – 35

Black

1.   4   2.   6   3.   2   4.   5   5.   3   6.   1

Blue

1.   1   2.   3   3.   2   4.   5   5.   4   6.   6

Colors 1

1.   5   2.   3   3.   4   4.   6   5.   2   6.   1

Colors 2

1.   2   2.   3   3.   1   4.   4   5.   6   6.   5

Colors 3

1.   1   2.   5   3.   3   4.   6   5.   4   6.

SECTION 4   –   DIRECTIONS   **Pages 36 – 39**

In and Out

1.   4   2.   6   3.   2   4.   5   5.   1   6.   3

Left, Right and Center

1.   3   2.   6   3.   5   4.   4   5.   1   6.   2

Up and Down

1.   2   2.   6   3.   1   4.   4   5.   3   6.   5

Way

1.   2   2.   3   3.   4   4.   6   5.   1   6.   5

SECTION 5   –   DIRTY   **Pages 40 – 42**

Dirt and Dirty

1.   4   2.   2   3.   1   4.   5   5.   6   6.   3

Dust

<u>1.</u>   6   <u>2.</u>   5   <u>3.</u>   4   <u>4.</u>   1   <u>5.</u>   2   <u>6.</u>   3

Mud

<u>1.</u>   3   <u>2.</u>   2   <u>3.</u>   5   <u>4.</u>   6   <u>5.</u>   4   <u>6.</u>   1

SECTION 6   –   EMOTIONS, FEELINGS AND PAIN   Pages 43 – 49

I'm Angry!

<u>1.</u>   2   <u>2.</u>   4   <u>3.</u>   6   <u>4.</u>   1   <u>5.</u>   5   <u>6.</u>   3

Ouch, That Hurts 1!

<u>1.</u>   6   <u>2.</u>   3   <u>3.</u>   4   <u>4.</u>   2   <u>5.</u>   5   <u>6.</u>   1

Ouch, That Hurts 2!

<u>1.</u>   5   <u>2.</u>   3   <u>3.</u>   1   <u>4.</u>   6   <u>5.</u>   2   <u>6.</u>   4

Ouch, That Hurts 3!

<u>1.</u>   1   <u>2.</u>   3   <u>3.</u>   5   <u>4.</u>   2   <u>5.</u>   6   <u>6.</u>   4

Soft, Kind and Gentle

<u>1.</u>   4   <u>2.</u>   2   <u>3.</u>   5   <u>4.</u>   1   <u>5.</u>   3   <u>6.</u>   6

Tired, Ashamed or Worn Out

<u>1.</u>   1   <u>2.</u>   3   <u>3.</u>   5   <u>4.</u>   6   <u>5.</u>   2   <u>6.</u>   4

Treated Badly

<u>1.</u>   2   <u>2.</u>   4   <u>3.</u>   6   <u>4.</u>   3   <u>5.</u>   1   <u>6.</u>   5

SECTION 7 – FOOD   Pages 50 – 60

Apples

<u>1.</u>   1   <u>2.</u>   4   <u>3.</u>   2   <u>4.</u>   3   <u>5.</u>   5   <u>6.</u>   6

Bananas

<u>1.</u>   6   <u>2.</u>   4   <u>3.</u>   5   <u>4.</u>   1   <u>5.</u>   3   <u>6.</u>   2

Eggs

<u>1.</u>   6   <u>2.</u>   3   <u>3.</u>   5   <u>4.</u>   4   <u>5.</u>   1   <u>6.</u>   2

Fruit

<u>1.</u>   3   <u>2.</u>   6   <u>3.</u>   1   <u>4.</u>   4   <u>5.</u>   2   <u>6.</u>   5

Fruits and Vegetables

<u>1.</u>   4   <u>2.</u>   1   <u>3.</u>   6   <u>4.</u>   2   <u>5.</u>   5   <u>6.</u>   3

In The Kitchen

<u>1.</u>   5   <u>2.</u>   4   <u>3.</u>   3   <u>4.</u>   2   <u>5.</u>   6   <u>6.</u>   1

Kitchen Utensils

<u>1.</u>   1   <u>2.</u>   5   <u>3.</u>   4   <u>4.</u>   2   <u>5.</u>   6   <u>6.</u>   3

Meals and Cooking

<u>1.</u>   4   <u>2.</u>   6   <u>3.</u>   1   <u>4.</u>   5   <u>5.</u>   2   <u>6.</u>   3

Tea and Coffee

<u>1.</u>   2   <u>2.</u>   1   <u>3.</u>   5   <u>4.</u>   6   <u>5.</u>   3   <u>6.</u>   4

Vegetables

<u>1.</u>   2   <u>2.</u>   3   <u>3.</u>   6   <u>4.</u>   4   <u>5.</u>   1   <u>6.</u>   5

Water

1. 6   2. 4   3. 1   4. 5   5. 2   6. 3

SECTION 8 – **HEAVEN, HELL and THE SUPERNATURAL Pages 61 – 69**

Death

1. 3   2. 4   3. 6   4. 5   5. 2   6. 1

The Devil

1. 3   2. 5   3. 6   4. 1   5. 2   6. 4

Dream

1. 5   2. 1   3. 4   4. 3   5. 6   6. 2

Ghosts and Scary Things

1. 1   2. 4   3. 3   4. 2   5. 5   6. 6

But For The Grace of God

1. 6   2. 5   3. 4   4. 3   5. 2   6. 1

Heaven 1

1. 2   2. 3   3. 6   4. 5   5. 4   6. 1

Heaven 2

1. 1   2. 3   3. 6   4. 2   5. 5   6. 4

Hell

1. 3   2. 5   3. 2   4. 1   5. 6   6. 4

Positive Energy

1. 2   2. 4   3. 6   4. 3   5. 1   6. 5

SECTION 9 – IMPLEMENTS Pages 70 – 76

Box

1. 3 2. 4 3. 6 4. 2 5. 1 6. 5

Rope

1. 2 2. 5 3. 1 4. 6 5. 3 6. 4

Stick

1. 3 2. 6 3. 4 4. 1 5. 2 6. 5
Stones and Rocks

1. 2 2. 4 3. 5 4. 6 5. 1 6. 3

Straw

1. 1 2. 5 3. 6 4. 4 5. 3 6. 2

String

1. 2 2. 6 3. 1 4. 3 5. 5 6. 4

SECTION 10 – LIFE AND LIVING Pages 77 – 80

Alert, Alive and Kicking

1. 5 2. 6 3. 3 4. 2 5. 1 6. 4

Life

1. 5 2. 1 3. 6 4. 3 5. 2 6. 4

Live, Life and Living

1. 5 2. 1 3. 6 4. 3 5. 2 6. 4

Living Dangerously

<u>1.</u>   5   <u>2.</u>   2   <u>3.</u>   6   <u>4.</u>   4   <u>5.</u>   1   <u>6.</u>   3

SECTION 11 – MONEY   **Pages 81 – 84**

Gambling

<u>1.</u>   3   <u>2.</u>   5   <u>3.</u>   4   <u>4.</u>   1   <u>5.</u>   2   <u>6.</u>   6

Money 1

<u>1.</u>   5   <u>2.</u>   4   <u>3.</u>   1   <u>4.</u>   3   <u>5.</u>   6   <u>6.</u>   2

Money 2

<u>1.</u>   5   <u>2.</u>   2   <u>3.</u>   1   <u>4.</u>   6   <u>5.</u>   4   <u>6.</u>   3

Penny

<u>1.</u>   5   <u>2.</u>   1   <u>3.</u>   6   <u>4.</u>   3   <u>5.</u>   2   <u>6.</u>   4

SECTION 12 – MOTHER NATURE   **Pages 86 – 100**

Air 1

<u>1.</u>   1   <u>2.</u>   5   <u>3.</u>   2   <u>4.</u>   3   <u>5.</u>   4   <u>6.</u>   6

Air 2

<u>1.</u>   2   <u>2.</u>   1   <u>3.</u>   6   <u>4.</u>   4   <u>5.</u>   3   <u>6.</u>   5

Burn and Fire

<u>1.</u>   1   <u>2.</u>   5   <u>3.</u>   6   <u>4.</u>   4   <u>5.</u>   2   <u>6.</u>   3

Cold, Icy and Chilling

<u>1.</u>   1   <u>2.</u>   3   <u>3.</u>   4   <u>4.</u>   2   <u>5.</u>   5   <u>6.</u>   6

Day

1.   5   2.   4   3.   6   4.   1   5.   2   6.   3

Fire

1.   2   2.   5   3.   6   4.   3   5.   1   6.   4

Hills and Mountains

1.   6   2.   4   3.   2   4.   1   5.   5   6.   3

Hot and Cold

1.   5   2.   2   3.   1   4.   6   5.   3   6.   4

Late at Night

1.   1   2.   6   3.   5   4.   2   5.   3   6.   4

Leaves, Trees and Branches

1.   1   2.   5   3.   6   4.   4   5.   3   6.   2

Sleep

1.   2   2.   6   3.   3   4.   5   5.   1   6.   4

Smoke

1.   3   2.   2   3.   6   4.   1   5.   4   6.   5

Time

1.   5   2.   1   3.   4   4.   2   5.   6   6.   3

Weather 1

1.   6   2.   5   3.   2   4.   4   5.   1   6.   3

Weather 2

1.   7   **2.**   1   **3.**   6   **4.**   2   **5.**   5   **6.**   3   **7.**   4

Wind

1.   4   2.   2   3.   1   4.   3   5.   6   6.   5

SECTION 13   –   MUSIC   **Pages 101 – 104**

Hip-Hop

1.   6   2.   1   3.   5   4.   3   5.   4   6.   2

Music and Musical Instruments

1.   4   2.   1   3.   6   4.   3   5.   2   6.   5

Sing and Song

1.   3   2.   6   3.   1   4.   2   5.   5   6.   4

Tune

1.   2   2.   5   3.   1   4.   3   5.   6   6.   4

SECTION 14   –   PEOPLE   **Pages 105 – 108**

Famous Names 1

1.   6   2.   4   3.   5   4.   2   5.   3   6.   1

Famous Names 2

1.   1   2.   2   3.   6   4.   5   5.   3   6.   4

Queens and Kings

1.   1   2.   6   3.   4   4.   2   5.   3   6.   5

Relatives

1.   5   2.   4   3.   1   4.   2   5.   3   6.   6

SECTION 15   –   PLACES   Pages 109 – 118

Corner

1.   5   2.   4   3.   6   4.   1   5.   3   6.   2

Edge

1.   4   2.   6   3.   1   4.   2   5.   3   6.   5

End

1.   1   2.   6   3.   2   4.   5   5.   3   6.   4

Famous Places 1

1.   5   2.   1   3.   4   4.   6   5.   2   6.   3

Famous Places 2

1.   4   2.   5   3.   2   4.   1   5.   6   6.   3

House

1.   4   2.   1   3.   3   4.   6   5.   2   6.   5

Medieval and Ancient World

1.   6   2.   3   3.   2   4.   5   5.   1   6.   4

Road and Street

1.   2   2.   5   3.   1   4.   3   5.   6   6.   4

School

1.   5   2.   6   3.   4   4.   1   5.   2   6.   3

World

1.   2   2.   6   3.   4   4.   1   5.   3   6.   5

SECTION 16 – <u>SCIENCE, ATOMS, ELEMENTS and NUMBERS</u>
<u>Pages 119 – 128</u>

<u>Astronomy</u>

<u>1.</u> 6   <u>2.</u> 5   <u>3.</u> 4   <u>4.</u> 3   <u>5.</u> 2   <u>6.</u> 1

<u>Atoms and Elements</u>

<u>1.</u> 6   <u>2.</u> 1   <u>3.</u> 5   <u>4.</u> 4   <u>5.</u> 3   <u>6.</u> 2

<u>Brass</u>

<u>1.</u> 3   <u>2.</u> 4   <u>3.</u> 2   <u>4.</u> 1   <u>5.</u> 6   <u>6.</u> 5

<u>Gold</u>

<u>1.</u> 4   <u>2.</u> 6   <u>3.</u> 2   <u>4.</u> 1   <u>5.</u> 3   <u>6.</u> 5

<u>Iron</u>

<u>1.</u> 3   <u>2.</u> 6   <u>3.</u> 5   <u>4.</u> 1   <u>5.</u> 2   <u>6.</u> 4

<u>Numbers</u>

<u>1.</u> 6   <u>2.</u> 4   <u>3.</u> 2   <u>4.</u> 5   <u>5.</u> 3   <u>6.</u> 1

<u>Oil and Gas</u>

<u>1.</u> 4   <u>2.</u> 6   <u>3.</u> 5   <u>4.</u> 3   <u>5.</u> 2   <u>6.</u> 1

<u>Ordinal Numbers</u>

<u>1.</u> 6   <u>2.</u> 1   <u>3.</u> 4   <u>4.</u> 3   <u>5.</u> 2   <u>6.</u> 5

<u>Science</u>

<u>1.</u> 4   <u>2.</u> 3   <u>3.</u> 6   <u>4.</u> 1   <u>5.</u> 2   <u>6.</u> 5

<u>Silver and Gold</u>

<u>1.</u> 1   <u>2.</u> 5   <u>3.</u> 2   <u>4.</u> 6   <u>5.</u> 3   <u>6.</u> 4

Marco Antonio Bussanich

SECTION 17   –   SPORTS AND GAMES   Pages 129 – 135

Ball 1

1.   2   2.   6   3.   1   4.   5   5.   3   6.   4

Ball 2

1.   6   2.   3   3.   5   4.   1   5.   4   6.   2

Game

1.   2   2.   4   3.   6   4.   5   5.   1   6.   3

Golf

1.   2   2.   5   3.   1   4.   6   5.   4   6.   3

Sports 1

1.   4   2.   3   3.   1   4.   5   5.   2   6.   6

Sports 2

1.   3   2.   4   3.   6   4.   5   5.   1   6.   2

Sports 3

1.   4   2.   5   3.   3   4.   1   5.   2   6.   6

SECTION 18   –   THE HUMAN BODY   Pages 136 – 162

Blood

1.   3   2.   1   3.   2   4.   4   5.   6   6.   5

Body Parts

1.   6   2.   5   3.   4   4.   1   5.   2   6.   3

Feet

1. 5   2. 4   3. 1   4. 6   5. 3   6. 2

Finger

1. 3   2. 5   3. 4   4. 1   5. 6   6. 2

Foot

1. 3   2. 1   3. 4   4. 6   5. 2   6. 5

Guts

1. 3   2. 6   3. 4   4. 2   5. 5   6. 1

Hair

1. 6   2. 3   3. 5   4. 1   5. 4   6. 2

Hand 1

1. 2   2. 4   3. 5   4. 6   5. 3   6. 1

Hand 2

1. 3   2. 6   3. 1   4. 2   5. 4   6. 5

Hand 3

1. 1   2. 6   3. 2   4. 5   5. 3   6. 4

Head 1

1. 6   2. 4   3. 5   4. 2   5. 3   6. 1

Head 2

1. 6   2. 5   3. 1   4. 2   5. 3   6. 4

Head 3

<u>1.</u>   6   <u>2.</u>   4   <u>3.</u>   5   <u>4.</u>   3   <u>5.</u>   1   <u>6.</u>   2

Heart

<u>1.</u>   4   <u>2.</u>   2   <u>3.</u>   1   <u>4.</u>   6   <u>5.</u>   3   <u>6.</u>   5

Lip

<u>1.</u>   2   <u>2.</u>   1   <u>3.</u>   3   <u>4.</u>   5   <u>5.</u>   6   <u>6.</u>   4

Mouth

<u>1.</u>   4   <u>2.</u>   6   <u>3.</u>   1   <u>4.</u>   2   <u>5.</u>   3   <u>6.</u>   5

Nose 1

<u>1.</u>   4   <u>2.</u>   6   <u>3.</u>   1   <u>4.</u>   5   <u>5.</u>   3   <u>6.</u>   2

Nose 2

<u>1.</u>   6   <u>2.</u>   5   <u>3.</u>   4   <u>4.</u>   1   <u>5.</u>   3   <u>6.</u>   2

Nose 3

<u>1.</u>   4   <u>2.</u>   2   <u>3.</u>   5   <u>4.</u>   6   <u>5.</u>   3   <u>6.</u>   1

Parts of the Face 1

<u>1.</u>   4   <u>2.</u>   6   <u>3.</u>   5   <u>4.</u>   3   <u>5.</u>   1   <u>6.</u>   2

Parts of the Face 2

<u>1.</u>   4   <u>2.</u>   6   <u>3.</u>   2   <u>4.</u>   1   <u>5.</u>   5   <u>6.</u>   3

Shoulders

<u>1.</u>   1   <u>2.</u>   6   <u>3.</u>   4   <u>4.</u>   5   <u>5.</u>   2   <u>6.</u>   3

Skin and Flesh

1.   3   2.   6   3.   1   4.   5   5.   2   6.   4

Sweet Tooth

1.   3   2.   1   3.   5   4.   2   5.   6   6.   4

Teeth

1.   6   2.   4   3.   1   4.   3   5.   5   6.   2

Thumb

1.   2   2.   5   3.   4   4.   6   5.   1   6.   3

Tooth and Teeth

1.   5   2.   1   3.   4   4.   2   5.   6   6.   3

SECTION 19 – THINGS   **Pages 163 – 175**

Big and Small

1.   4   2.   5   3.   2   4.   3   5.   6   6.   1

Chip and Chips

1.   2   2.   1   3.   5   4.   6   5.   4   6.   3

Flags

1.   5   2.   6   3.   3   4.   2   5.   1   6.   4

Hit and Break

1.   6   2.   3   3.   5   4.   4   5.   2   6.   1

Line 1

1.   5   2.   2   3.   1   4.   6   5.   4   6.   3

Line 2

1.	6	2.	1	3.	4	4.	3	5.	2	6.	5

Mark

1.	4	2.	5	3.	1	4.	6	5.	2	6.	3

News

1.	5	2.	6	3.	2	4.	4	5.	1	6.	3

Order

1.	5	2.	3	3.	2	4.	6	5.	1	6.	4

Point

1.	2	2.	6	3.	1	4.	3	5.	4	6.	5

Questions and Answers

1.	6	2.	1	3.	4	4.	5	5.	2	6.	3

Shot

1.	5	2.	4	3.	6	4.	3	5.	2	6.	1

Word

1.	4	2.	3	3.	5	4.	6	5.	1	6.	2

Work

1.	1	2.	3	3.	5	4.	2	5.	4	6.	6

SECTION 20 — VICES AND VIRTUES   Pages 176 – 191

At the Bar 1

1.	5	2.	3	3.	1	4.	2	5.	4	6.	6

At the Bar 2

1.	5	2.	1	3.	4	4.	6	5.	2	6.	3

Dating and Marriage

1.	5	2.	3	3.	6	4.	4	5.	2	6.	1

Drinking

1.	2	2.	3	3.	1	4.	6	5.	5	6.	4

Dumb, Stupid or Idiotic

1.	4	2.	6	3.	5	4.	3	5.	1	6.	2

Fall

1.	1	2.	5	3.	4	4.	2	5.	3	6.	6

Getting Drunk

1.	5	2.	4	3.	2/1	4.	6	5.	3	6.	2/1

Gossip and Silence

1.	4	2.	1	3.	3	4.	2	5.	5	6.	6

In Trouble

1.	6	2.	3	3.	2	4.	5	5.	4	6.	1

Lie and Lying

1.	2	2.	6	3.	3	4.	5	5.	1	6.	4

Noise and Silence

1.	5	2.	1	3.	4	4.	3	5.	6	6.	2

## On the Dole	(Unemployed)

1.	4	2.	3	3.	6	4.	2/1	5.	5	6.	2/1

Pregnant

<u>1.</u> 3   <u>2.</u> 5   <u>3.</u> 4   <u>4.</u> 6   <u>5.</u> 1   <u>6.</u> 2

Steal or Cheat

<u>1.</u> 6   <u>2.</u> 3   <u>3.</u> 1   <u>4.</u> 4   <u>5.</u> 2   <u>6.</u> 5

Trick

<u>1.</u> 3   <u>2.</u> 5   <u>3.</u> 1   <u>4.</u> 6   <u>5.</u> 4   <u>6.</u> 2

Truth

<u>1.</u> 2   <u>2.</u> 6   <u>3.</u> 3   <u>4.</u> 5   <u>5.</u> 1   <u>6.</u> 4

MEANINGS

0

1. A **zero** sum game
   - there can only be a loser and a winner, and an advantage to one person comes at a disadvantage to another person

1

1. **One** love
   - all humanity is the same and everyone should love everyone else
2. Get to **1ˢᵗ base**
   - to begin to see progress in the carrying out of a plan

2

1. Put **two** and **two** together
   - to make a correct guess, based on available information

3

1. **Three strikes** against someone (and now you're out)
   - laws that punish people severely who commit 3 separate crimes

5

1. Give me **five**
   - to slap hands together without someone else

6 & 7

1. At **sixes** and **sevens**
   - refers to someone who is confused and disorganized

8

1. Get **86'ed**
   - to be bounced or thrown out of a bar or club

19

1. Talk **nineteen** to the **dozen**
   - to talk very quickly, without pausing

A

ACE

1. Have an **ace** in the hole
   - to have a secret asset that can be used to your advantage

2. Play your **ace**
   - to do an unexpected thing, giving you an advantage over others

ACID

1. The **acid** test
   - a test that determines how effective or valid something is

AIR

1. A breath of fresh **air**
   - a person whose sincerity and honesty is welcome or appreciated
2. Left hanging in the **air**
   - refers to an issue or question which is not discussed or answered
3. Full of hot **air**
   - refers to a person who is insincere and cannot be believed
4. Out of thin **air**
   - something that appears suddenly or unexpectedly
5. Be walking on **air**
   - to feel very happy or very excited
6. Up in the **air**
   - something whose outcome is uncertain
7. Clear the **air**
   - discuss something so as to make divisions or problems go away
8. Free as the **air**
   - to be completely free and/or to have no problems or worries
9. Hot **air**
   - something that is not sincere or truthful
10. Into thin **air**
    - something or someone that vanishes completely, so that no one knows where that thing or person is
11. Pluck something from the **air**
    - to say something spontaneously without considering if it is factual
12. Put on **airs**
    - behave as if you are better or more important than others

ANGELS

1. On the side of the **angels**
   - to do, or to support, the morally correct course of action

ANSWER

1. Have a lot to **answer** for
   - refers to a person that is now coming under pressure to take responsibility for something bad that has happened
2. Dusty (or dirty) **answer**
   - a negative or unpleasant answer
3. Won't take no for an **answer**
   - won't accept the fact someone refuses to do what you asked of them

ANTE
1. Up the **ante**
   - take greater risks, or make greater demands on yourself or others

APPLES
1. A bad **apple**
   - a dishonest, unpleasant person who influences others poorly
2. How do you like them **apples?**
   - a taunting comment, made to someone as a retort
3. As sure as God made little green **apples**
   - something that is 100% certain
4. Upset the **apple** cart
   - to ruin someone's plans
5. Polish someone's **apples**
   - to flatter someone else
6. **Apple**-pie order
   - something that is very tidy and in proper order
7. **Apple** of someone's eye
   - refers to someone who is treasured and loved by someone else

ARK
1. Out of the **ark**
   - something that is very old, or very old-fashioned

ARMOR
1. A **knight** in shining **armor**
   - a person who bravely rescues someone from danger
2. A chink in someone's **armor**
   - a weakness that someone has that can be taken advantage of

AXED
1. Get **axed**
   - to be fired from a job

B

BABY
1. Left holding the **baby**
   - to be blamed for something that was not your fault
2. **Baby bumps**
   - the visual sight of the enlarged stomach of a pregnant woman
3. Have a **baby**
   - to react irately and/or with anger at someone or something

BACK
1. Cover your **back**
   - to take measures to protect yourself, against things like criticism, or accusations of wrongdoing

BACK-HANDED
1. A **back-handed compliment**
   - a critical comment, which at first seems complimentary

BALL
1. **Ball** and chain
   - something that limits a person's, or a thing's, freedom
2. A crystal **ball**
   - something that is used to predict the future
3. Drop the **ball**
   - to make a mistake or do something that is considered foolish
4. Have a **ball**
   - to have a great time
5. Keep the **ball** rolling
   - to make sure that a thing that you are involved in keeps on going
6. On the **ball**
   - to deal with something in an quick, intelligent and alert manner
7. Pick up the **ball** and run with it
   - use a plan or idea someone else started, and develop it further
8. Play **hardball**
   - to try to force someone into doing what you want them to do
9. Start the **ball** rolling
   - be the person to start a process which other people join in on later
10. A whole new **ball** game
    - something that is totally different than the thing that preceded it
11. Break someone's **balls**
    - create problems for a person to make him lose his confidence
12. Keep **balls** in the air
    - deal with a number of different matters at the same time
13. **Ball** someone out
    - to castigate someone for something they did, by scolding them
14. The **ball** is in your court
    - it is now your responsibility to make the next decision or move
15. Play **ball**
    - refers to someone who makes you do what they want you to do
16. Throw someone a **curve ball**
    - refers to something done unexpectedly, which then can cause \ problems
17. A **ballpark** figure
    - a rough estimate

BALLISTIC
1. Go **ballistic**
   - to become very angry

BANANAS
1. Go **bananas**
   - to become very upset or angry
2. Slip on a **banana** peel
   - the act of doing something that makes a person look foolish
3. Second **banana**
   - the second most important person in a group or organization
4. Go **bananas** over something
   - to become very enthusiastic about doing something
5. **Banana** oil
   - an insincere thing that is said in order to gain an advantage
6. **Banana** republic
   - a small, poor country with a corrupt government

BANK
1. Break the **bank**
   - to have something cost too much money
2. Laughing all the way to the **bank**
   - to make a lot of money very easily

BASE
1. Get to 1st **base**
   - to begin to see progress in the carrying out of a plan

BAT
1. Like a **bat** out of hell
   - refers to a place that someone goes to very quickly, or to something that happens, or that is done, very, very quickly

BEE
1. The **bee's** knees
   - refers to someone, or something, that is very good at something
2. A **bee** in your bonnet
   - to feel strongly about some thing, and to talk continuously about it

BEET
1. Red as a **beet**
   - to blush because you have been embarrassed

BELLY
1. **Belly-ache**
   - to consistently complain about something or someone

BETS
1. All **bets** are off
   - a situation where it is impossible to know the outcome

BIG
1. **Big** frog in small pond
   - an important person in a small group
2. **Big** tuna/ big cheese/ big kahuna
   - an important or powerful person, or, the boss
3. Too **big** for your britches
   - a person who feels they are more important than they really are

BIRDS
1. **Birds** of a feather flock together
   - people who have similar likes and inclinations will congregate and and then spend time together, often doing the things they both like

BITE
1. **Bite** your lip
   - to be quiet about something, especially when you would rather express an opinion or have a say on some matter
2. **Bite** your head off
   - to angrily reprimand someone for something they have done
3. **Bite** your tongue
   - to stop from saying something that you really want to say

BLACK
1. Not as **black** as painted
   - someone who is not as awful as other people think he/she is
2. **Black** and **blue**
   - to have a badly bruised body
3. **Black** and **white**
   - to judge something in an extreme sense so it is at either one of two extremes. There is no middle ground, or mid point of view.
4. In the **black**
   - to be free of debt or to not owe any money to anyone
5. The new **black**
   - a thing or a color is the new black if it is now fashionable
6. A **black** cloud
   - when a black cloud hangs over someone's head, then they are encountering a string of bad luck
7. In **black** and **white**
   - refers to something that is so extremely and plainly obvious

BLOOD

1. Bad **blood**
   - the bad feelings that exist between people due to past arguments
2. Be after **blood**
   - a desire to punish someone for something they have done to you
3. Get **blood** out of a stone
   - where it's very difficult to get a person to give you something
4. New **blood**
   - new people who are brought into a group to added needed energy
5. Have **blood** on your hands
   - a person who is responsible for a death, or a bad thing happening
6. **Blood** on the carpet
   - trouble that's a result of a struggle between members of a group

BLUE

1. Feel **blue**
   - to feel sad or depressed
2. A bolt from the **blue**
   - a thing that happens unexpectedly, coming as a complete surprise
3. **Blue** blood
   - refers to someone with royal or aristocratic blood, or upbringing
4. Until you are **blue** in the face
   - refers to a long period of time
5. **Blue** collar
   - a person from the working class
6. Cuss a **blue** streak
   - to curse a lot
7. Out of the **blue**
   - refers to something that happens unexpectedly

BOOTS

1. Get the **boot**
   - to lose your job
2. Put the **boot** in
   - to say something that is very critical or unkind
3. Be quaking in one's **boots**
   - to be very frightened about something
4. **Boots** and all
   - to do something with a lot of energy and enthusiasm
5. Fill your **boots**
   - to get as much of something as a person can
6. Lick someone's **boots**
   - to suck up to a powerful person, or to say something nice to them, because you want to please them
7. Tough as old **boots**
   - a person with strong character who does not get easily upset

BOTTLE
1. **Hit** the **bottle**
   - to drink too much

BOUNDS
1. Out of **bounds**
   - a place where people are not allowed to go to

BOX
1. The first out of the **box**
   - to be the first person to do something
2. Black **box**
   - a reference to something that produces an output or a result, but without knowing how the output or result is obtained
3. A **box** of birds
   - a reference to someone who is very healthy
4. Come out of the **box**
   - a reference to how someone or something starts something
5. Out of your **box**
   - someone who is very drunk, stupid, or acts foolishly
6. Think outside of the **box**
   - to have new or revolutionary ideas, or new ways of doing things

BRAIN
1. Grab a **brain**
   - a negative comment said to someone who cannot understand something, probably because they are either naïve, or stupid
2. Have a **brain** like a sieve
   - refers to someone who is bad at remembering things
3. Get your **brain** into gear
   - start to think more clearly, so you can accomplish a certain task

BRANCH
1. Hold out an olive **branch**
   - do or say something in an attempt to end a disagreement with someone

BRASS
1. The **brass** ring
   - a very successful or profitable thing or venture
2. Cold enough to freeze the balls off a **brass** monkey
   - a reference to extremely cold weather
3. Get down to **brass** tacks
   - to discuss the most important or fundamental points of an issue

4. A **brass** farthing
   - something that has to do with the paying of money. It is often used in a negative way. If, for example, you do not want to give money to someone, you say, I won't that person a brass farthing
5. The **brass**
   - high-ranking military or civilian officials
6. Bold as **brass**
   - bold, impudent or shameless

BREAD
1. Know which side your **bread** is buttered
   - to know who or what the best possible situation is for yourself, and then to who to please in order to arrive at this situation
2. **Bread** and **butter**
   - a person's most important source of income or talent

BREAK
1. **Break** the ice
   - do something to make people feel more relaxed, in what is originally a tense environment
2. **Break** the news
   - (a) to be the person to tell bad news to someone, because that person doesn't realize something that is truly obvious
   - (b) to tell someone some bad news, even though it will be hurtful
3. **Break** his/her/my word
   - to purposely break a promise that you originally intended to keep
4. **Break** a leg
   - to wish an actor or performer good luck, before they goes on stage

BREAKFAST
1. Have someone for **breakfast**
   - refers to someone who's stronger or more aggressive than another person, so the 1st person can dominate the 2nd person

BROTHER
1. Not your **brother's** keeper
   - a saying that express the fact that you don't know where someone is, and that you shouldn't have to know where that person is

BROWN
1. **Brown** as a berry
   - to have skin that's very tanned because you've been in the sun
2. **Brownie** points
   - to receive praise or admiration for doing something

BUCK
1. **Buck** the trend
   - refers to a person that takes an alternative path to what is popular
2. The **buck** stops here
   - when someone says, "The buck stops here", they mean that they are taking total responsibility for an issue or a matter
3. Pass the **buck**
   - if someone passes the buck, they're not taking responsibility for something, and they're expecting someone else to deal with it

BUGS
1. Bitten by a **bug**
   - become very eager or enthusiastic to do something. After being bit by the bug, the person will start doing this thing a lot
2. Snug as a **bug** in a rug
   - to be very comfortable and warm

BULL
1. Like a red flag to a **bull**
   - something that always makes a person, or an entity, very angry
2. A **bull** in a china shop
   - a person who says or does things rashly or quickly, without considering the damage this will cause
3. A red flag to a **bull**
   - refers to something that always makes a particular person angry
4. Take the **bull** by the horns
   - to act swiftly, and with determination, to take control of a situation
5. Don't take any **bull** (from someone)
   - to not take abuse or maltreatment from someone else, or to not accept their lies

BUM
1. **Bum** a smoke
   - borrow a cigarette

BUN
1. **Bun** in the oven
   - to be pregnant

BURN
1. **Burn/burning** the midnight oil
   - to stay up late, to either study, or to work
2. **Burn** my/his/her bridges
   - to destroy all previous business or personal contacts
3. **Burnt** out
   - to be extremely and totally fatigued, and in need of rest

BUST
  1. **Bust** your balls
     - to harass someone with the intention of breaking their spirit
  2. **Busting** your chops
     - to say something to someone so as to harass them

BUTTERFLIES
  1. Get **butterflies**
     - become nervous

BUTTON
  1. **Button** your lip
     - to keep silent, although there is a great urge to say something
  2. On the **button**
     - something that is exactly on time, or is the right amount of cash

C

CAKE
  1. Have your **cake** and eat it too
     - it's not possible to enjoy the benefit of two conflicting situations: a person can only have 1 of these things, not both at the same time
  2. Take the **cake**
     - a person, or a form of behaviour, that is the most extreme example of a bad thing

CANDY
  1. Like taking **candy** from a baby
     - something that is very easy to do

CANNED
  1. Get **canned**
     - to be fired from a job

CAP
  1. Put on your thinking **cap**
     - to think deeply about a problem in order to solve it
  2. Set your **cap** at someone
     - refers to a situation where a woman wants a man to notice her, and especially if she wants him to marry her

CARBON
  1. **Carbon** copy
     - two things that are very similar or almost identical

CARD
1. Get **carded**
   - to be required to present your identification for age verification

CARROT
1. Offer someone a **carrot**
   - offer an inducement, incentive or reward to others so as to influence them to make them do what you want them to do

CASH
1. A **cash** cow
   - something that makes a lot of money

CASTLES
1. **Castles** in the air
   - refers to someone who's unrealistic, and who has no chance of success

CAT
1. The **cat's** whiskers
   - someone or something that is very popular, appealing or desirable
2. Has the **cat** got your tongue?
   - something that is said to someone when they are quiet, when they should be talking or saying something
3. Let the **cat** out of the bag
   - to reveal a secret that was not intended to be told to someone
4. There's more than one way to skin a **cat**
   - there's more than one way to do something, rather than the traditional or most popular way
5. Play a game of **cat** and mouse
   - occurs when a person attempts to deceive or confuse someone else to gain advantage over them, so they can defeat them
6. **Fat** cat
   - a description of a politician or a businessman, who it has been concluded, unfairly uses their wealth or their power
7. **Cat** nap - a short nap
8. Who's she, the **cat's** mother?
   - this is used to show that you think it is rude when someone refers to someone as she, instead of using the person's real name
9. Raining **cats** and **dogs**
   - when it rains a lot
10. When the **cats** away the **mice** will play
    - people will behave mischievously when their boss, or a person of authority, is absent
11. Put the **cat** amongst the **pigeons**
    - if the cat is put amongst the pigeons, then this signifies that an action will cause a group a lot of worry or angst

12. Fight like **cats** and **dogs**
    - refers to two people who fight a lot, and who often fight violently
13. Like the **cat** that ate the **canary**
    - to feel satisfied to have accomplished something you are proud of

CENTER
1. Take **center** stage
    - to become the most significant person in a situation
2. **Left, right** and **center**
    - a statement used to show that something is being done a lot

CHEEK
1. **Cheek** by jowl
    - refers to a situation where two people are very close to each other, but in a very strange situation
2. Turn the other **cheek**
    - to not take action when someone tries to hurt or harms you

CHEMISTRY
1. Have **chemistry**
    - a situation where two people are a perfect match for each other

CHERRIES
1. A bowl of **cherries**
    - refers to a life or a lifestyle that is enjoyable and pleasant

CHICKEN AND EGGS
1. **Chicken** and **egg**
    - a situation where it is impossible to know which of two events came first, or which of the events caused the other
2. Run around like a **chicken** with its head cut off
    - a situation where a person is acting illogically or irrational
3. **Chicken**
    - refers to a person who is a coward, or who is afraid
4. **Chickens** come home to roost
    - when all of your bad karma, mistakes and bad returns pile up, which leads to bad luck, or to bad consequences
5. **Chicken** out
    - to become afraid and intimidated, causing you to either stop doing something, or even not do it all
6. **Chicken** feed
    - a very small amount, especially in comparison to something else
7. No spring **chicken**
    - refers to a person who is no longer young

225

CHILLING
1. **Chill** out
   - to relax and take it easy
2. **Chill**
   - something said to an angry person to make them calm down

CHIN
1. **Take it** on the **chin**
   - to accept criticism or defeat in a very brave way

2. Keep your **chin** up
   - to try to stay cheerful in a difficult situation

CHIP and CHIPS
1. A **chip** off the old block
   - a person who is similar to their parents in character, behaviour or appearance
2. Have a **chip** on your shoulder
   - a person who is resentful or angry, and who feels like they are being treated unfairly
3. Have had your **chips**
   - to fail completely in a person's attempt in doing something
4. Call in your **chips**
   - to use influence and connections to gain advantages over others
5. Cash in your **chips**
   - to sell something, such as an investment, in order to get money
6. When the **chips** are down
   - a reference to how someone behaves when they are placed in a difficult or dangerous situation

CLAM
1. Shut up like a **clam**
   - become quiet and stop talking to others, usually because you are mad or angry about something

CLEANERS
1. **Take** someone to the **cleaners**
   - use illegal or dishonest ways to make someone lose lots of money

CLOUD
1. Under a **cloud**
   - refers to someone who is not trusted because of recent behaviour

COATTAILS
1. Ride someone's **coattails**
   - to use a person, or a person's success, to get success for yourself

COFFEE
1. **Coffee**-table book
   - a book that is more suited for display rather than for being read
2. Wake up and smell the **coffee**
   - to tell someone to be become more realistic and/or aware of the realities about themselves

COLD
1. Give someone the **cold** shoulder
   - to ignore someone deliberately
2. **Cold** feet
   - become nervous or anxious about something you may want to do, and then do not do it
3. Leave someone out in the **cold**/ Left out in the **cold**
   - ignore someone, and do not include them in your plans
4. Blow **hot** and **cold**
   - describes when someone is sometimes very enthusiastic about doing something, but then suddenly becomes very uninterested in it
5. **Cold** turkey
   - to quit smoking suddenly
6. **Cold** as ice
   - refers to someone who shows little feelings or emotions
7. **Cold** comfort
   - a statement that when said to someone, doesn't make them feel any better

COLORS
1. Sailing under false **colors**
   - to deliberately deceive other people
2. Nail your **colors** to the mast
   - refers to a person who states their opinions or beliefs very clearly and openly
3. With flying **colors**
   - to achieve something or accomplish something very easily
4. **Color** me something
   - to state your preference quite clearly

COMPLIMENT
1. A **back-handed** **compliment**
   - a comment that's critical, even though it may seem complimentary

COOKIE
1. Catch someone with their hand in the **cookie** jar
   - to catch someone doing something wrong or illegal

2. That's the way the **cookie** crumbles
   - a saying that implies a person must accept the way something turns out, even if the end result isn't what the person wanted

COOKS
1. Too many **cooks** spoil the **broth**
   - if too many people work on one thing together, it will be hard to be successful, because the ideas of the different people can conflict

CORNER
1. In a **corner**
   - to be in a difficult predicament, which is difficult to escape from
2. In someone's **corner**
   - to be supportive of someone
3. Just round the **corner**
   - something that is going to happen very, very soon
4. Paint yourself into a **corner**
   - to do something that will ultimately create difficulties for you
5. Turn the **corner**
   - to start to recover from a troubling situation or an illness
6. Cut **corners**
   - to not follow the correct rules or procedures to get something done, in an attempt to save time, effort or money

COVER
1. **Cover** charge
   - to pay an entrance fee before entering the bar

COW
1. Have/had a **cow**
   - to become extremely upset, or very, very angry
2. A sacred **cow**
   - something that people are unwilling to criticize or change, because it has a long-standing tradition

CRAB
1. **Crabby**
   - someone who is cranky, or who is usually in a bad mood

CROCODILE
1. **Crocodile** tears
   - refers to someone who pretends to shows sadness or who cries over something, but who doesn't really care about the situation or thing

CROW
1. As the **crow** flies
   - refers to the shortest linear distance between two points
2. Eat **crow**
   - to admit your wrongdoing, in a humble way

CUCUMBER
1. As cool as a **cucumber**
   - to be calm and relaxed, especially under pressure

CUP OF TEA
1. Not your **cup of tea**
   - refers to some thing, or some person, which you don't like, or which you are not good at

CUPBOARD
1. The **cupboard** is bare
   - there is nothing more available because everything has been used, whether this be money, or some other material thing

D

DAISIES
1. Pushing **daisies**
   - refers to someone who is dead

DARK
1. In the **dark**
   - to be denied knowledge about something, so that the person knows very little about the thing

DATING
1. A **blind date**
   - to have an arranged date with a person you've never met before

DAY
1. Carry the **day**
   - to win an argument or a competition
2. The **day** of reckoning
   - to face the time when a person has to deal with an unpleasant thing, because the person has delayed facing it in the past
3. Don't give up your **day** job
   - a negative comment, implying to someone that they are not very good at doing something

4. Have had your **day**
   - refers to when a person's best achievements are in the past, and the person can no longer achieve to the same level
5. Late in the **day**
   - to do something in the final stages of a situation
6. Seize the **day**
   - to do something at the very instant that you want to do it, and then not worry about the future consequences of the action
7. Late in the **day**
   - refers to something that is done at the last possible moment
8. Like night and **day**
   - refers to two or more things that are completely different

DARK
1. In the **dark**
   - to be denied knowledge about something, so that the person knows very little about the thing

DEATH
1. At **death's** door
   - refers to a person that is very ill, and that will soon die
2. **Death** and taxes
   - when something is compared to death and taxes, this mean this thing is impossible to avoid
3. Fight to the **death**
   - refers to something a person has to fight extremely hard to get
4. Come back from **death's** door
   - refers to someone who has recovered from a very serious illness
5. A living **death**
   - refers to someone whose quality of life is very low
6. Sign someone's (or your own) **death** warrant
   - to cause someone else's ruin, or to cause your own ruin
7. **Cheat death**
   - to escape serious injury, or even death, in a dangerous situation
8. **Dice** with **death**
   - take risks that will put your life in danger

THE DEVIL
1. A **devil** of a job
   - a job that is very difficult to do
2. Better the **devil** you know
   - you would rather deal with a person you already know, rather than someone you don't, because the other person may be worse
3. Play **devils** advocate
   - to purposely disagree with someone to make people think deeply about a topic, or to make a discussion more interesting

4. The **devil** take the hindmost
   - do what is best for yourself, without considering other's interests
5. Speak of the **devil**
   - used when someone you've been talking about suddenly appears
6. Between the **devil** and the deep blue sea
   - used when a person is in a difficult situation, and where 2 equally difficult courses of action are either difficult or bad

DICE
1. The **dice** is loaded against you
   - a situation where things purposely arranged to your disadvantage
2. No **dice**
   - to refuse to do what is asked of you

DINNER
1. Done like **dinner**
   - to be defeated by an opponent, in a way that may be unfair

DIRT
1. Dig up **dirt**
   - to look for harmful information on someone
2. Dish the **dirt** on someone
   - to tell other people harmful information about someone
3. Treat someone like **dirt**
   - to treat someone very badly, or to betray them
4. **Dirt**
   - unpleasant or bad personal information

DIRTY
1. Do the **dirty** on someone
   - to betray someone, or treat them badly
2. Air your **dirty** linen in public
   - to publicly talk about private matters that should be kept private

DOGS
1. A **dog's** life
   - an unpleasant or difficult life
2. In the **dog** house
   - to be in trouble with someone, so they punish you
3. Put on the **dog**
   - to act as if you are rich or important
4. Every **dog** has its day
   - Everyone will be successful at some point in their life
5. Let sleeping **dogs** lie
   - not talk about problems or issues that have happened in the past

6. A **dog's** dinner
   - something that is very unappetizing, and that looks so bad that it should only be fed to dogs
7. Call off the **dogs**
   - to stop criticizing or attacking someone

DOLE
1. On the **dole**
   - to be receiving government issued unemployment insurance

DOLLARS
1. Bet your (my) bottom **dollar**
   - you are saying that you are absolutely certain that something will definitely happen, or that something is definitely true
2. **Dollars** to doughnuts
   - a saying used to convey the impression that if you think that something will happen, then you are certain that it will happen
3. The $64,000 **dollar** question
   - a question that is very, very important, but is difficult to answer

DONKEY
1. **Donkey** years
   - refers to something that's being happening for a long, long time

DOO-DOO
1. In deep **doo-doo**
   - to be in serious trouble for something you did

DOWN
1. **Down** and dirty
   - refers to a person who behaves unpleasantly or dishonestly
2. **Down** the tubes (drain)
   - a situation that is getting worse, and will probably not get better
3. **Down**
   - to be supportive of someone or something

DREAM
1. The American **Dream**
   - an idea from America that states that anybody can achieve success, no matter how poor they are or were in the beginning
2. A **dream** ticket
   - a pair who it is thought will be very successful working together, especially in the field of politics
3. Like a **dream**
   - to do something very wells
   - a reference to something that works very well

4. Work like a **dream**
   - something that works very well or is done very well
5. Beyond your wildest **dreams**
   - something that is much better than can ever be hoped for
6. In your **dreams**
   - a saying that implies that some thing will never happen, or, that it will happen only in their dreams

DRINK

1. Belt down a **drink**
   - to drink rapidly
2. **Drink** someone under the table
   - to have the ability to drink more than someone else
3. **Drink** like a fish
   - drink a lot of alcohol
4. I'll **drink** to that
   - to agree with something
5. Knock back a **drink**
   - swallow an alcoholic drink
6. Drive someone to **drink**
   - make another person anxious and unhappy

DRUM

1. Bang the **drum**
   - to support someone or something publicly, in a very forceful and open way

DRUNK

1. **Drunk** as a skunk
   - very drunk
2. Dead **drunk**
   - Extremely drunk
3. Punch **drunk**
   - To be very tired and confused

DUMB

1. **Dumb** as a doornail
   - a person who is very, very stupid

DUMPS

1. **Down** in the **dumps**
   - to feel very depressed

DUST

1. Bite the **dust**
   - something that stops existing, fails or dies

2. The **dust** settles
   - to pause or allow a time of reflection after an argument or a big change
3. Eat someone's **dust**
   - to be thoroughly defeated, or be a long way behind a competitor
4. Gather **dust**
   - something that isn't used or talked about for a long period of time
5. Not see someone for the **dust**
   - refers to a person who has left a certain place very quickly
6. Shake the **dust** of some place off your feet
   - to leave a place behind forever

E

EAT

1. **Eat** someone alive
   - (a) to purposely say bad things, or do bad things, to another person, in order to cause them grief, pain or suffering
   - (b) to decisively defeat an opponent

EAGLE

1. The eyes of an **eagle**
   - to watch things very carefully, and to be good at noticing or analyzing things

EDGE

1. On the **edge** of your seat
   - to be excited about something, to the point that you are eager to know what will happen next
2. At (on) the cutting **edge**
   - something that is the most developed or advanced development in its field
3. Lose your **edge**
   - to lose a skill or ability that once made a person successful in their field
4. On **edge**
   - to be anxious or nervous
5. Rough around the **edges**
   - something or someone that is good, but not perfect
6. Take the **edge** off (something)
   - to lessen an unpleasant feeling or situation, to the point that it is not as bad as it once was

EEL

1. Slippery as an **eel**
   - something, or someone, that is difficult to take hold of, or catch

EGGS

1. Have **egg** on one's face
   - to become ashamed or embarrassed because of something you have done
2. **Egg** on
   - to encourage someone to do something, which is thing that this person would not normally do
3. Put all of your **eggs** in one basket
   - to put all of your efforts or resources in one thing or place, so that you won't be able to do anything else if this one thing is not successful
4. Lay an **egg**
   - to complete and utterly fail in an endeavor
5. Walk on **eggshells**
   - a situation where a person has to be very careful in what they say or do, because they don't want to offend or upset someone else
6. A good **egg**
   - a kind, gentile, trustworthy or reliable person

ELBOW

1. **Elbow** grease
   - to expend great effort and wo hard at something

ELEPHANT

1. See the **elephant**
   - do something especially extreme, especially if it is waging war
2. A white **elephant**
   - something that is completely useless, even though it cost a lot

END

1. The **end** of the rainbow
   - a desired place where a person may want to get to, but that is hard to reach
2. Make **ends** meet
   - find it difficult to have enough money to pay for life's necessities
3. Keep your **end** of the deal (bargain)
   - to do what you have either promised, or are expected, to do
4. Dead **end**
   - a place from where a person can go no further
5. Do an **end** run
   - something that you do in order to avoid something else
6. Go off the deep **end**
   - to behave like a crazy person

EYEBALL
1. **Eyeball** to **eyeball**
   - refers to a situation where two people are very close to each other and arguing, while staring into each other's eyes
2. Up to your **eyeballs**
   - when you are very deeply involved in an unpleasant situation

F

FALL
1. **Fall** on hard times
   - face difficult personal or financial situations
2. Take the **fall**
   - take the blame for something
3. **Fall** on your face
   - fail in something miserably
4. **Fall** for
   - fall deeply in love with someone
5. Heading for a **fall**
   - refers to a situation where a person is doing things in a way that will soon make them have problems, or that will lead to failure
6. **Fall** over oneself (to do something)
   - refers to a situation where a person is extremely enthusiastic to do something, or accomplish something
7. Fall **flat** on your face
   - to fail embarrassingly when attempting to do something

FAMOUS NAMES
1. In like **Flynn**
   - to do something quickly, and with a lot of enthusiasm
2. **Hobson's** choice
   - a decision that must be made, when in reality, there is no other choice
3. Keeping up with the **Joneses**
   - to deliberately, buy, do or act like the successful people around you, so that you also appear successful as well
4. Happy as **Larry**
   - refers to a person that is very, very happy
5. **Joe** Schmoe
   - refers to an everyday, ordinary, average person
6. Living the life of **Riley**
   - someone who is living a very enjoyable life, because they have very few problems, and have a lot of money
7. **Achilles** heel
   - a thing that causes a person problems, because it is a weakness, so it often gives others the chance to criticize or attack it

8. The Real **McCoy**
   - something that is original, authentic, and of the best quality
9. Before you can say **Jack Robinson**
   - refers to something that happens very quickly or suddenly
10. **Joe** public
    - a saying used to describe ordinary people
11. Typhoid **Mary**
    - refers to a person who tries to bring bad luck or harm to people
12. Robbing **Peter** to Pay **Paul**
    - to use money that was meant to be used for something else

FAMOUS PLACES

1. Be/being sent to **Coventry**
   - to be ignored by others because they disapprove of what you have done
2. Not whistling **Dixie**
   - if someone is not whistling Dixie, they are being honest and should be listened to
3. Go **Dutch** treat
   - to share the cost equally between two people when they have a meal or share an evening out together
4. A **Trojan** horse
   - a situation where something appears useful, but is really intended to harm you in the long run
5. When in **Rome**
   - people should adopt the customs and behaviour of the place they are in
6. **Rome** was not built in a day
   - an expression used to convey the idea that it can take a long time to complete a task, and that all things cannot be done quickly
7. Not for all the tea in **China**
   - refers to something that a person will never do
8. **Dutch** courage
   - to feel brave or confident because you've consumed alcohol
9. In **Dutch**
   - to be in trouble
10. Pardon my **French**
    - a humorous apology made when a person swears or uses a rude word
11. Its all **Greek** to me
    - refers to something that is totally unintelligible, or not understandable
12. As **American** as apple pie
    - something that is typical of the American way of life

FAST ·

1. Live life in the **fast lane**
   - live life vigorously, and to the fullest, by doing exciting things

FATHER
   1. **Father** time
      - refers to the passage of time, which makes a person older, and therefore less able to do things they once used to do

FEET
   1. Find your **feet**
      - to learn what to do in a new situation and become more confident in doing it
   2. Get cold **feet**
      - to become nervous or anxious over a planned endeavor, and to either not do it anymore, or have doubts about doing it
   3. Get one's **feet** wet
      - to begin a new endeavor, and try it for the first time
   4. Have two left **feet**
      - Do not have the talent or ability to dance
   5. Stand on your own two **feet**
      - to be independent, without relying on anyone else
   6. Vote with your **feet**
      - To show displeasure over a place, a situation, or an event, by leaving it

FIDDLE
   1. Fit as a **fiddle**
      - to be very fit and healthy
   2. On the **fiddle**
      - To obtain something by doing illegal or dishonest things

FINGER
   1. Point your **finger** at someone
      - to blame someone for something
   2. Put your **finger** on something
      - to determine the root cause of something
   3. Get your **fingers** burned
      - to face unpleasant consequences for something you have done
   4. Have your **finger** on the pulse
      - to understand something very well, or to know have thorough knowledge about something
   5. Wrap someone around your **finger**
      - to be able to make someone do anything that you want them to do
   6. Have a **finger** in every pie
      - to be involved in a lot of activities or things

FIRE
   1. **Fired** up
      - to be extremely excited, sometimes to a point of over-agitation

2. Light/relight my **fire**
   - to excite, or re-ignite someone's interest in something, because their life has become very boring
3. **Fire** sale
   - to sell things at extremely low prices because the person or business is desperately in need of money
4. **Fire** on all cylinders
   - to utilize all of your capabilities or capacities, to the fullest
5. Play with **fire**
   - doing something that is very risky, and that may lead to further problems
6. Draw **fire** (from someone)
   - to be criticized strongly by someone else
7. Fight **fire** with **fire**
   - to attack someone or something forcefully, after you have been attacked
8. Breath **fire**
   - to be very angry about something
9. Light a **fire** under someone
   - to motivate someone, to try to force them to do something with more energy or vigor

FISH
1. A big **fish**
   - an extremely important or powerful person or individual
2. A big **fish** in a small pond
   - an important person that is a member of a small group
3. A cold **fish**
   - a person that is uncaring, or who has no feelings
4. A **fishing** expedition
   - to secretly try to find out facts
5. There are more **fish** in the sea
   - there are many more people that you can have a relationship with, rather than the person you are now dating, or no longer dating
6. Neither **fish** nor fowl
   - something that's in between two extremes, making it difficult to categorize
7. Like a **fish** out of water
   - refers to a person in an unfamiliar situation, or in a situation where they aren't comfortable in, or a situation where they cannot do well in
8. Drink like a **fish**
   - to drink a lot of alcohol, quite regularly
9. Have bigger **fish** to fry
   - ignoring one situation, or doing nothing about one particular thing, because you have another, or other, more important things to do
10. A **fishing** expedition
    - trying to secretly find out facts, without letting others know what you're doing

11. **Fishy**
   - something or someone that is suspicious, hard to believe, or untrustworthy
12. Like shooting **fish** in a barrel
   - competing in something where it is very easy to win

FLAG
1. A red **flag**
   - a warning about an impending bad situation
2. Fly the **flag**
   - when someone flies their flag, they are showing support for their country, or for a group they belong to
3. Keep the **flag** flying
   - show support for your country or a thing you believe strongly in
4. Wrap yourself in the **flag**
   - trying to make others believe you're doing something good for the country, when you're really doing it for your own political benefit
5. Run something up the **flagpole**
   - to make a suggestion about something, so that you can gauge other people's opinions about it
6. This is like waving a red **flag** before a bull
   - to purposely do or say something, that makes someone angry

FLAT
1. Fall **flat** on your face
   - to fail embarrassingly when attempting to do something

FLAVOR
1. **Flavor** of the month
   - to be very popular at the present time

FLESH
1. In the **flesh**
   - if a person meets or sees a person in the flesh, then they actually see or meet a famous person
2. Press the **flesh**
   - to be in a crowd and talk with people, or shake their hands
3. Put more **flesh** on something
   - add detailed information to a particular thing

FLOWERS
1. **Flower** power
   - a saying from the Hippie era, where the emphasis was on love and peace

FLY

1. A **fly** in the ointment
   - a bothersome person, who prevents something from happening, or from being successful

FOOD

1. **Food** for thought
   - a thing that makes you think very deeply about it

FOOT

1. Get a **foot** in the door
   - to start in a lower position than you desire in a company that you want to work for, for the purpose of eventually being promoted and then getting your coveted position
2. Get off on the wrong **foot**
   - to start a relationship in a negative or bad way
3. One **foot** in the grave
   - to be gravely ill, and be near to death
4. Put your best **foot** forward
   - to show your best quality or to work as hard as you can
5. Put your **foot** down
   - to act with force, telling someone they must stop a certain activity
6. Shoot yourself in the **foot**
   - to say or do something, which harms your future chances of success, or which causes you problems in the future

FORELOCK

1. Tug your **forelock**
   - to show a lot of respect to a person who has a high position or standing in society

FORK

1. Stick a **fork** in it
   - advice given to someone who should cease doing a particular thing

FORT

1. Hold down the **fort**
   - something you ask someone to look after, while you are away

FRAZZLE

1. Wear yourself to a **frazzle**
   - to become exhausted and tired through overwork

FRITZ

1. On the **fritz**
   - refers to something that does not work well anymore

FROG
1. **Frog** in your throat
   - find it difficult to speak, usually because you are coughing.
2. Big **frog** in a small pond
   - the most important person in a small group, or a person who has outgrown their particular situation, and would be more suitably placed in a larger, more important situation

FRIED
1. **Fried**
   - to be stoned or very drunk

FRYING PAN
1. Out of the **frying pan** and into the fire
   - to go from a bad situation to an even worse situation

FUNERAL
1. Its your **funeral**
   - a warning issued to someone who does dangerous or life threatening things

FURY
1. Fury drop
   - to throw or drop something in order to relieve stress

FUSE
1. Blow a **fuse**
   - to become angry and then be unable to control your anger

G

GAME
1. The **game** is up
   - refers to a situation where a person can no longer continue to do things illegally, because the illegality has been revealed
2. Ahead of the **game**
   - to know about all recent developments with respect to something, and then to use this knowledge to keep ahead of others
3. New to the **game**
   - to have no experience in a certain area or activity you are now involved in
4. Beat someone at their own **game**
   - to defeat someone, or do something better than them, in an activity that this person was thought to have an advantage in
5. Play a waiting **game**
   - to wait out a situation, for the purpose of seeing how it will develop

6. Give the **game** away
   - to reveal something which others have been trying to keep secret

GAS

1. He's/she's a **gas**
   - to be a very funny person
2. Run out of **gas**
   - to run out of energy or to lose interest in something
3. I'm **gassed**
   - to be very, very tired

GENTLE

1. A **gentle** giant
   - refers to a person who is very large, but who is kind or gentle

GHOSTS

1. Give up the **ghost**
   - to stop doing something because you can no longer succeed
2. A **ghost** of a chance
   - something you have little chance in completing, or succeeding in
3. White as a **ghost**
   - to look pale and white, because you are very, very frightened

GLOVES

1. The **gloves** are off
   - a reference to two groups, who are prepared to fight or compete aggressively, often after a compromise has failed to be reached

GOALPOSTS

1. Move the **goalposts**
   - to suddenly change the rules or something about a situation, suddenly making it more difficult for other people to compete in

GOAT

1. **Scapegoat**
   - a person that is unfairly blamed for something
2. Act the **goat**
   - to behave in a silly or inane way
3. Get someone's **goat**
   - to annoy someone

GOD

1. Play **God**
   - To believe that you have the ultimate say in saving or taking a person's life

2. **God's** gift to something
   - refers to someone who thinks they are the best in doing something, or are very skilled in it

GOLD
1. All that glitters is not **gold**
   - refers to something, or someone, that may not be as good as first thought
2. As good as **gold**
   - refers to someone, or something, who does something very well, is very good at something, or that behaves very well
3. Pot of **gold**
   - a large amount of money that a person hopes to get in the future
4. Strike **gold**
   - to become rich by being successful, or through chance
5. There's **gold** in them thar hills
   - refers to the possibility of making money in a particular place, or by doing a particular activity in that place
6. Worth its weight in **gold**
   - something that is very, very valuable, given its smallish size
7. **Gold** digger
   - refers to someone who's only interested in someone else's money
8. **Gold** mine of information
   - someone or something that's a great source of information
9. **Golden** handshake
   - refers to a person who receives a large sum of money to leave a job years before they are scheduled to retire

GOOSE
1. Cook your own **goose**
   - to do something which spoils your chances for success

GOSPEL
1. Take something as **gospel**
   - to believe that something is 100% true, when in actuality, it is not

GRACE
1. A saving **grace**
   - a good or redeemable quality in a person that prevents them from being totally bad

GRAPES
1. Sour **grapes**
   - refers to a person who is bitter and jealous over other people's success, and who criticizes these other successful people

GRAPEVINE
1. Hear something through the **grapevine**
   - to be told information from a second hand source

GREEN
1. **Green** as grass
   - to have little experience, and to too easily trust what is told to you
2. **Green** with envy
   - to really covet something that another person has, so as to be very envious of this thing, or of this person

GROOVE
1. In the **groove**
   - to perform well at something

GUTS
1. **Gut** feeling
   - to know that you are right about something, without having proof to justify your feelings
2. A **gut** reaction
   - to have an immediate and strong reaction to something or someone, without thinking it through or knowing the reasons for your reaction
3. **Guts**
   - if a person has guts, they possess courage
4. Hate (someone's) **guts**
   - to dislike or hate someone very much
5. Spill your **guts**
   - confess to something, or talk about a thing that is secret or private
6. Work your **guts** out
   - work very hard at something

H

HAIR
1. Split **hairs**
   - to emphasize or argue about very, very small details, even when they are not important enough to argue about
2. Tear your **hair** out
   - refers to someone who is very upset or anxious about something
3. In your **hair**
   - refers to someone or something that is either annoying you, or that is interfering with what you are trying to do
4. Let your **hair** down
   - to relax, usually after something hectic or stressful has happened
5. A **hair's** breadth
   - something that is within the smallest of margins

6. Make your **hair** curl
   - refers to something that causes you great worry, or that shocks you

HAND

1. Bite the **hand** that feeds you
   - betray or do a bad thing to someone who helps or supports you
2. Force someone's **hand**
   - to force someone to do something they do not want to do
3. Get out of **hand**
   - refers to a situation that has gotten out of control
4. Give with one **hand** and take with the other
   - to help someone in one way, but then to do something else that hurts or hinders them
5. **Hand** in glove
   - to work very closely with someone or some thing
6. **Hand** over fist
   - to make or lose a lot of money very quickly
7. Have to **hand** it to someone
   - implies that someone admires something someone else has done
8. Have someone eating out of the palm of your **hand**
   - refers to a situation where someone will do anything you want them to do, because they either like or admire you a lot
9. Have a **hand** in something
   - to be one of the people involved in doing or creating something
10. Have your **hand** in the till OR **hand** in the till
    - to steal from an employer, or a group you belong to
11. In the palm of your **hand**
    - to keep someone under control, by using your wits or personality
12. Know something like the back of your **hand**
    - to know something very, very well
13. An old **hand**
    - someone that has a lot of experience in something
14. The right **hand** doesn't know what the left hand is doing
    - the people in section of something do not know what people in the other section are doing, leading to a confusing situation
15. Show your **hand**
    - to reveal to other people what your intentions are
16. Take someone in **hand**
    - to take control of someone, to help them with their own situation
17. Throw in your **hand**
    - to give up on something because you realize you will not succeed
18. The upper **hand**
    - to be in a dominant or superior position over someone else

HANG

1. **Hang** your **head**
   - to feel ashamed or embarrassed for something you have done, or after a recent failure

HAPPY

1. **Happy** hour
   - the period of time (6–7 PM, for example) that drinks are half-price.

HAT

1. Eat your **hat**
   - a reference to a particular thing that someone thinks will not happen. As an example, a person can say, "I will eat my hat if Jim passes the test", means that the person believes Jim has no chance of passing the test.
2. Go **hat** in hand to someone
   - to very humbly ask someone else for help or for money
3. Picked out of a **hat**
   - refers to a random event, where the chance of any particular person winning or being chosen is completely random
4. Thrown your **hat** into the ring
   - to enter or take part in a contest or competition
5. Old **hat**
   - something that is out of date and not very original
6. Pull a rabbit out of the **hat**
   - to do something with the result that something is unexpectedly solved, or something is unexpectedly achieved
7. All **hat** and no cattle
   - to talk about something which at first seems impressive, but then you later realize that this thing is not as impressive as first thought
8. Keep something under your **hat**
   - to keep something a secret, and not tell anyone else about it
9. Knock something into a cocked **hat**
   - when one thing knocks a 2nd thing into a <u>cocked hat</u>, then the 1st thing is much better than the 2nd thing
10. Pass the **hat** (around)
    - to collect money for something
11. Be talking through your **hat OR** Talk through your **hat**
    - to say silly or nonsensical thing
12. Take your **hat** off to something
    - to express admiration for something that someone has done

HAWK

1. Watch someone like a **hawk**
   - to pay very close attention to someone, with the aim of making sure they do not make mistakes, or do something wrong

HEAD

1. Hang your **head**
   - to look and feel ashamed
2. In over your **head**
   - to be in situation that is too difficult to deal with
3. Have your **head** screwed on backwards
   - to be unsensible and unrealistic
4. Go over (someone's) **head**
   - open a line of communication with someone in a superior position to the person who has authority over your actions
5. Keep your **head** down
   - to avoid being noticed
6. Off the top of your **head**
   - to say something without knowing much about it, or without checking the facts in regard to this thing
7. Lose your **head**
   - lose your calm and cool, and to panic in a difficult situation
8. Bang your **head** against a wall
   - to feel frustrated, because it seems that you are not making progress in the thing that you are trying to do
9. Laugh your **head** off
   - to laugh a lot
10. Scratch your **head**
    - to be puzzled and uncertain about something
11. Keep your **head**
    - to remain cool and calm in a tense or difficult situation
12. Put your **head** in a noose
    - do something deliberately that puts you in a difficult or dangerous situation
13. Bury your **head** in the sand
    - to refuse to accept the truth about an unpleasant thing
14. Get your **head** around (something)
    - to try to succeed in accepting or understanding something
15. Fall **head** over **heals**
    - to fall suddenly and completely in love with someone
16. Get into someone's **head**
    - to be able to know or understand what someone is really thinking
17. Go to your **head**
    - a situation where someone starts to believe that they are more intelligent or better than other people
18. Keep your **head** above water
    - to have just enough money to survive, either in a personal sense, or for a business

HEART

1. Bleeding **heart**
   - a person who has sympathy for poor or disadvantaged people

2. Cross my **heart**
   - to make a very solemn promise that can be believed
3. Lose **heart**
   - to feel that you will be unsuccessful in doing something
4. Take something to **heart**
   - to be greatly influenced and/or upset by a particular thing
5. Have your **heart** set on something
   - to want or desire something very much, and then to put a great amount of effort into achieving this thing
6. Wear your **heart** on your sleeve
   - to openly display your feelings about an issue to other people
7. **Heart** of the matter
   - the most important part of an issue or matter

HEAVEN

1. In seventh **heaven**
   - refers to someone who is extremely happy or content
2. Move **heaven** and earth
   - do everything possible to make sure something happens
3. The **heavens** open
   - when it begins to rain very heavily
4. Like manna from **heaven**
   - refers to a situation where a person gets something that they really need, but when they are not expecting to get it
5. Stink to high **heaven**
   - to smell horribly bad
6. A marriage made in **heaven**
   - a very happy and harmonious marriage
7. Stink to high **heaven**
   - a suspicious situation where someone feels that something is very wrong
8. **Heaven** forbid
   - a strong statement regarding a person's feelings that they will do anything possible to prevent some particular thing from happening
9. **Heavens** to Betsy!
   - a proclamation of extreme surprise
10. In **heaven's** name
    - this statement is used to question why people are doing a particular thing
11. **Heaven** help us
    - a statement used in a hopeless situation, so that intervention from heaven is the only thing that can remedy the problem
12. A match made in **heaven**
    - refers to the happy and harmonious union between two entities

HELL

1. All **hell** breaks loose
   - a situation that is uncontrollable, often with a lot of fighting and/or arguing

2. Go to **hell** and back
   - to have a terrible experience
3. A living **hell**
   - an extremely unpleasant place or situation
4. Raise **hell**
   - to cause trouble, especially when a person gets drunk, with the person destroying things or causing property damage
5. There'll be **hell** to pay
   - a warning issued to someone if they don't do something, or, if they do something that is essentially forbidden
6. Until (when) **hell** freezes over
   - (a) refers to something that a person thinks will not happen
     (b) refers to something that a person thinks will happen for a very, very long time, or that will happen forever

HERRING
1. A red **herring**
   - something that is used to take people's attention away from something else, or to divert attention away from the real issue

HILL
1. A **hill** of beans
   - refers to something that's insignificant, or very small in quantity
2. Over the **hill**
   - refers to someone or something that is very, very old, and that does not perform as it once did

HIP-HOP
1. **Hood**
   - a person's neighborhood
2. **PHAT** (Pretty, hot and tempting)
   - refers to a female who is extremely beautiful
3. **Dog**
   - a reference to someone's good, male friend
4. **Crib**
   - a person's home
5. **Hater**
   - a person who constantly says negative things about other people
6. **Dis** OR **Dissed**
   - to disrespect someone else

HIT
1. **Hit** the books
   - to study hard
2. **Hit** the hay/sack
   - to go to sleep

3. **Hit** and miss
    - used to describe something whose quality varies from good to bad, or from bad to good
4. **Hit** on someone
    - to make a pass at another person in the bar

HOGS
1. In **hog** heaven
    - to be extremely happy because of your situation
2. Be living high on the **hog**
    - to have a lot of money, and to live a good life
3. Go the whole **hog**
    - to do something to the fullest extent possible

HOME
1. Hit a **home run**
    - to do something successfully, or to have an unexpected gain

HORSES
1. One **horse** race
    - describes a situation where a person, or a thing, is much better than anything or anyone else, and will surely win
2. Get on your high **horse**
    - when someone gets on their high horse, they behave as if they know more about a particular thing, (or many things) than everyone else
3. Dark **horse**
    - a person or thing that wins something, when they are not expected to
4. One **horse** town
    - a town that is very small and not interesting
5. Trojan **horse**
    - describes something, like a proposal or an idea, that seems to have a specific purpose, but one that really is put forward to deceive, or that is meant to harm something in the future
6. Hold your **horses**
    - when you are being told to hold your horses, you are being told to pause, and reflect on your course of actions, or on what you are saying, because you have not thought them through adequately

HOT
1. Sell like **hot** cakes
    - refers to something that is bought by many people in a short time
2. In the **hot** seat
    - a situation where a person has to make important decisions
3. Blow **hot** and **cold**
    - describes an occurrence when someone is sometimes very enthusiastic about doing something, but then suddenly become very uninterested in it

HOUSE
    1. Bring the **house** down
       - refers to an audience that cheers and claps loudly, for a long time, because the audience has enjoyed the performance
    2. Eat someone out of **house** and home
       - a person that eats so much, so that it costs a lot to feed them
    3. Get on like a **house** on fire
       - refers to two people who become good friends very quickly
    4. A **house** of cards
       - describes something that is about to fail or collapse
    5. Put your **house** in order
       - to make sure that all of your affairs and problems are dealt with and taken care of
    6. A **household** name
       - refers to a person who is famous and well known
    7. On the **house**
       - refers to a drink that is free

HUSH
    1. **Hush** money
       - money paid to someone to make them keep quiet, and to not reveal a secret

I

ICE
    1. On **ice**
       - to delay something

ILL GOTTEN
    1. **Ill gotten** gains
       - The use of illegal methods to gain a monetary advantage

IN
    1. **In** a flash/ **In** a jiffy
       - very, very, quickly
    2. **In** good with (someone)
       - a situation where a person has earned the total trust of someone else, so much so, that the 2nd person completely trusts the 1st
    3. **In** good faith
       - refers to a situation where a person places an inordinate amount of faith in another person, placing a lot of trust in the 2nd person

INSULT
    1. Add **insult** to **injury**
       - make a bad situation worse by doing another bad thing to someone

IRON
1. **Iron** fist
   - to do something with great force
2. Cast **iron**
   - something that can be believed in and is totally, absolutely certain
3. Strike while the **iron** is hot
   - to act quickly and absolutely when the right opportunity presents itself, and when the best chance to succeed is offered
4. An **iron** fist in a velvet glove
   - something that looks gentile or benign, but which has a lot of force
5. Pump **iron**
   - to lift weights
6. Have a lot of **irons** in the fire
   - to have a number of different plans or opportunities, so that some of them will likely succeed, even if others fail

J

JACKPOT
1. Hit the **jackpot**
   - to earn a lot of money by being successful at something, or to unexpectedly come across a good fortune, or some good luck

JOCKEY
1. **Jockey** for position
   - to try to get in a better position than your competitors

JOKER
1. The **joker** in the pack
   - refers to a person who is different from others, which means that no one will know how they will act or behave

K

KICK-OFF
1. For a **kick-off**
   - refers to just the first thing in a long list of things that can be entioned about a particular occurrence

KILL
1. Move in for the **kill**
   - to make a decisive, final move, in order to defeat an opponent

KIND
1. In **kind**
   - to pay for goods or services in goods or services, and not money

2. Kill someone with **kindness**
   - to treat someone with too much kindness, especially when they do not want, or do not need, to be treated with this much kindness

KING
   1. Fit for a **king**
      - something that is of the best quality
   2. **King** of the hill
      - the top or number one person in a group
   3. Pay a **king's** ransom
      - to be willing to pay a lot for something or to overpay for something

KNEE
   1. **Knee** jerk reaction
      - a quick, senseless reaction to something

KNICKERS
   1. Get your **knickers** in a twist
      - to be very upset about something, or worry too much about it

KNIFE
   1. Twist the **knife**
      - to inflict more pain on a person who is already experiencing pain or some sort of difficulty
   2. You could cut the atmosphere with a **knife**
      - implies that the atmosphere in a particular place or in a particular situation is very tense
   3. The **knives** are out
      - when people try to criticize cause further problems for a person
   4. Put the **knife** in
      - to deliberately say bad things to another person, to upset them

KNIGHT
   1. A **knight** in shining **armor**
      - a person who bravely rescues someone from danger

KNOCKED
   1. **Knocked** up
      - To become pregnant, usually by illegitimate means, or by accident

KNOT
   1. Tie the **knot**
      - to get married

L

LAST
1. **Last** call
   - when last call is announced, no more drinks can be bought after this

LEAD
1. **Lead** foot
   - refers to someone who drives too fast
2. Get the **lead** out
   - to tell someone to start working faster or moving faster
3. Go down like a **lead** balloon
   - an idea or concept that's very unpopular and that people don't like

LEAF
1. Fig **leaf**
   - something that is used to hide an awkward or embarrassing situation
2. Turn over a new **leaf**
   - to try to improve to make yourself better than before
3. Take a **leaf** out of (someone's) book
   - copy or mimic someone's behaviour, in order to become successful as they are

LEAVE
1. Leave a **tip**
   - to leave a gratuity for the waitress, waiter or bartender

LIE
1. Live a **lie**
   - to live life in a dishonest or false way
2. Give the **lie** to (something)
   - prove that something is not true
3. A white **lie**
   - to say something that is not true, to prevent from upsetting someone, or to protect that person

LIFE
1. Cannot for the **life** of me
   - something a person cannot do, no matter how hard they try
2. Get a **life**
   - a reference to someone who's life is boring, or who cares about what seems to be unimportant things
3. **Life** in the fast lane
   - refers to a person whose life is exciting, active and highly pressured
4. **Life** is a bowl of cherries
   - life is enjoyable and pleasant

5. You bet your **life**
   - to say yes, in a very forceful way
6. Take your **life** into your hands
   - to take a lot of risks by doing something that may be dangerous
7. Larger than **life**
   - someone who has a strong personality and sands out in a crowd
8. **Live** the **life** of Riley
   - someone whose life is very enjoyable, problem free, and who seems to have a lot of money

LIGHTNING
1. **Lightning** doesn't/does strike twice
   - to imply a person has either been very lucky, or very unlucky, because the same good thing, or bad thing, will not happen again
2. Like greased **lightning**
   - to do something very quickly

LINE
1. The bottom **line**
   - the most important issue when dealing with something
2. Cross the **line**
   - to begin to behave in an offensive or improper manner
3. Draw the **line**
   - choose a point where something begins to be unacceptable
4. Walk a fine **line** (between something)
   - refers to a thing that is proper or acceptable, but could become unacceptable or improper with the slightest change or variation
5. In the **line** of fire
   - refers to person in a position such that he or she could easily come under criticism, or be subject to attack
6. Put yourself (your neck) on the **line**
   - to do something that is personally, very risky
7. Come on **line**
   - refers to some thing, or some endeavor, that starts to operate, usually at its full capacity
8. Down the **line**
   - refers to something that will happen at a later time
9. Along the **line**
   - refers to something that will happen, but at a later time, that cannot be predicted or identified
10. Sign on the dotted **line**
    - sign a document, signifying you formally agree to some thing
11. Get a **line** on (someone)
    - to get information about a certain person
12. Lay it on the **line**
    - to say something truthfully, often in rather difficult circumstances

LION
1. Fight like a **lion**
   - to fight very bravely, fiercely or aggressively
2. The heart of a **lion**
   - someone who has a lot of courage, heart or determination
3. Put your head into the **lion's** mouth
   - to deliberately place yourself in a dangerous or difficult situation
4. The **lion's** share
   - refers to the largest part, or largest share, of something
5. Throw someone to the **lions**
   - subject someone to danger, or to place them in a difficult situation
6. Walk into the **lion's** den
   - to enter into a situation, where you will either have to face danger, or where you will be exposed to difficulty

LIPS
1. Pay **lip** service to
   - to be in favor of something, without saying anything to support it
2. A stiff upper **lip**
   - to hide one's emotions, not letting other people see you are upset
3. Loose **lips** sink ships
   - the revealing of secrets to others can be harmful or dangerous, as others can use the secrets you reveal against you
4. Licking your **lips**
   - to look eagerly forward to something that is coming up
5. Read my **lips**
   - refers to an issue that a lot of people are talking about
6. My **lips** are sealed
   - to state that you will keep a secret that has been told to you

LIQUOR
1. Can't hold your **liquor**
   - get drunk very easily

LIVE
1. **Live** on the edge
   - live an exciting life, that is full of danger and peril
2. Nine **lives**
   - a situation when someone survives, and even prospers, after managing to get out of many difficult circumstances
3. **Live** and breathe something
   - spend a lot of time on a thing that you are very enthusiastic about
4. **Live** the **life** of Riley
   - an enjoyable and problem free life, with a plentiful supply of money

LIVING
1. Think that someone owes you a **living**
   - the thought that government, or that parents, should furnish you the money to allow you to continue to live, without you working

LOSE
1. **Lose** your **head**
   - to lose your calm, and to panic, in a difficult situation

LOVE
1. All's fair in **love** and war
   - any form of behaviour is acceptable, even in love or war. This may equate the state of relationships to being like warfare
2. Puppy **love**
   - love that is not considered serious, like the love between children

3. **Love** me, **love** my dog
   - This implies that if you love someone, then you must love everything about them, including their friends

LUNCH
1. Out to **lunch**
   - a person who does not understand or comprehend a situation
2. There's no such thing as a free **lunch**
   - a person cannot expect to get things for free
3. Love me, love my dog
   - This implies that if you love someone, then you must love everything about them, including their friends

M

MARK
1. Hit the **mark**
   - to accomplish something or be accurate in your predictions
2. A black **mark**
   - a situation where people form a bad opinion about something, due to something bad being done by one person, or by a group of people
3. Leave a **mark**
   - to leave an impression or to have a lasting effect
4. On the **mark**
   - to be accurate or totally correct
5. Quick off the **mark**
   - to be quick in starting something, or to responding to something
6. Way off the **mark**
   - something that is totally wrong or inaccurate, or something that is rude or inappropriate when said

MARS
1. Men are from **Mars** and women are from **Venus**
   - men and women have completely different mind frames

MEDICINE
1. A taste of your own **medicine**
   - to give someone the same bad treatment they have been giving you

MILK
1. The land of **milk** and **honey**
   - a prosperous land with abundant resources, and lots of jobs

MOM
1. **Mom** and **pop** store
   - a small, corner side grocery store, that is run as a small family business

MONEY
1. Made of **money**
   - if a person is made of money, then they have a virtual unlimited ability to spend money for anything
2. Even **money**
   - refers to two possible outcomes, which are equally likely

MONKEY
1. **Monkey** around
   - to act or behave silly, foolishly or inane
2. A **monkey** on/off your back
   - an emotional burden a person carries. When the burden is finally lifted, then the person has take the monkey **off** their back.
3. **Monkey** business
   - dishonest or suspicious activities
4. Make a **monkey** out of someone
   - do something to make someone else look stupid, silly or idiotic
5. If you pay peanuts, you get **monkeys**
   - if low wages are paid, the quality of the staff will be low
6. **Monkey** see, **monkey** do
   - a critical comment on someone who copies another person's actions, without thinking through what actions they are copying

MOON
1. Ask for the **moon**
   - to ask for something that is unattainable

MOTHER
1. Be tied to your **mother's** apron strings

259

- refers to a person who is still dependent on their mother, when they should, in fact, be independent

MOUNTAIN
1. A **mountain** to climb
   - the great effort that will be needed in order to complete a big task
2. If Mohammed will not come to the **mountain**
   - if someone doesn't come to you, you then have no choice but to go to them
3. Move **mountains**
   - to succeed in doing something difficult through much hard work
4. Make a **mountain** out of a **molehill**
   - to complain about something that is unimportant, in a way that makes it seem that you think it is important

MOUTH
1. Foam at the **mouth**
   - become very angry
2. Shoot your **mouth** off
   - refers to someone who brags or boasts about their abilities
3. Speak out of both sides of your **mouth**
   - to give different opinions or points of view on a subject
4. Put one's foot in one's **mouth**
   - embarrass one's self
5. Live hand to **mouth**
   - live from paycheque to paycheque, without much money on hand
6. **Mouth** to **mouth**
   - a method used to revive a person who has stopped breathing

MUD
1. Clear as **mud**
   - something that is very difficult to understand or comprehend
2. Dragged through the **mud**
   - says bad things about a person, in an effort to ruin their reputation
3. Like a pig in **mud**
   - refers to someone who's extremely happy doing a particular thing
4. **Mud** that sticks **OR Mud** has stuck
   - refers to a situation when something bad is said about someone, leading people to believe that it is true, even though it is not
5. A stick in the **mud**
   - refers to someone who is dull, boring and doesn't try new things
6. Throw **mud**
   - when someone throws mud at someone, then they say bad or harmful things about this person

MUSIC

1. Face the **music**
   - to accept responsibility for something you have done wrong, and to prepare yourself to accept punishment for the wrongdoing
2. **Music** to my ears
   - to be very happy when you hear a piece of good news

N

NECK

1. Stick your **neck** out
   - do something for someone, even if it may cause you harm or pain

NEWS

1. Bad **news**
   - refers to a person who is troublesome and has a bad character
2. To be **news** to someone
   - be surprised about something you didn't know about before
3. Break the **news**
   - tell someone about a bad occurrence or event
4. No news is good **news**
   - a positive statement, meaning that if bad news has not yet come, then nothing bad has happened
5. No news is bad **news**
   - a negative statement, meaning that if good news has not yet come, then something bad has happened
6. Be the bearer of bad **news**
   - to tell someone something they didn't know about before

NEWT

1. Pissed as a **newt**
   - refers to a person who has become extremely drunk

NICE

1. **Nice** as pie
   - refers to someone who is friendly, pleasant and gracious

NIGHT

1. A **night** owl
   - a person who does things late at night or who likes to stay up late
2. A **night** on the tiles
   - to go out late, to a night club or bar, and to also come home late

NOSE

1. Follow your **nose**
   - to seek something by using intuition, and not by following a plan

2. Get up someone's **nose**
   - refers to someone who irritates you greatly
3. Keep your **nose** clean
   - to behave properly and avoid getting into trouble
4. Keep your **nose** out of (something)
   - to abruptly tell someone to not interfere in your personal business
5. Keep your **nose** to the grindstone
   - work hard on something, and not devote any time to anything else
6. Lead someone around by the **nose**
   - control another person, making them do whatever you want
7. Cut off your **nose** to spite your face
   - refers to a situation where someone does something to punish another person, but in doing so, actually hurts themselves more
8. Give someone a bloody **nose**
   - to defeat or harm someone when engaging in a competition
9. Look down your **nose** at (something)
   - to look down upon someone or something disrespectfully
10. A **nose** for (something)
    - a person who has a good ability to recognize or find something
11. Not see beyond your **nose**
    - refers to a person who is concerned only with their own personal satisfaction, rather than other people, or other possible outcomes
12. On the **nose**
    - a person who is exactly on time, or exactly correct in a prediction
13. Plain as the **nose** on your face
    - something that is very obvious, and is easy to see or understand
14. Put someone's **nose** out of joint
    - to offend someone by treating them with disrespect
15. Rub someone's **nose** in it
    - talk about something that someone else would rather forget
16. Thumb your **nose** at someone
    - to show a lack of respect for someone
17. Turn your **nose** up at something
    - to reject someone or something, and show disrespect towards it, because you believe it is not good enough for you
18. Under your **nose**
    - something which happens right in front of you, but you can do nothing to stop it, even though it is obvious that it is happening
19. Pay through the **nose**
    - to pay too much for something

O

OFFSIDE
1. **Offside**
   - refers to a particularly rude comment or gesture

OIL
1. The good **oil**
   - good or reliable information
2. No **oil** painting
   - to comment on somebody that is not attractive
3. Strike **oil**
   - to become suddenly successful, or to come into a lot of money

ONIONS
1. Know your **onions**
   - to know a lot about a particular thing

ORDER
1. A tall **order**
   - something that is very difficult to do, achieve, or get
2. Out of **order** (1)
   - refers to something that is no longer working or operating
3. Out of **order** (2)
   - a reference to someone's unacceptable or rude behaviour
4. Marching **orders**
   - instructions that someone is given so they can carry out a plan
5. Give someone their marching **orders**
   - tell someone to leave
6. Pecking **order**
   - a ranking showing you place, or are arranged, in a hierarchy

OUT
1. **Out** of line
   - refers to behaviour that is improper or inappropriate
2. **Out** to lunch
   - refers to a person who is very stupid, or to a person that has absolutely no awareness about a thing or a situation
3. **Out** of the woods
   - a person that has solved most of their problems, so that they are no longer in a precarious, difficult or dangerous situation
4. **Out** on a limb
   - in a dangerous, precarious or untenable situation

OXEN
1. As strong as an **ox**
   - someone or something that is very strong
2. As stupid as an **ox**
   - someone or something that is very stupid

P

PANTS
1. Be caught with your **pants** down
   - caught in an embarrassing situation you are not prepared to face
2. By the seat of your **pants**
   - achieve something, or win something, by the thinnest of margins
3. Beat the **pants** off someone
   - to totally defeat another person in a competition or contest
4. Wear the **pants**
   - to make all of the important decisions, usually in a relationship

PAR
1. **Par** for the course
   - a thing which is not really good, but as good as can be expected
2. On **par** with
   - something that is of the same standard as something else
3. Under **par**
   - a thing that is not on as high as a level as it could be

PARROT
1. **Parrot** fashion
   - refers to something that is learned by repetition, but which is also only memorized, without really understanding its meaning

PEAS
1. Two **peas** in a pod
   - refers to two people who have similar appearances or characteristics

PENNY
1. The **penny** drops
   - the time when someone finally realizes the truth about something
2. A pretty **penny**
   - Something that costs a lot of money
3. A **penny** for your thoughts
   - a thing said when someone really wants to know what you're thinking
4. **Penny** wise and **pound** foolish
   - refers to someone is very frugal about small amounts of money, but who is then careless about spending large amounts of money
5. In for a **penny**, in for a **pound**
   - to demonstrate that you will definitely continue on with some endeavor, even if it will require more money or more effort
6. Not have a **penny** to your name
   - to be totally and utterly broke

PIG
1. Make a **pig's** ear of something
   - to do something very, very badly

2. A **pig** in a poke
   - to buy something that is of very poor quality, because you failed to examine its quality before buying
3. A **pig** in the middle
   - to be caught in a situation in between two people that are having an argument, and you have to try to settle the argument
4. Like a **pig** in mud
   - to be in an ideal situation, causing a person to be very happy

PINK
1. In the **pink**
   - to be very healthy

PITS
1. The **pits**
   - refers to something is in low or extremely bad working order

PLANET
1. What/which **planet** are you from?
   - a reference to someone who has unrealistic expectations, or who is not aware about some simple issues or facts

PLAY
1. **Play** the field
   - date a number of people, without intending to settle down
2. **Play by play** description
   - to give a detailed analysis or description of something
3. A level **playing field**
   - where no one has an unfair advantage over anyone else

POCKETS
1. Dig into your **pocket**
   - to pay for something with your own money
2. In someone's **pocket**
   - to control someone so they do whatever you want them to do
3. Have deep **pocket**
   - to have a lot of money
4. Line your **pockets**
   - to make a lot of money dishonestly or unfairly
5. Live in each other's **pocket**
   - refers to two people who spend a lot of time together
6. Out of **pocket**
   - something a person pays for, but then is reimbursed for later

POINT
1. Labor the **point**

- keep explaining something even though people already understand it
2. Reach a boiling **point**
   - refers to anger, or an emotion, that can no longer be controlled
3. Not put a fine **point** on it
   - what will be said will not be pleasant for someone else to hear
4. A sore **point**
   - something that makes someone feel upset, angry or embarrassed
5. A sticking **point**
   - a topic people can't agree upon, so progress is not achieved
6. **Point** blank
   - say something very directly and bluntly, without feeling apologetic

POP
1. **Mom** and **pop** store
   - a small cornerside grocery store, that is run as a small family business

POSTAL
1. Go **postal**
   - to become angry and then lose control of your emotions

POTATOES
1. Meat and **potatoes**
   - the basic or important part of something
2. Couch **potato**
   - a lazy person who watches TV a lot
3. Hot **potato**
   - a delicate issue, that people find it hard to agree upon

PRAYER
1. Not have a **prayer**
   - a person who has no chance to complete or accomplish a task

PUP
1. Be **sold** a **pup**
   - buy or get something free, that is not as good as advertised

Q

QUARTERBACK
1. Monday morning **quarterback**
   - a person who criticizes something from a distance, after having the benefit of hindsight to analyze the situation

QUEEN
1. **Queen** bee
   - the top person or leader, who is a female, in a group

2. **Queen** for a day
   - a situation where a female is pampered for a short period

QUESTION
1. Only a **question** of time
   - something that will eventually happen
2. Beg the **question**
   - something that makes people want to ask a question about it
3. Pop the **question**
   - to ask someone to marry you

QUIET
1. **Quiet** as a mouse
   - refers to a person, or persons, who are very quiet

R

RAINBOW
1. The end of the **rainbow**
   - something that a person would like to achieve, or a place that a person would like to get to, but that is very difficult to do

RAT
1. Smell a **rat**
   - a situation in where a person believes something is wrong, or that something is amiss, and that something bad will happen
   - have a premonition that someone is trying to deceive, harm you, or do something improper

RED
1. See **red**
   - to suddenly become extremely angry over a thing that happens
2. A **red**-letter day
   - refers to a day when something important happens

RIGHT
1. **Right** as rain
   - a person who is now healthy, after going through a long illness
2. **Right**-hand man
   - a close assistant who is trusted by the boss
3. **Left, right** and **center**
   - a statement used to show that something is being done a lot

RINGSIDE
1. A **ringside** seat
   - to have a clear view of what is happening

ROBBERY
1. Highway **robbery**
   - a situation where a person is vastly overcharged for something

ROCK
1. Hit **rock** bottom
   - reach a situation or a level from where a person can go no lower
2. Between a **rock** and a hard place
   - refers to a difficult situation, where someone has to choose between 2 equally difficult options
3. **Rock**
   - something that is awesome, or totally wonderful
4. On the **rocks**
   - drinks that are served with ice cubes in the glass

ROPE
1. Give someone enough **rope** to hang themselves
   - give someone the freedom they want in accomplishing something, because you know they are likely to fail in their endeavor
2. At the end of one's **rope**
   - to be no longer able to handle or deal with a difficult situation
3. Money of/for old **rope**
   - an easy way to earn money
4. Learn the **ropes**
   - to learn how to do something
5. On the **ropes**
   - refers to someone who is very close to failing or being defeated
6. Show someone the **ropes**
   - to show someone how to do a particular job or task

ROSES
1. **Rose-tinted** glasses
   - an unrealistic assessment that comes from viewing only positive or good things, and not the bad things around them
2. Everything is coming up **roses**
   - a description of someone whose life is very successful
3. No bed of **roses**
   - a situation which is not all pleasant

ROUND
1. Buy a **round**
   - to buy drinks for everyone in your circle of friends

ROYAL
1. Given the **royal** treatment
   - to be treated extremely well, as if one were royalty

RUSSIAN ROULETTE
1. Play **Russian Roulette**
   - to take great risk by doing something dangerous

S

SAW
1. **Saw logs**
   - to snore

SCHOOL
1. To **school** someone
   - to beat someone in something by a large margin, thereby teaching this person a lesson in how to do this particular thing
2. Old **school** ways
   - refers to the old traditional values or ways of doing things
3. Old **school** ties
   - refers to people who use their previous personal ties with friends from their old school, to enhance each other's personal positions
4. The **school** of hard knocks
   - refers to instances where lessons are learned the hard way
5. A **school** of thought
   - a particular point of view on a subject or topic
6. Ole **skool**
   - refers to things that were popular in the past, like older music

SCIENCE
1. Its not **rocket science**
   - refers to something that should not be difficult to do
2. Blind someone with **science**
   - describe a thing in a technical way, making it hard to understand

SCORE
1. Settle an old **score**
   - to get revenge for something done to you in the past

SCREW
1. Have a **screw** loose
   - refers to a person who is not sane

SHADOW
1. Afraid of your own **shadow**
   - refers to a person who is very nervous or anxious, and/or very shy

SHEEP

1. Black **sheep** (of the family)
   - a person who is considered to behave badly, or to have their acts or actions disapproved of by the others in a group
2. Separate the **sheep** from the **goats**
   - examine something and separate the good parts of it from the bad
3. Like a **lamb** to the slaughter
   - to go to an unpleasant or dangerous place, in a gentle way, and without protest, either you are not aware where you are being led, or because you have no power to prevent the situation

SHIRT

1. Keep your **shirt** on
   - to stop being angry and calm down
2. The **shirt** off your back
   - signifies everything that a person owns
3. A stuffed **shirt**
   - a formal and boring person
4. Bet your **shirt** on something
   - risk lots of money because you're certain something will succeed
5. A hair **shirt**
   - someone wearing a hair shirt chooses to be unpleasant by not experiencing anything that can give them pleasure
6. Lose your **shirt**
   - lose everything you have, either in an investment or by gambling

SHOES

1. Be waiting for the other **shoe** to drop
   - to be waiting for a bad thing to happen, after another bad thing has already happened
2. Drop the other **shoe**
   - to complete a task or chore by doing the last part of it
3. If the **shoe** fits
   - to tell someone, that unpleasant or unflattering remarks that have been made about them, are reasonable or truthful
4. A goody two **shoes**
   - to attempt to please a person in authority, often in a way that is looked on disapprovingly by other people
5. In someone's **shoes**
   - to describe how you might feel or act if you were in the same situation as another person
6. Step in someone's **shoes**
   - to begin to do someone else's job
7. On a **shoestring**
   - to do something using very little money

8. Dead men's **shoes**
   - a situation where a person cannot make progress in their career

SHOT
1. Like a **shot**
   - do something or have something done, eagerly and immediately
2. A cheap **shot**
   - to criticize something unfairly or in an unpleasant way
3. A big **shot**
   - an important person
4. A **shot** in the arm
   - help given by someone or something, when the help is direly needed
5. A **shotgun** wedding
   - a wedding that takes place quickly, because the woman is pregnant
6. Call the **shots**
   - to make all of the important decisions

SHOULDER
1. Rub **shoulders** with someone
   - spend time with someone important
2. Look over your **shoulder**
   - refers to someone who is anxious because he or she thinks that others are trying to harm them or do bad things to them
3. Give someone the cold **shoulder**
   - ignore someone deliberately
4. Straight from the **shoulder**
   - to say something directly and with complete honesty
5. A **shoulder** to cry on
   - a person who is sympathetic to your problems, and offers support
6. Stand **shoulder** to **shoulder**
   - work cooperatively together with others to achieve the same goal

SIDELINES
1. On the **sidelines**
   - to watch something happen without being involved in it

SILENCE
1. **Silence** is golden
   - silence and quiet are wonderful and blissful things

SILVER
1. On a **silver** platter
   - refers to something that is given to someone, without that person having to work hard for it
2. A **silver** lining
   - a good or positive thing, in an otherwise bad situation

3. Born with a **silver** spoon in your mouth
   - a child who has very rich parents, and who is usually very spoiled

SING
1. **Sing** a different tune
   - refers to someone who changes their mind, and expresses an different than the one they only recently expessed
2. **Sing** from the same song sheet
   - to publicly express an opinion that is the same as someone else's
3. **Sing**
   - refers to a criminal who finally reveals information to the police, when in the beginning the criminal tried to withhold the information

SKELETION
1. A **skeleton** in your closet
   - a secret that a person would like to keep secret, because it would cause a great deal of embarrassment if it were revealed

SKIN
1. By the **skin** of your teeth
   - to accomplish or do something by the barest of margins
2. Get under your **skin**
   - refers to someone that has the ability to annoy you
3. Have a thick **skin**
   - to be unbothered in any way by any type of criticism

SKY
1. **Reach** for the **sky**
   - be ambitious and give much effort in accomplishing a difficult thing
2. The **sky's** the limit
   - a motto that states anyone can be very successful at what they do

SLEEP
1. **Sleep** like a log
   - to sleep very soundly
2. **Sleep** on something
   - to give yourself time to think something over
3. **Sleep** something off
   - to use sleep to recover from something
4. Not **sleep** a wink
   - to not sleep at all

SLEEVE
1. Have something up your **sleeve**
   - to have a secret advantage, that can be used as leverage over someone else

SMALL

1. **Small** fry
   - a way to address a child
2. **Small** potatoes
   - not important
3. Make someone feel **small**
   - insult someone in front of others, to make them feel stupid

SMOKE

1. **Smoke** signals
   - a hint sent by someone to suggest something is about to happen
2. The big **smoke**
   - refers to the biggest city in a particular country
3. Blow **smoke**
   - to deliberately confuse or deceive someone
4. Where there's **smoke**, there's fire
   - refers to a rumor that has to be true, or partially true, because the rumor would not have happened if it wasn't true or partially true
5. **Smoke** and mirrors
   - something that is said that is meant to confuse or deceive people
6. Go up in **smoke**
   - refers to an important thing that does not happen or come to fruition

SNAKE

1. A **snake** in the grass
   - refers to a person who pretends to be your friend, but who says bad things to others about you, or that secretly tries to cause you harm
2. **Snake** oil salesman
   - someone who tries to persuade you to buy something of no value

SNOW

1. A snow **job**
   - attempt to deceive someone by telling them lies about something

SOCKS

1. Put a **sock** in it
   - to tell someone, in an abrupt way, to stop talking
2. **Sock** it to someone
   - to do something to someone in a very forceful way
3. Knock the **socks** off someone
   - to impress someone else
4. Knock someone's **socks** off
   - to be impressed by someone else
5. Pull up your **socks**
   - to imply that someone that they must improve their behavior

273

6. Work your **socks** off
   - to work extremely hard

SOFT
1. **Soft** money
   - money that is obtained without the use of much effort
2. A **soft** option
   - the easiest or least painful option or choice available to a person
3. **Soft** as shit
   - a person with a weak character, who can be easily pushed around

SOLD
1. Be **sold** a **pup**
   - buy or get something free, that is not as good as advertised

SONG
1. For a **song**
   - to buy something for very little money
2. Make a **song** and dance
   - to react excitedly or nervously to something that is not important
3. On **song**
   - refers to an athlete who is playing very well

SOUND
1. **Empty vessels** make the most **sound**
   - people who talk a lot, and who think they know a lot about many things, are often the ones who know very little about a subject
2. **Sound** hollow
   - something that does not seem to be true or sincere

SPLEEN
1. Vent your **spleen**
   - to express your anger about some thing

SPOON
1. A greasy **spoon**
   - a type of diner that specializes in fried food
2. The wooden **spoon**
   - a prize people get when they are worst, or last, in an activity

SQUEAKY WHEEL
1. The **squeaky wheel** gets oiled
   - the one who complains the most gets their complaints addressed

STAB
1. **Stab** someone in the back
   - to betray someone, in a secret, non-overt way

STARS
1. Reach for the **stars**
   - to try to achieve a very difficult thing, or to have high expectations
2. Have **stars** in your eyes
   - to be excited and enthusiastic about your future expectations

STEAMED
1. **Steamed**
   - to be in a very angry state

STICK
1. Carry a big **stick**
   - have a lot of power, and be able to use it to get what you want
2. Get the short end of the **stick**
   - to be in an inferior or worse position than others around you
3. Make something **stick**
   - to continue to make something successful or effective
4. Get a lot of **stick**
   - to be blamed a lot for something, even if you are not at fault
5. More things than you can shake a **stick** at
   - have an inordinately large number of things
6. **Stick** in your throat
   - refers to someone that is annoying you

STONE
1. Leave no **stone** unturned
   - use every effort to do something, or to achieve something
2. Kill 2 birds with 1 **stone**
   - achieve 2 different goals with 1 single effort
3. Set in **stone**
   - a thing that is completely decided upon and cannot be changed

STORM
1. Weather the **storm**
   - to survive a difficult situation, without being harmed by it
2. Take something by **storm**
   - to be incredibly popular, or amazingly successful at something

STRAW
1. The **straw** that breaks the camel's back
   - the last event, in a series of events, that makes something untenable, or that makes something fail

2. A **straw** in the wind
   - a sign, or an omen, which signifies the way that things will go
3. The last **straw**
   - the latest event, in a series of events, that makes a person unable to deal with a particular situation any longer
4. Draw the short **straw**
   - to be the person that is chosen to do something, from amongst a group of people, that nobody else in the group wants to do
5. Draw **straws**
   - to which person, from a group of people, will do a particular thing
6. Grasp at **straws**
   - try desperately to do a thing you have no chance succeeding in

STRIKES
1. **Three strikes** against someone (and now you're out)
   - a law in America that punishes a person very severely if they commit three separate crimes

STRING
1. Add another **string** to your bow
   - add a skill a person can use if their primary skill is unsuccessful
2. Have someone on a **string**
   - have the ability to make someone do whatever you want them to
3. Pull **strings**
   - to use connections or friendships that a person has with powerful people, to get what they want
4. Pull the **strings**
   - control someone, without other people noticing what you're doing
5. With no **strings** attached
   - an offer that **DOES NOT** require a reciprocal favor or act in return
6. With **strings** attached
   - an offer that **DOES** require a reciprocal favor or act in return

SUN
1. The **Sun** is over the yardarm
   - it is now late enough to have an alcoholic beverage

SWAN
1. **Swan** song
   - the very last performance in a person's long career

SWING
1. In full **swing**
   - something that has been operating fully for some time, rather than it just beginning, or just starting up

SWORD
1. The **sword** of **Damocles** hangs over someone
   - a situation where bad things can happen to someone at any time

T

TAB
1. Run a **tab**
   - to pay for your drinks at one time at the end of the night, instead of paying for them each time the server brings them to you.

TABLE
1. **Under** the **table**
   - to earn money in an illegal way, by not paying taxes on it

TEA
1. **Tea** and sympathy
   - the kindness and sympathy you show to someone who is upset
2. Not for all the **tea** in China
   - let it be known that you will not do a certain thing, no matter what
3. Tempest in a **teapot**
   - something that is blown out of proportions, as it is not important
4. Not my cup of **tea**
   - something that is not a person's preference

TEE
1. To a **tee**
   - something that is perfect or 100% right
2. Down to a **tee**
   - something practiced many times, so you can now do it perfectly

TEETH
1. Gnash your **teeth**
   - to show your annoyance or anger at something or someone
2. Grind your **teeth**
   - to be angry, but to hold your anger back and not show it
3. Grit your **teeth**
   - to accept a fate, or to continue doing something, even if it is painful to do so
4. Have **teeth**
   - to have the necessary authority to be able to enforce a law, or to force people to do something
5. Lie through your **teeth**
   - to tell an obvious lie without feeling embarrassed about doing so

6. Show your **teeth**
   - to show others that you have the will and the power to enforce something, or the will and power to defend yourself
7. Armed to the **teeth**
   - to have many weapons
8. Cut your **teeth**
   - to gain the experience of doing a particular thing for the first time
9. Sink your **teeth** into something
   - to do a particular thing with a lot of enthusiasm

THORN
1. A **thorn** in your side
   - a person who continuously annoys or causes trouble for another person

THUMB
1. Have a green **thumb**
   - to be good at gardening
2. Stick out like a sore **thumb**
   - to be different and noticeable, especially in comparison to others
3. Under a person's **thumb**
   - to be under the control of another person
4. All **thumbs**
   - to be a very clumsy person
5. Give something the **thumbs** down
   - to give or show disapproval towards something
6. Twiddling your **thumbs**
   - to be idly wasting time, with nothing to occupy you

TIE
1. **Tie** one on
   - to drink a lot, to get drunk

TIME
1. Ahead of its/one's **time**
   - some thing that is so new and modern, or some person whose ideas are so new and modern, that it is hard for others to accept the idea or the person because the idea is so ground breaking
2. Living on borrowed **time**
   - refers to someone or something that is not expected to survive very long
3. In your own **time**
   - to not be hurried into doing something, but doing it at your own pace
4. Make **time**
   - create time to do an activity or thing, even though you thought you you had no time to do this activity or thing in the first place
5. Play for **time**
   - create a delay, so as to have more time to prepare for something

6. **Time** will tell
   - only the passage of time will reveal if a choice was the right one

TIN
1. A little **tin** god
   - a person who behaves as if they are more important than they really are
2. Have a **tin** ear
   - to be unable to understand or hear music well

TONE
1. Lower the **tone**
   - to make a place seem less respectable

TONGUE
1. Set **tongues** wagging
   - have things said about you because of a thing you said or did

TOOTH
1. Fight **tooth** and nail
   - to fight as hard as one can to achieve a goal
2. Long in the **tooth**
   - refers to someone or some thing that is particularly old
3. Sweet **tooth**
   - to enjoy, like or love eating sweet things

TREE
1. Bark up the wrong **tree**
   - follow incorrect actions usually because your beliefs are erroneous
2. Up a **tree**
   - to be in a difficult situation

TRIAL BALLOON
1. Float a **trial balloon**
   - to suggest an idea or a plan, and circulate it as a rumor (at times), to see what other people think about the idea

TRICK
1. A one **trick** pony
   - refers to someone or something that is only good at one thing
2. Do the **trick**
   - something that achieves want a person wants done
3. Up to your same old **tricks**
   - a person who continues to behave in the same dishonest, foolish or irrational way that they always have behaved in before
4. Use every **trick** in the book
   - refers to someone who uses every possible way to achieve their goal

5. The oldest **trick** in the book
   - a common or understandable thing that most people understand, but that completely fools or deceives a naïve person
6. Not/never miss a **trick**
   - to take advantage of a situation because you are very knowledgable

TRUMPET
1. Blow your own **trumpet**
   - to tell people good or positive things about yourself

TRUTH
1. Economical with the **truth**
   - to deceive others by not telling them the whole truth
2. Stretch the **truth**
   - to purposely manipulate the facts, and present this as the truth
3. A grain of **truth**
   - even the smallest amount of truth

TUNE
1. Call the **tune**
   - control a situation and have an ability to make important decisions
2. Can carry a **tune**
   - to have the ability to sing a song with the right note
3. Change your **tune**
   - express an opinion that is different than one previously expressed
4. To the **tune** of
   - a saying that is used before quoting a sum of money, especially when the amount of money is large
5. Dance to someone else's **tune**
   - to do whatever someone else tells you to do
6. March to a different **tune**
   - behave differently or have different morals than most other people

TWIST
1. **Twist** an arm
   - to try hard to persuade someone to do something

U

UNCLE
1. Bob's your **uncle**
   - this saying used to express that a certain thing is easy to achieve
2. A monkey's **uncle**
   - an expression used by someone to express surprise at something they should have known about, but did not know about

UNDER
   1. **Under** the **table**
      - to earn money in an illegal way, by not paying taxes on it

UP
   1. **Up** against it
      - a situation where a person has a difficult problem to deal with
   2. **Up** and running
      - something that has begun or started, and that is functioning well
   3. On the **up and up**
      - a person or activity that is honest and/or legal

V

VACUUM
   1. In a **vacuum**
      - a thing happening in isolation, not being affected by other things

VEGETABLES
   1. **Veg** out
      - to take it easy, and to relax

VEIL
   1. Draw a **veil** around something
      - make a deliberate effort to keep something quite because it is private

VIOLET
   1. A shrinking **violet**
      - a reference to a person who is very shy, or who wilts when confronted, or when under pressure

W

WALLABY
   1. On the **wallaby** track
      - to be unemployed

WATER
   1. Blown out of the **water**
      - refers to something that is destroyed or defeated completely
   2. Dead in the **water**
      - refers to someone or something that failed and no longer works
   3. In deep **water**
      - to be in trouble, or to be in a difficult or dangerous situation
   4. In hot **water**
      - do something wrong, so that others are angry at you

5. Like **water** off a duck's back
   - a reference to criticism that does not have any effect on the person that is being criticized
6. Not hold **water**
   - an incorrect theory or argument that can proven to be incorrect

WAVELENGTH
1. On the same **wavelength**
   - to have the same line of thought or method of thinking as someone else

WAY

1. The easy **way** out
   - choose an easy way to get out of a situation, even though this may not solve the problem
2. Go back a long **way**
   - refers to two people who have been friends for a very long time
3. Look the other **way**
   - ignore a bad thing, instead of dealing with the problem
4. No **way**
   - an emphatic way to say, "definitely not"
5. Pave the **way**
   - a thing that happened that made it easier for a 2nd thing to happen
6. Rub someone the wrong **way**
   - refers to someone who annoys someone else

WHALE
1. A **whale** of a story
   - a story that is too incredible, so it is hard to believe

WHITE
1. **Whiter** than **white**
   - refers to actions or behaviour that is completely moral and honest
2. In **black** and **white**
   - refers to something that is so extremely and plainly obvious

WIND
1. Blowing in the **wind**
   - a thing being considered but which no decision has been made on
2. Get **wind** of
   - to find out information, even if that wasn't your original intention
3. Gone with the **wind**
   - something that has gone and disappeared forever, never to return
4. In the **wind**
   - something that will most likely happen very soon

5. Spitting in the **wind**
   - doing a thing that is waste of time, as it has no chance for success
6. Twist in the **wind**
   - refers to someone who puts another person in a difficult situation by controlling them, or the outcome of the situation

WINKS
1. 40 **winks**
   - a quick nap

WOMEN
1. Make an honest **woman** out of someone
   - this happens when a man marries his girlfriend

WOOL
1. **Pull** the **wool** over someone's eyes
   - deceive someone, so as to take advantage of them

WORD
1. Eat your **words**
   - state publicly that what you once said is completely wrong
2. The last **word**
   - to be able to make the final decision, or to win an argument
3. At a loss for **words**
   - refers to a situation where a person is speechless, because they do not know what to say, because of what has just transpired
4. Put **words** into someone's mouth
   - to tell someone what their opinion should be, instead of listening to what that person's opinion is
5. Take the **words** out of someone's mouth
   - to say something that someone else is about to say
6. Not mince your **words**
   - state your opinion openly, even if this means offending others

WORK
1. Do someone's dirty **work**
   - to do some difficult or unpleasant thing for someone, because they do not want to do it themselves
2. Make light **work** of someone
   - to defeat an opponent decisively
3. A nasty piece of **work**
   - refers to an unpleasant or nasty person
4. Have your **work** cut out for you
   - to have a very big and/or unpleasant task to deal with
5. A piece of **work**
   - refers to a very unusual, impressive or surprising person

6. **Work** your arse off
   - to work very, very hard
7. Nice **work** if you can get it
   - a job that you do not have, but that you would like to have, because it is either easy, or because it pays well

WORKMAN

1. A **bad workman** blames his tools
   - a person who does a bad job, then blames the quality of the tools or equipment, instead of admitting that they didn't do the job well

WORLD

1. Come down in the **world**
   - refers to a person that is not as rich as they used to be, or that does not have the same social status as they once had
2. It's a small **world**
   - when people bump into each other in an unexpected place
3. Not the end of the **world**
   - a person shouldn't take too any bad happening too seriously
4. On top of the **world**
   - to feel very, very happy, or to have achieved a great feat
5. Out of this **world**
   - to feel a sense of excitement over any incredibly exciting thing
6. The **world** is your oyster
   - refers to a person who can do anything or go wherever they want

WORM

1. The **worm** has turned
   - a situation where a person has put up with bad treatment, but6 then finally decides they will no longer accept the situation anymore

WRAPS

1. Keep something under **wraps**
   - to keep something secret

Y

1. **Yellow** belly
   - refers to a person who is a coward, or who behaves in a cowardly way